PuNK
MaRketinG

PUNK MARKETING

Get Off Your Ass and Join the Revolution

RICHARD LAERMER and MARK SIMMONS

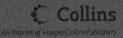
Collins
An Imprint of HarperCollinsPublishers

Punk Marketing logo by 86 The Onions
Illustrations by David Creek

HarperCollins books may be purchased for educational, business, or sales promotional use. For information, please write to: Special Markets Department, HarperCollins Publishers, 10 East 53rd Street, New York, NY 10022.

Designed by Timothy Shaner, nightanddaydesign.biz

Library of Congress Cataloging-In-Publication Data

Laermer, Richard, 1960–
    Punk marketing: get off your ass and join the revolution / Richard Laermer and Mark Simmons.
        p.cm.
    Includes index.
    ISBN: 978-0-06-115110-1
    ISBN-10: 0-0-6-115110-6
        1. Marketing. I. Simmons, Mark, marketing analyst. II. Title.
    HF5415.L253 2007
    658.8–dc22   2006049748

07 08 09 10 11 ❖ 10 9 8 7 6 5 4 3 2 1

Dedicated to everyone
who's ever shit-canned us . . .
and their spouses.

Kitchen Table of Contents
The Darkness That Lies Within

Acknowledgments ix

First Words xi

Authors' Note of Pure Promotion xiii

Prologue Welcome to the Revolution *Don't Blame Us, Just Thank Us* xv

Chapter One The Punk Marketing Manifesto
You Read—We Make Your Life Better 1

Chapter Two Kill the Middlemen *Do So before They Kill You* 19

Chapter Three Brand Not Bland *How to Stand Out so You Are "The Chosen"* ... 41

Chapter Four Who's Eating Your Lunch? *Make Them Spit It Out* 59

Chapter Five The Sell Phone *Use and Abuse of the Cell Phone for Marketing* ... 77

Chapter Six The Captive Consumer *Callous Corporations Con Customers* ... 93

Chapter Seven Now It's Story Time
The Art of Making a Case through Storytelling 109

Chapter Eight Leave Me Alone, Will Ya! *Too Much Stuff, Too Little Time* 121

Chapter Nine Lies Lies Lies: *The Truth about Truth And Factoids about Facts* 135

Chapter Ten As Seen on TV *Place It, Baby, Place It* 149

Chapter Eleven At Last, a Job in Hollywood! *You Are the Content* 167

Chapter Twelve Game On *No One Is a Loser* 177

Chapter Thirteen It's More Than Just Us *Hard as That Is to Believe* 195

Who Are Your Leaders? 212

Notes 214

Index 217

Final Words 226

Acknowledgments

Punk Marketing wouldn't have been possible without the help of an establishment to rail against. We'd like to thank all of the mud-stickers, dullards, and dimwits who have stood in the way of the inevitable for too long.

And thanks to our two spouses.* They're adorable.

Richard Laermer & Mark Simmons

---

* To be fair, we tip our hat to Scott J. Milne, the most *Gumby* person on earth, Larry Vein (who introduced us before we knew any better!), and the always-on Erin Mitchell! Who said the world isn't fair?

FIRST WORDS

Reluctantly the panic begins
To catch fire
                    —The Clash

Authors' Note of Pure Promotion

This is a nonfiction work. That means fact, opinion, wholly unnecessary commentary, interviews, and anecdotes overheard and taken advantage of. On PunkMarketing.com, you will find *regular* updates on each topic covered in these pages.

What's there?

- Extended footnote information based upon what we started. We're itching to tell the inside stories, and we will. Oh, we will.
- Rants.
- More rants. A couple of tantrums too.
- A directory of Punk Marketing practitioners (so accredited) by us dudes.
- The bios and inside details of us, and whom we work with, and why.

In the book you will stumble onto online destinations to further explain our M.O. These include PunkMarketing.com/punkthink, the AwardsAwards.com site, PunkPR.com (for campaigns we adore), CaptiveConsumer.com, ArticleFifteen.com, where the reader/participant gets prizes, and the strictly irrelevant religious site called PunkisGod.com.

If you need us, have a question burning at you, or feel like saying hello, write anytime: richardandmark@punkmarketing.com. Peace, love, virtue, sell.

Use our sites to add your voice to the revolution. *Vive la Révolution!*

Richard Laermer & Mark Simmons

Prologue

Welcome to the Revolution
(Don't Blame Us, Just Thank Us)

I. Welcome to Our World

There's a revolution brewing.

The relationship that consumers have with brands has gone through a seismic shift over the past few years, and a new approach to marketing is long overdue.

The assumptions that established marketing methods are based on have been proven invalid, and while many marketers instinctively feel things aren't quite right, no new approach to doing things differently has emerged. We're here to say stop it.

But first let's go back.

All the marketing industries—from advertising to PR to direct to online to anyone who has ever sold a damn thing—have gone through a rough patch since just a few short years before the century started. The advertising agencies were roaring kings of a marketing jungle—brand guardians responsible for advising everyone and their assistants how to spend a budget. Of course, that translated to an entire budget being spent via *them*. The glory days of 15 percent meant agencies were remunerated based on how much money was spent: pay me a piece of the action for lazy-ass me spending your money.

But as agencies began unbundling services, and media planning and media buying were spun off into disparate companies or divisions, marketers thought it better to pay agencies a flat fee for services rather than commissions on purchased media. Clients were no longer shelling out a single fixed percentage of their budgets, and now were able to drive down the fees agencies got paid. Out went the

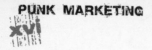

system based upon the amount of money spent on work in favor of one based on the amount of time agencies spent working!

Agencies were expected to justify the time and rates of employees servicing an account, just like a regular service business.

Gee.

An agency in fee negotiations with a prospective client would recommend who of the, ahem, team was required to do what on an account and for how long. Using actual salaries of team members or average industry salaries of people with their skill levels, plus an agency's markup for overhead (lightbulbs and coffee), plus profit (cash in pockets), a figure would be derived.

fee = sum of each individual's time x cost of time including overhead & profit

Clients and agencies subsequently haggled over the number necessary in a team and for how much time, while the client quietly assumed the agency padded these massive figures. It was assumed that the value of services that an agency provided to a client was in direct proportion to the time spent toiling away.

Suddenly, cracks started to show in the foundation. First there was a downturn in marketing spend in the midnineties, then a decline of the economy in the early 2000s. An acute oversupply of advertising talent led agencies to accept lower fees to win or retain clientele. If they didn't succumb, they got cannibalized by someone willing to do it at the price a powerful client felt like paying. Shoe on other foot. Agencies were forced to grin and bear it. Some of them cut overhead until, in many cases, they just closed the door.

Agencies got rid of people, stopped hiring, and lowered salaries for new recruits. Morale suffered, as security and pay went to hell, and the quality of those joining up declined.

Bright young graduates who would once have said becoming the new Darrin Stephens was their top career wish now turned their needy eyes toward other professions that offered cash and prospects—not to mention a better reputation. Talented veterans who were sorely needed just crapped out.

Over a short few years this industry that had once promised a sexy mix of business and creativity and perks lost all allure.

As the slowdown happened, a brief reprieve for the industry, in the guise of the .com error (*sic!*), took hold, and start-ups silly with VC cash began to pay big money for nothing. For a sobering example, you could, until a few years ago, go to San Francisco's AT&T Park and see plaques from dozens of companies. All dead.

Just as the last glowing embers caught by a rogue wind flared up into a full blaze of hope, marketing crashed and burned.

By April 2000, Ad World was a ghost town.

But this did not mean there were no longer talented people in advertising. Most were merely dejected by what had happened over the last years. Now all they wanted was to keep their jobs. Most good men and women tacitly realized that while smart advertising meant taking risks and often arguing with less knowing clients and bosses, this certainly was not the time for that. They would do what they were asked and smile through gritted teeth. So what if pay was not high, at least the hours were!

The work churned out wasn't good; it was passable in a "Get what you pay for" economy. And marketers became a joke—especially in the spiteful media who remembered how uppity we all were when we were making more money than everyone at the Last Supper.

The ad business was not a creative business in 2000. It had become only about conning the dupable public into buying things they had no use for. Even ad campaigns that broke through to consumer consciousness were dissociated from the brands themselves. Talking dogs and frogs were adorable, but what were they selling?*

"Got Milk?" had become so plagiarized that it has nothing to do with dairy products any longer. Got Punk?

Meanwhile, orphan media-buying firms cast adrift to fend for themselves during the ad heyday were doing okay, thanks. They were no longer dependent on ad agencies and did not have to recommend that a brand manager purchase gads of wasteful ads. They could look at a mix of options available—the buffet was

---

* The Chihuahua was Taco Bell's advertising mascot, while frogs and the like were used by Anheuser-Busch for Budweiser beer. Both were summarily fired. So was the chimp for E*TRADE, which one of us got to take on a national tour. Those were the days. Sorta.

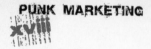

wide-open—and make impartial, well-informed recommendations on how to spend someone's money.

Would you like a little sponsorship to go with that promotion? Some direct mail on the side! There's a sauce of new online banners to tuck into, or even branded product placement instead of any fattening ads for dessert.

Media buyers, when they were ad agency employees in the back of the room, had been used and abused—an afterthought. Boy did they have power now! In the early 2000s the buyers were in charge of the big picture and had the ear of the senior clients. What they said went.

To top if off, that ad agency lifeblood, the thirty-second spot on which they bet everything, was now being dubbed the deadest of the dead.

One day, while we were sleeping, people who had a DVR (digital video recorder, or TiVo-type machine) used it to avoid watching ads. And it was clear why: People hated them. An industry that had been comatose for a long time was snapped into a quick panic. This was really bad. It was one thing to realize that advertising is not the only game in town, and, sure, we'll take a smaller share of the budget pie, and—heavy sigh—I guess we need to follow strategies created by outsider media agencies or those idiot consultants. But to be told that TV ads are no longer cutting it, that has to be the last straw! Walk me to the window.

Ad industry executives needed to consider other options—those previously unbeknownst to them, "nontraditional" advertising mechanisms—that they simply had no skills to produce. They couldn't even find it on dictionary.com!

Smart marketers and all of us businesspeople who rely on marketing realized with a jolt that all was not right in this ever-branded world we paid mightily to live in. The thinking and methods that once worked so effectively to influence the behavior of consumers were simply not cutting it anymore.

II. Changing Brandscape

It's difficult to exaggerate how much has changed in terms of consumers' relationships with brands in the last few years. *Everything* is different now: from how brands are viewed, to the mechanisms through which we find out about them. When did the change really start? Let us ponder.

Was it the day in 1993 when Marlboro dropped its prices by 40 percent to compete with the cut-price cigarettes that were eating away at its market share, thus sending investors into a panic that lopped nearly $50 billion off the value of twenty-five top brand-makers?

Was it when a nascent World Wide Web became a tool for instant swapping of info, enabling each of us to instantly see the truth about all available choices of product?

. . . When the TV market fragmented into hundreds of smaller channels, each wanting a piece of the viewer's time?

. . . When technologies like TiVo made it possible for viewers to avoid watching commercials altogether?

. . . When Enron and others collapsed in a stinking mass of deceit and consumers lost faith in corporations and what they sold?

. . . When incomprehensible events on September 11 made us reassess values and beliefs?

Choose all of the above. For the most part the marketing industry hasn't kept apace of the changed relationship consumers have with brands. Marketers and their advisers are largely still thinking and working in the same way that they always have: buying media and creating messages that interrupt, rather than connect with, consumers. Why? Because that's the way it has always been, and it's comfy to pretend that poor results are due to wars or consumer confidence and that things will "return to normal" before too long.

But what if they *never* go back to the way they were? The changes are fundamental and permanent. The interaction between brands and consumers is significantly different from even a decade ago. Intense media fragmentation has made it difficult to reach the target consumer in any number; consumers find it convenient and desirable to avoid marketing messages and are paralyzed by too many similar choices and too little time to choose.

Never has the need been greater for a cohesive new approach to marketing based on some radically revised assumptions on the way consumers interact with brands.

III. The Good Old Days

It used to be possible to reach potential consumers easily. According to an analysis by Willard Bishop Consulting, lo, back in 1995 it took the airing of a TV

commercial just three measly times to reach 80 percent of eighteen-to-forty-nine-year-old ladies. But five years later, reaching the same demographic required airing that awful commercial ninety-seven times.[1] The media market has fragmented beyond recognition, making it impossible to build any brand awareness quickly through buying via a so-called traditional campaign, other than on the Super Bowl, the last bastion of watercooler advertising.

Here's another demographic of consumers: according to a study from 2003, teenagers and young adults spend more time on the Internet than watching television. The survey demonstrated how young people on average claimed to spend nearly seventeen hours online each week, not including time used to read and, oh, yeah, send e-mail, compared with fourteen hours spent watching television and

twelve hours listening to the radio.[2] It's not that they are not tuning into TV—a 2005 study showed they have the box on *at least* as much as ever—it's that they are tuning out more as other, newer media grab their wandering attentions.[3]

Reaching a target audience by running a campaign in one place—whether TV, radio, print, outdoor, Web, etc.—has become incredibly difficult. Nay, impossible.

Then, as if that isn't bad enough news, as fragmentation made it difficult to reach people in any numbers to write home about, consumers were handed the ability to avoid at a swipe TV advertising, the single most powerful form of marketing.

And while you and we *could* blame it on TiVo and its bastard stepsisters, it was the remote control that made commercial avoidance simple. The remote was without a doubt the first poster child for consumer control. It's no surprise we could not locate one major study on how people use their remote controls to switch over during commercials*—and Nielsen has no interest in trying to include such data. Imagine the depressing numbers!

But still, studies have been done ad nauseam on how people use their TiVos to time-shift programs and toilet-shift the commercials in the breaks, which is how TiVo became the symbol of change.

All this talk of consumers having the power to avoid commercials begs the question: Why do they have to avoid them in the first place? One theory is the commercial itself is poorly targeted; simply buying air based upon audience data of the programs commercials run during, and the networks on which they run, is way too blunt an instrument. The same spots will be seen by everyone watching in a particular DMA†, and for many of those folks, who don't fit into the general demographic profile, the ad is irrelevant.

So we turn your attention to a system developed by INVIDI Technologies Corporation that gives advertisers a canny ability to target commercials much more precisely. Their software can profile households with 95 percent accuracy solely based upon their use of the remote, and after only twenty to twenty-five clicks, all commercials for, say, a denture adhesive product are beamed *only* to viewers over fifty-five years old. In this scenario, Mr. X "enjoys" a different commercial from his

---

* But, hey, we're fallible. If you know of one, drop us a line at yousowrong@punkmarketing.com.

† Shorthand for Nielsen Media Research's *Designated Market Area.*

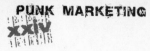

These Guys Defined Punk So We Tribute Their Actions

When the Sex Pistols were inducted into the Rock and Roll Hall of Fame in 2006, they behaved exactly how we expected them to. They didn't just snub the ceremony by not showing up, but took a metaphorical crap on the establishment in a grammatically challenged letter read at the ceremony by Jann Wenner. The band's statement was simple: "Next to the Sex Pistols, rock and roll and that hall of fame is a piss stain. Your museum. Urine in wine. We're not coming. We're not your monkeys. If you voted for us, hope you noted your reasons. Your [sic] anonymous as judges but your [sic] still music industry people. We're not coming."

It finished with this little gem: "Your [sic] not paying attention. Outside the shit-stem is a real SEX PISTOL."

Wow. After all this time the band that brought an underground music movement to the forefront of pop culture hasn't changed an iota, and we love them for it. Part of being punk for real, it reminded us, is never wavering in your conviction and/or vision.

The media treated this like a harsh statement on the state of rock 'n' roll or a pox on the corporate scum that run the music industry or in a few cases the continued arrogance of Johnny Rotten. Well, maybe it was any of these, but the only true message that you will notice as a marketer is that the band used a gimmick that worked! It's the same gimmick they've used since day one: be outrageous, get attention.

SIDEBAR

Who knows if the Sex Pistols put any thought into it, but it sure got them a lot more press than just showing up and saying thank you, we love you. It's a risky endeavor to be so anti-everything-we-know-to-work-it. That's the risk-taking needed to really have an impact though, isn't it?

neighbor Mrs. Y, even though both watch the same show on the same station. It's our favorite nascent form of discrimination.

But if people to whom the message is targeted still seek to avoid it, what then? One idea is to strap them into their armchairs with eyelids pried open as in *A Clockwork Orange*. Perhaps Nielsen or Comcast does a deal with La-Z-Boy to develop the fabulous new Strapomatic to Guarantee Comfortable Uninterrupted Viewing!

Ah, forget it. The problem is that commercials suck. Maybe the biggest assumption this revolution needs to destroy is that consumers are happy being bombarded with ill-conceived marketing messages that treat them as idiots. In words of oft-quoted David Ogilvy, "The consumer is not a moron: she is your wife." Somehow such ageless common sense is lost on many in these businesses.

So that's what we are here to do: slap some creativity into marketing and make it less of a nice-to-have and more of a necessity. Let's add good old-fashioned thinking to all the fancy shmancy new gadgets and know-how. How about instead of fascinating ways to trick consumers, we go for unbelievable ways to *engage* them!

IV. Enter Punk Marketing

In the late seventies, punk was a shot heard around the radio as a beyond-refreshing change from the tired old formulaic music of the time. It was a call to action, a demand for revolt delivered in our own language. The punk rock that burst rudely onto the scene with bands like The Stooges, The New York Dolls, the Sex Pistols, and The Clash was replete with energy and vitality and shook the complacent music industry to its core and scared the crap out of disco-infused freaks that were running/ruining the whorish record business.

The new scene gave voice to scores of teens on both sides of the Atlantic too. The records were raw and unstructured and had the unmistakable feel of something created with glee *by* the people *for* the people.

Likewise, marketing has reached the point at which a groundswell from the consumer up is engulfing the established industry thinking. Punk Marketing is not founded upon a single idea or technique. It is a defined approach to doing things differently based upon a clear set of principles for how marketers—whether in large corporations, agencies, or small businesses—can use the shift in power to the consumer to their advantage.

V. Who's Your Daddy, Ahora?

The consumer is, *chico.*

But today, Mr. and Mrs. Buyer and their Buyerlings have the willingness as well as the means to switch on, tune in, and turn off as never before. We as humans

get what we want when we want it. When we with arms folded do not want it and still it won't stop talking to us (is AOL listening?), we get really pissed off. And turn off. Sometimes we go so far as to create sites and post well-read gripes that tell the world how off them we are.

Want to know how much that CEO of the bank you're thinking of opening an account with earns? No problem. We can check his salary on Google or WiseNut in a few minutes. Hey, and along the way we will see subtle paid-for sponsored links by four other banks wanting to get our business. Interested in learning about a new *Jetsons*-esque TV on the market? Of course! Epinions.com will get us the inside track—opinions from other owners and information on where to buy it the cheapest—and blow the carefully managed press release and advert from the manufacturer (whoosh!) right out of the water.

Tired of radio that plays the same chart music slotted in between annoying commercials? The alternatives are endless! Download a podcast, subscribe to, rent, buy, or steal tunes digitally; or use multimedia cell phones to listen while you surf preset satellite radio and cue up the blog that's written by a stranger we call pal.

This is the revolution. A fundamental shift in power from big to small: from top-down to bottom-up.

The days when dull marketing could be pushed at passive consumers are gone. Consumers have been slapped out of their obedient stupor and, now dazed but enthused, are armed to the tits and ready with remote controls, TiVos, self-made blogs, and Googley sites in which to choose what to consume and to play a godlike part in its creation.*

---

* This is Web 2.0, simple. As John Markoff in the *NY Times* said in July 2006: "Web 2.0 [coined by O'Reilly Media] is a new generation of Internet software technologies that . . . plug together, much like Lego blocks, in new and unexpected ways." What we call it: thin client computing where any user can get whatever he needs from a browser. And now it's being used as a way to get free content as "people collaborate," meaning put their content on sites that make money off it. It has created new language for an enamored world—among our favorites "folksonomies," which is the opposite of taxonomy. For more, see "The Real Deal" on PunkMarketing.com.

VI. Boiling Point: The C's

You probably think Convergence is a cliché, but we say no longer. Now is the time of Collusion among three worlds that up till now have stuck to traditional roles and respected self-appointed boundaries: those of Commerce, Content, and Consumers.

Commerce has till now been the world of business that makes products and sells them to Consumers through marketing; this often relies upon attaching itself to Content.

Content is all the news and entertainment created by media companies Consumers seek out and into which Commerce has been piggybacking itself to reach them.

Consumers are the people—all of us—who hold purse strings but who have until recently been treated less like individuals and more like a giant mass.

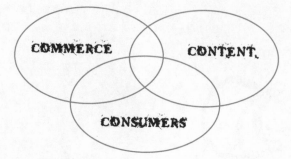

Note that those roles are no longer so clear-cut—or even that interesting.

Thanks for listening. A shift in power to the consumers, with technology as a catalyst, has led this setup to break down. The breaking down has important consequences for what marketing must do to be effective; how to engage consumers in a world where choice is infinite; and how to introduce the concept that integrity is It.

Marketing industries have to wake up to one fact: slowly but surely the situation has changed while we ignored the signs. Now, everything's reached the boiling point. Wake up to a quiet revolution that's not so quiet anymore. Get on the bandwagon and enjoy getting up each morning with verve and gusto.

The time is now. You too can be saved! Welcome to our world. . . .

VII. How to Use This Book

Well, maybe as a doorstop or way to prop up a wobbly table.

But if you do get around to reading it, might we suggest you don't read it as you would other business books. We want you to have fun and scream, maybe giggle, maybe roll your eyes a little, even shout at us occasionally for being so not in our minds.

In short we want you to have as much of a good time as we had writing the damn thing.

We mean it.

Each chapter is written as a stand-alone piece that doesn't live or die on arguments put forward in previous chapters; they don't have to be read in order. Dip into one. Pick out something at random and see where it leads. We point along the way to other chapters or side thoughts that are, perhaps in some Kundera-esque way, connected.

There is no single idea in this book on which all else hinges. Books with one idea read often like magazine articles and run out of steam by the third chapter and then repeat themselves so much you end up tossing the damn things into a fireplace.

But here instead we proffer one theme to tie everything together: power has been transferred from corporation to consumers, and so marketing must be both brave and intelligent to succeed.

The information within is not timeless. Technology changes daily and with it often come new ways of marketing. We think the deeper principles hold true—principles that have existed forever but should now be followed with urgency to win back the consumer.

So tear it apart, write notes within the paragraphs—not just on the margins. Doodle on our faces on the page in the back. Rip out the pages you like—rip up the pages you hate! Put your coffee cup on it and leave rings. We're so sick of people saying *books should be treated with reverence*. Use this as you would a user manual for your car, not some literary tome. Because it ain't that.

Oh, and by the way, you'll notice there are a lot of references to examples of marketing from the other side of the Atlantic. This is for no other reason than that the practitioners of marketing in the UK have in the past been willing to take risks, sometimes leading to failure but other times to phenomenal success. From these we can all learn. So if you find us being veddy British, we swear, it'll be worthwhile. Plus, you can read those sections in a fake accent.

One

The Punk Marketing Manifesto
You Read—We Make Your Life Better

Karl Marx had one. As did Simón Bolívar. Now you do too. Congratulations.

Be proud. Copy it onto vellum, and read it out loud from the wreckage of your overturned desk.

What's a revolt without something to hold in your hands?

We feel marketers need a manifesto to change the thinking from a set of outdated ideas to another, more relevant set. There's nothing better to establish the guiding principles by which like-minded revolutionaries can live.

The Punk Marketing Manifesto* consists of fifteen articles, each of which should be followed without fail for the revolution to carry you along with it and not leave you trampled underfoot. So with no further ado:

The Articles of the Revolution

Article One: Avoid Risk and Die

In times of change the greatest risk is to take none at all.

Risk is one of those words that to some sound bad and to others good. It's easy

---

* Not to be confused with "Punk Manifesto," an essay from 1998 by Dr. Gregory Walter Graffin III, better known as Greg Graffin, singer and founder of punk rockers Bad Religion. It's a good read, though, worth being confused with.

1

to ask others to take a risk but not so easy to take one yourself. (What's that Joe Jackson line about giving advice but never taking any yourself?) But in this revolution—no, actually, in *all* revolutions—risk is a necessity for anyone who wishes to come out from behind the barricades as the winner.

The trick is to take calculated jumps and share them among all stakeholders with your own blend of saucy verve and gusto.

So what's a calculated risk in these days of careful conglomeration? Not necessarily one checked out with consumers (if research were a prerequisite, would Sony *ever* have launched the Walkman or Ted Turner started CNN?—conventional wisdom says nah*) but one that has properly been thought through and discussed with those people involved with actually creating the thing. This is where sharing among the risk-taking stakeholders group is most needed.

Article Two: Why Not Ask "Why Not?"

Assumptions are just that. They are in no way true. Anything you assume is usually a half-truth or a generalization that once served a useful purpose but now hinders truly creative solutions.

One of the most innovative pieces of thinking in marketing in recent years was for Dove and its strangely titled Campaign for Real Beauty. Dove's dad, Unilever, took the fundamental rule of the beauty-products category—that women featured in marketing must be stick-model perfect to be effective role models—and asked why not try something made for controversy: use models that are unconventionally good-looking, even curvy? The result was a campaign that made women everywhere feel special about not conforming to conventional views of perfection.

Article Three: Take a Strong Stand

Trying to be all things to everyone inevitably results in meaning little to anybody.

---

* Turner once said: "There's never a reason for a study if your idea is conceptually sound. You have to have confidence in your own ideas. I never did a market study on CNN. I do my own marketing analysis." Finally some sense, Ted. (From South Africa's *Young Magazine*.)

Why did John Kerry lose that election? Many reasons, but more than anything we'll call it the way his rival strategists at the GOP played on the fear of the voters to keep a firm course of don't-screw-with-us action. But many observers said a significant reason for his death at the polls was Kerry's desire to be liked by everyone and his habit of flopping from one viewpoint to another with each situation that popped up in his hyperactive sight line. One minute he's talking about green issues until he's blue in the face, the next he's defending his family's ownership of gas-eating SUVs ("Gee whiz, it's my wife's").*

---

* Kerry told his supporters that he truly disliked gas-guzzling SUVs because they are just so poor for the environment. During a conference call with reporters, Kerry was asked whether he owned a Chevrolet Suburban. He replied, I don't own an SUV.... "The family has it. I don't have it."

Deciding what you want your brand to stand for must come from a firm set of well-thought-out beliefs you are prepared to defend on any battleground. So what if not everyone likes you? Most people don't like you anyway–they certainly don't dig us. Make those who *do* your loyal friends forever, and if you still need to be loved by newcomers, go out and start a new brand with equally strong but different positioning for those other wannabe lovers. Procter and Gamble lives by that credo and it works for them.

Article Four: Don't Pander

Customers are important but they are not necessarily right.

The really good news about being resolute is that people respect you for it even if they don't admit it. Respect from those who buy things is tough to get. Let us tell you a little secret: consumers like to be told what to do. They're actually slightly submissive and want a brand to take charge, push them into a corner, stand proud, thump its chest and say, "This is me and this is what I've got to offer."

What they don't like is being asked what they want–because they don't know! Henry Ford said it many years ago and it still holds true: "If I had asked my customers what they wanted, they'd have told me, 'a faster horse.'" (One of us owned that horse in the form of a Fiesta.)

Of course people like to be given choices, but that's different from coming off as being desperate to please everyone. Like, what's with these incessant price promotions, incentives, and cash-back offers that are all the rage with U.S. automakers? Distress marketing makes consumers think there's something wrong, pure and simple. Avoid it and folks will respect you again.

Article Five: Give Up Control

Consumers now control brands–end of debate. Smart marketers recognize this and embrace it rather than fight the powerful truth.

A long time ago (the nineties), there was a one-way process by which marketers and those providing content delivered their product to consumers. Consumers sat in front of their TVs or radios and were entertained. The marketing messages were a necessary evil, to fund what they enjoyed.

Then when the faceless TiVo machine and its offspring came along, viewers had a way to opt out of commercials altogether. At the same time the rise of alternative forms of content and ways of getting it let consumers become participants rather

than recipients, forcing more of a two-way conversation with the marketers and media moguls.

The once unspoken contract between providers and consumers has expired, and a new version has been written by the latter. No more cheap entertainment in exchange for their attention to what we sell! Thus any marketer needs to make its message as enjoyable as the content it funds and consumers will choose rather than just endure it—or click off.

Article Six: Expose Yourself

A relationship of trust between brand and consumer, like that between two people, is built upon honesty.

How strange that honesty has become such a rare commodity in relationships between commerce and consumers! We live in a bargain-hunting culture that has encouraged marketers to become hucksters and talk incessantly about the deal: how much money can be saved from a product or service that is the most unbelievable . . . thing . . . ever.* Unbelievable because, well, it's not really true. It's hype! Truth has become a powerful filter, and brands that don't pass muster are quickly disregarded for ones that pass it.

Prior to the mass immediate sharing of what-we-know that the Internet gave us, this was hardly a big deal; if the lowly buyer felt the product didn't live up to its hype, he or she might complain to the seller or maker. Today, via instant feedback on sites like Shopping.com and Buy.com, plus consumer opinions basically everywhere via blogs et al., you can instantly outweigh the impact of any carefully crafted marketing campaign by just shouting about how *It stinks* (e.g., PunkStinks.com).

The success of eBay is due to trust created between buyers and sellers through those damning or glorifying user-feedback ratings. Why would you pay money to perfect strangers if you saw they were *imperfect*?

Honesty, once a way to stand out, is now the point of entry! You, the smart

---

* Song Airways was a bust. Such a gorgeous idea: buy cheap plane tickets and have a glorious time. We know why Delta killed it! Bankrupt and pissed, Delta was getting crappy press while Song got huzzahs. Don't screw with Mama—or never look better than she does in the media.

revolutionary marketer, can earn the trust of cynical consumers and show you are open to feedback from them. As semiretired billionaire Bill Gates once muttered, "Your most unhappy customers are your greatest source of learning."

Amen, Billy.

Article Seven: Make Enemies

All brands need to position themselves against an alternative.

It may seem counterintuitive but having an enemy is a good thing for a brand.

One British workaholic, Richard Branson, is a master beyond comprehension at positioning his Virgin brands against the market leader in whatever category he dives into; so those competitors become his archenemy without fail. And what do you do to enemies? Fight them off with big sticks! When Sir Richard launched Virgin Cola in the United States, he took a full-page ad in the *New York Times* to challenge Coca-Cola's CEO to an arm-wresting match (loser quits the U.S. market, ha!).* Then he, Mussolini-like, drove a tank down Manhattan's Fifth Avenue to seek him out—cameras trailing him everywhere. Talk about serious cojones going against his enemies in this manner. We like.

Oh, and need we tell you? Sometimes the enemy need not be so obvious. For the antismoking campaign created by ad agency emeritus Crispin Porter + Bogusky for the busy State of Florida, the chosen foe was not the health risks of smoking—since a teen target audience already knew these and assumed the risks were greater than they actually were—but evil fibs spread by Big Tobacco. (See chapter 9 for more on the "Truth" campaign.)

Article Eight: Leave Them Wanting More

Avoid the temptation to reveal all of your assets at once. Or as the masters have said, you don't teach them everything you know. You teach them everything *they* know.

---

* Research has failed to uncover this ad, but we remember it, or think we do, or at least dreamt about it happening.

  If anyone has a copy, do send it along.

The temptation is for marketers to shout out all the brand's strengths rather than let consumers discover them over time. This always forsakes one of the most powerful marketing tools, the one we used back in high school to get sex: we're talking about the tease!

Reveal bits and pieces about who you are over time and leave some to the imagination. Ah, yes—mystery. Then you have a buyer who's "in" and will subsequently need to seek out more. Think of the skillful stripper slowly showing more of her assets and leaving an audience panting.

Putting salaciousness aside, just look: a brand has the same power to draw people in so that consumers want to pull and don't need anyone to push.

A big bad beast of a brand, Nike has learned to hold back to increase sexy appeal. The Air Force 1 sneaker is one of its biggest sellers, and still Nike manages supply carefully by keeping it real tight and releasing collectible versions just as Disney does with *Bambi*.

Article Nine: Outthink the Competition

Think smarter than the other dude.

Do not be led into temptation by the fast buck, Freddie; and don't outspend them. That is the definition of fool's gold.

A friend described advertising as the one remaining legal way to beat the crap out of your competition. Marketing executed by the best will always beat the pants off the lesser equivalent, no matter how gargantuan the opponent's budget.

Having a huge budget to play with merely tempts marketers to do two things they shouldn't: take only tried and tested (and, truthfully, dull) approaches; and treat consumers as a mass rather than a collection of individuals with tough-to-attend-to tastes.

See, when you're trying to reach large numbers of people, the temptation is to go after the lowest common denominator since that takes less work, which ultimately necessitates watering down any ole message until it is incomprehensible.

Why were online BMW films of a few years ago so life affirming when they first hit us smack on the head? Because they were created to reach a few thousand of the exact *right* sort: people with the money to buy a car like a BMW who were into performance and were avid Internet browsers and wanted a cheap (yeah, sure, okay,

Communication 101:
How to Stay Popular in an Age of Zero Talking

In a 2006 article in the *New York Times*, an editorialist mentioned that we are all too tied to the buzzing and ringing of our many devices. The line she used was "We are always pushing buttons."

No one is communicating anymore. We push out instead of speak to. We hope for a connection. We e-mix mail with calls and text messages and browsing. We're all doing something else when we should just be doing some talking. I guess we think we'll get our point across . . . somehow.

What can we do to communicate with substance in a world with so many choices and distractions? Businesspeople must rise up and take back subtlety:

1. Get a vibrating phone. Leave the noise pollution to construction sites and traffic jams.
2. Get a silent keyboard for the PDA.
3. During dinner, just sit there. Put down the device and pay attention to the person you're with. Maybe we can get to know each other better. We've become a society addicted to escape; it has to stop.
4. Do yourself a favor and don't prove yourself a bad speller. Especially with the spelling bee craze taking over pop culture. Spell-check e-mails. Take some time and let the person on the other end know you have a brain, even if it's working a mile a minute.
5. When you call someone on a VoIP (Internet) phone, remember these phones are not ready for prime time. You can't have an overlapping casual conversation on a VoIP phone, so if you are calling to, say, break up with someone, use a landline. You know it from *Seinfeld*, we get our examples from RL (real life).
6. If BlackBerrying while walking and you bump into someone, apologize. Say, "I'm sorry," and explain you are truly self-important and promise to work on it.
7. If you're asked a question, put everything down! Give undivided attention. It is an amazing way of showing someone you care about them. Respond after giving it some thought and in a complete, coherent sentence. You'll see quick appreciation for this, and you will have

SIDEBAR

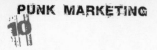
more success at getting your point across. You do have a point, right?

8. Stop using language you read in *Fast Company*. Buzzwords and catchphrases say, "I'm not sure what I'm talking about, but here are some cool words to make you feel like the idiot here."

9. When an e-mail comes in that you want to respond to, either high-flag it or send back an answer. Now. Do whatever it takes to remember to write someone back, or risk burning a bridge. People hate being snubbed as much with electronic communication as in the in-person world.

10. When you discover someone is not listening to you, *bust* them. Shake your head. The more we tolerate poor communicative behavior, the more people will continue.

11. Skipping town is no excuse to stop checking e-mail. If you still haven't gotten a proper WAP-enabled mobile device, we will wait while you go to a local coffee shop. Or pick up a laptop. You can get those little suckers for around four hundred bucks.

12. Don't answer your mobile, "Hi, Mark," because you know who it is. Considering everyone has caller ID it is no longer a novelty act. It is not only jarring and obnoxious, but also a terrible attempt at trying to get "hand," as Costanza said.

13. Stop making it all about you. (It's all about us.) The one you're communicating with is smarter than you think. When you write someone and they see "Ah, he wants something from me," they move on. Try meaning it when you ask someone, "How are you?" When people reply, remember to listen. See number 11.

14. When e-mailing a friend or colleague, choose one topic and end it. People have trouble responding to more than one thought.

15. Everyone should do a conference call standing up! Plus, IM-ing is tremendously helpful for reminding folks they are due at a conference call or to tell someone his fly is open. But otherwise it's something that gives us, ah,  you know, continual partial . . . What was I going on about? Oh—CPA. Continual partial attention.

16. Why send people things *you* want them to read? Chain letters and viral e-mails are irksome time-wasters. If you think a heartbreaking tale of a Nigerian village boy who needs a thousand dollars to reach our homeland to see his family again is true . . .

17. *Don't make it tough to reach you.* Create a free e-mail account (We vote for Gmail. Not AOL. It doesn't exactly scream "We mean business!") and make it public. If you're really so important and busy, you should be thankful that anyone wants to know you.

18. If you really want to upset someone, then don't respond after they say something nasty. . . .

19. If you want to reach someone, and you get nothing after lobbing an e-mail, it doesn't mean you're *snubbed*. If you really want to reach someone, pick up the phone and you'll get "I didn't see your mail." E-mailing is not the final word.

20. Use the mute key. No one wants to hear you snort or chortle.

21. Now review these. We'll wait.

SIDEBAR

expensive) thrill in driving. BMW was not targeting regular drivers who saw autos as appliances.

Of course those shorts got mentioned endlessly via editorial coverage, which was really what BMW wanted. Even if this didn't translate into large numbers of people downloading them, it started a trend. Everyone wanted to be an innovative company like BMW. Earned media coverage via PR canceled out the many millions their marketing group shelled out to produce these minimasterpieces; the company claims to have far exceeded their sales goals.

Article Ten: Don't Be Seduced by Technology

The *media* is not the message anymore. The message is the message is the message.

As we have said and will often say again, technology is the catalyst for the shift of power from commerce and content providers to consumers. But—but!—the content is always most important and not the medium by which it is delivered. Please reread that sentence, satellite radio.

For instance, many marketers have embraced the blog (or the video blog) as a modern way to reach consumers, and yet while certainly a way of reaching some of the fragmented target, its effectiveness as a marketing tool is in doubt by everyone (even the honest bloggers). The power of a blog is only as strong as the credibility of its content and the intake of its participants. If the content is created by a marketer,

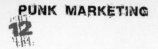

for instance, it is no more believable than a pathetic *ad*. Just because the format is new doesn't mean the cynicism is withheld.

Article Eleven: Know Who You Are

If you don't understand what it is that you are good at, you might be tempted to try to be something you are plainly not.

Many if not most brands reach a crescendo where they become so successful that they forget why people bought them in the first place. Gap Corporation created well-made, affordable basics for years and added an element of style to the brand through iconic advertising reflecting simplicity—there were loads of T-shirts for people who just enjoyed life and their ads were musical, funny, and, to use a cliché that fits, snappy. The whole idea was "We accessorize you. Buy from us instead of doing laundry." Brilliant! They were peerless for a while but then their perceived competition intensified—particularly from big-box retailers Target, Wal-Mart, and even small boxes like Kohl's—so they shifted their product offering to be fashion-conscious and, splash, missed the boat. Even with superstylish marketing the brand lost touch with a simple reality: their clothes weren't that cool.

Von Dutch Originals took a cool, underground label and brought it to mainstream by branding everything and everyone that they could with the VD logo and opening up single-minded stores. Sure enough, poof, Puff Diddy stopped caring or wearing, everyone got sick of seeing them everywhere, the shops were sloppily designed by kids, and Von Dutch killed any chance of long-term success with a quick killing.

That in business is known as Rape, Pillage, and Plunder. And it's sure messy.

Article Twelve: No More Marketing Bullshit

Get to the point. Express it clearly and simply. Einstein said—we believe he meant marketers—"Things should be made as simple as possible, but not any simpler."

Our duty to consumers (and to our makers) is to cut through and make sense of an increasingly complex world before *choice paralysis* sets in.

Let's start by using clear language and terms for the Punk Marketing Revolution, which you are free to share with friends and close enemies.

PUNK—an attitude of rebellion against tradition.

MARKETING—the practice of encouraging consumers to buy products.

PUNK MARKETING—a new form of marketing that rejects the status quo and recognizes the shift in power from corporations to consumers.

PRODUCT—something a marketer is trying to sell.

BRAND—something a consumer buys into. In other words, the brand is how consumers perceive the product.

CONVERGENCE—increasing blurring of the lines among commerce, content, and consumers.

CONSUMERS—the people in control.

STAKEHOLDER—those who should share the marketing problem and its inherent solution.

CREATIVITY—part of marketing mistakenly reserved for the end of a process but that is better used from the very start.

Article Thirteen: Don't Let Others Set Your Standards

Sorry to tell you this, but good no longer means anything, while mediocre does more harm than doing nothing. We'll repeat that: mediocre does more harm than doing nothing.

The cry that the thirty-second spot is plain dead is likely exaggerated (even though it was just mentioned) and has almost led to a giant baby being thrown out with much soapy water. In fact, the dirty water that deserves to be thrown out are those intrusive ads that plague consumers wherever they go, be they in front of the TV, in the cinema, in their cars listening to the radio, at the 7-Eleven, walking down the street, waiting on the telephone, watching a game at the stadium, etc.

That baby is advertising.

The problem is the amount of *bad* advertising that is allowed to air.

Just watch CNN for half an hour and witness how appalling almost everything is—ads, showbiz-infused content, bad hair, fake friendly talking *at* us, everything. The breaks are endless. The ads are repeated and they scream, "We advertisers have our thumbs up our asses!" Everything is insulting to our intelligence.

Go to the multiplex, sit through the ads, and see how used and abused you feel by the start of the movie. Then go to a cinema in the UK and notice that most people turn up to view those commercials. Because they are actually fun—sensible and intriguing and full of messages that make people applaud. Yes, shout out with glee! These are entertaining, funny, well-produced, and cool. Four terms you'd never use to describe an ad at movies in the US of A today.

This shows us consumers will actually go out of their way to watch good ads. Here in the United States at least 95 percent* of TV, cinema, and radio commercials are so bad, it's surprising people haven't done more than just boo and hiss; we keep hoping for legislation to stop the madness!†

Therefore, it is our duty as marketers to raise standards of our advertising and all marketing efforts to no less than excellence. This merits marketing based on ideas that are really smart and involve some sweat and effort. Our ads have to have a point and a reason for folks to wish they'd come on. The execution must be flawless! We will treat our audiences with respect! And not a little fear!

Our Punk advice: sacrifice quantity of runs for quality of product.

One fabulous ad run a handful of instances is so much more powerful than a mediocre one run so many times that people roll their eyes upon its reemergence.‡

---

* This is a made-up figure as *good* and *bad* are subjective terms, but in our view we're being overgenerous and the actual figure is nearer 99 percent!

† In mid-2006, an episode of *The Closer* on TNT earned 8.6 million viewers, more than any drama show on basic cable—ever. Why? There were no ads shown, and it was heavily promoted as such.

‡ An August 2005 study by MediaCheck, called Project Wanamaker (after department-store magnate John Wanamaker, who reputedly said, "Half the money I spend on advertising is wasted; the trouble is I don't know which half"), found a significant number of TV spots reach saturation long before they finish airing.

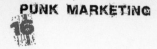

Piss-poor ads—those that dumb down messages for that maligned "audience"—not only harm the brand, they make it less likely that consumers will ever care.

Article Fourteen: Use the Tools of the Revolution

Go write your own manifesto. Remind yourself of its articles whenever you lack resolve.

Every marketer needs a manifesto tailored to the brand. Like your new pal, the Punk Marketing Manifesto, which you can steal from since you paid for it,* it has to state with clarity and ferocity the guidelines by which your marketing should and will live.

Accept that change is always difficult to bring to fruition when it involves taking some bizarre attempt at newness, which is finally what good marketing should always do. Marketing as an avocation from 8 a.m. to 8 p.m. has suffered because the field has forced itself to become a pseudoscience to bridge the sometimes-felt chasm between business and creativity. There will always be a leap of faith where measurement and metrics fail, and this makes decisions in marketing vulnerable to anyone requiring a fact-based life.

As a true marketing revolutionary you need to create your own resource tool chest of the best information and people.

The old tools are blunt and ineffective. For instance, it is no longer possible to use only media that can be measured in reach and frequency, for two valid reasons. One, the measurement system is still, despite Nielsen's attempts to improve it, hardly perfect. It can at best yield a rough approximation of how many people may be viewing a TV show live. At this reading it includes TV shows watched later, but does not account for the attention paid to messages by viewers—again, only who turns away during which three-minute pee breaks. Second, only a few mediums have metrics, and each uses different and subjective criteria of measurement, making it beyond tough to compare one with the other. But, more important, useful mediums are plumb ignored, resulting in the temptation to see them as too risky to dive into as an advertiser. Gee, Beav, that's like looking for mislaid car keys only in places where the light is really bright because it's too hard to search in the dark.

---

* If you borrowed us, sorry, go to PunkMarketing.com/beggar.

But this is not to discount the role of hard data about our consumers, our brand, our market, our competitors, and about how real-time convergence is changing the game on a weekly—no, scrap that, daily . . . no, wait, hourly—basis!

Yet we must avoid becoming anesthetized by information overload and being tempted to flee back to old methods of marketing that in the past served us so well.

Oh, and surround yourself with the smartest people you can find. Throughout this tome we'll highlight those sources relevant to each topic and companies that are creating examples that are the best in their class. You can view a list of resources at PunkMarketing.com/friends. Yeah, we send you to a lot of places on the Web to find stuff. Work it, baby.

Article Fifteen: The Question Mark, O Participant

This is where you help. The point of this revolution is to make it about interaction and not dictation; so tell us what you think the last article should be. Post to PunkMarketing.com/article15; or see articlefifteen.com for the full list.

Punk is . . .

Introducing some managed chaos into the
workplace to unshackle people's thinking.

Taking a day out of the office (with the CrackBerry
off, please!) to do something completely different
but stimulating—an art gallery, a movie, a hike—
and let your mind make creative connections
to go at problems in a new way.

[to be continued]

Tasty Morsels

- One of the major prizewinning flicks at the 2004 Sundance Film Festival cost about $7,000 to make.

- Crafty consumers are using home computers to create ads that rival those created by big agencies and posting them on sites like YouTube and Metacafe.

- There are tens of millions of blogs on the Internet, and the number is growing exponentially.

- Companies use the feedback from blogs to aid product development—and doesn't that mean that we consumers are powerful?

- Buyers can make money by selling ads in blogs and other places online in which companies can reach small, pertinent groups of like-minded consumers.

- Podcasting too, where anybody can create audio content on and for MP3 players when they want to (make it or listen to it or watch it), is changing the role of traditional media as the gatekeepers to consumers.

- Warm man Al Gore's barely watched Current TV lets viewers make programming and create ads that run during it.

- Social network sites such as Xanga, MySpace, Bebo, Grouper, and FaceBook are attracting huge numbers of young users. MySpace is of course one of the most popular sites on the Web, wholly gotten to this point in history through fabulous, time-released PR.

Kill the Middlemen
Do So before They Kill You

What a joy it is to see those two iconic iPods as they spin across the screen, perfectly choreographed to the music track "Tiny Machine" by eighties pop band Darling Buds. The sixty seconds viewed is a celebration of the tiny MP3 player's size, looks, and music-playing ability. Golly, the agency sure did a fantastic job making it desirable no matter what mood you are in.

Except it wasn't Apple's ad firm that made this thing! It didn't come from an ad agency at all, but rather was the work of George Masters, a talented high school teacher from the real O.C. He teaches Web design and graphics, and in his spare time, an hour here, an hour there, over five months he created that ad of all that huffing and puffing with the machines having the time of their lives . . . then he dropped it on his personal site.

After influential blogs started shouting about it, a viral hoopla pushed the bit to those big mouths of the world. People started noticing and within weeks tens of thousands had seen George's hobby.

Of course Apple hasn't yet given the advertising account to Masters, nor have they stopped to shout, "Stop! TM infringement!" or to criticize the gall of George. And why would anyone in his right mind? The piece is wonderful, clearly a celebration of one of their products. We smart marketers see the Web as one big wet T-shirt proclaiming a slogan.

Let's take the case of nineteen-year-old Minneapolis-bred Tyson Ibele, who created a Sony "commercial" as a way to nab a job at a production company. Tyson

posted it on his site and it got the attention of many senior executives at Sony, who were duly impressed if not dumbfounded by how talented he was. Tyson's strategy worked. He now has a job at Minneapolis-based animation and visual effects production house MAKE LLC.

In an interview with *Ad Age*, Sony's marketing chief, Mike Fasulo, shouted out, "Agencies beware. It's a great reinvention. . . . These are the folks we want to tap into speaking to each other—let's put them to work on their terms, not ours."[1]

More and more—and even more—consumers are now not consumers but content creators and distributors of really good material too; they simply avoid all traditional channels to let their voices be heard. The role of the middleman who manages the stream of communication is so much less important now, if not redundant or purely quaint.

It's called disintermediation, and it is the avoiding of that man in the middle. The D word became popular during the first dot-com boom as people used the Internet to reach out without going through what was perceived to be the same old channels.

All of us have a slew of technologies at our call and beck that let us create and distribute content—and pan content we hate—that would only a few years ago have been dreamy.

We like to remind folks how the software needed to create the special effects on the 1995 movie *Babe* was apparently available to amateurs on their home PCs at the time the sequel came out three years later. Also, *Primer*, a surprise winner of 2004's Sundance Festival Dramatic Grand Jury Prize, beat some high-profile competitors such as Zach Braff's mightily hyped *Garden State,* and yet according to auteur Shane Carruth the former cost about as much as a used car.*

Pretty soon all we'll have to do is license the synthetic likeness of our favorite actress to create a flick on our home computer that looks the same or better than her usual Hollywood blather.

It's not that your home-produced film will automatically get a big distributor—there aren't many Shane Carruths. But there are easy ways to get your film

---

* Reportedly around $7,000.

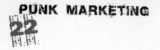

shown on the Web. At MTV Networks' AtomFilms.com, like so many home-baked Web sites, filmmakers can get their movies seen by a potentially large audience simply by uploading it, and qualifying films get an advance payment and royalties each time they're viewed just as with an Amazon.com affiliate.*

AtomFilms even funds ideas from filmmakers they dig. Simply pitch them by e-mail. Even if these actions do not replace Hollywood, they are fine training grounds for those who have a vision; some of AtomFilm's alumni have gone on to big things. In an example replete with nepotism, Jason Reitman directed star-studded and critically acclaimed *Thank You for Smoking* in 2005 (Ivan of *Ghostbusters* fame is Dad) after a few shorts appeared à la Atom.

Budding filmmakers can upload their own movies on iFilm.com and YouTube.com, the Google-owned site that "allows" users to upload, tag, and share personal video clips proudly displayed—and subsequently distributed around the Internet. In just a year after launching, it shot up to become one of the most visited sites on the planet and now cashes in on that interest through advertising revenue and deals with the likes of NBC Universal to promote TV shows. On the site you can create your own personal video network of films to share with friends and family as you once did with e-mail chains and photo spreads. See such delights as *The Easter Bunny Hates You*, a short home video of the Easter Bunny attacking innocent bystanders viewed nearly a million times. Or comedian Judson Laipply's *Evolution of Dance*, which was posted early April 2006 and by mid-June had been viewed 25 million times. This for a clip six minutes long that cost nothing but video-by-phone time to make.

Marketers, ignore this at your peril. Sticking with content created by the media megaliths just won't cut it anymore. Consumers now have the means to create their own content, and the smart marketers can either find ways to join them or be trampled underfoot. In 2004, Nike Inc. subsidiary Converse Shoes chose a new ad agency in Butler, Shine, Stern & Partners, who had a brilliant, if not lazy, idea to get consumers to create the ads for them. It was pretty clever too! The BSSP

---

* Every Tom, Dick, and hairy creature online has an affiliate deal with the big A. That's why your name pops up so often when you Google yourself. Via affiliation, each sale "gotten" through a site on the way to Amazon gets the site owner a fraction of a penny. Those of you who've ever published a word and had it sold by Amazon know that already.

invited consumers to create twenty-four-second films celebrating "the spirit of Converse and the Chuck Taylor All-Star Shoe." The appearance of the sneaker in submitted films was not mandatory. Makers of mini-spots subsequently selected to appear on TV—which had a Converse tag added to them—were given ten grand (or "no money at all" in advertising).

The campaign was huge for the sneaker manufacturer and led to a 40 percent spike in site traffic and a striking 12 percent increase in sales during the quarter immediately following the launch of this gimmick.

There were some gripes in the blogosphere that the Converse films weren't all consumer-generated since it was found that one film posted on the contest site was indeed created by the originating agency itself. But that bit of whining aside, lots of positive buzz was created about the brand in one fell swoop.

So it gave Converse a serious choice here: Do they keep a firm grip on the brand's wholly outdated "Who cares?" message of we're the best sneaker, or take a risk and allow consumers to shape the brand anew?

But a brand is formed in the eye of the beholder—the consumer—and is not the property of the marketer. The marketer is simply a temporary caretaker who has newly awakened to the fact that the lord of the manor just came home.

Converse went far with this, and it paid off handsomely. The campaign was a recipient of a prestigious EFFIE Award in 2005* for its effectiveness in increasing sales, and two years after its launch the "Brand Democracy" campaign is still running. Some of the hundreds of films submitted can be viewed at converse.com/gallery.

They have not been the only ones to enlist consumers as barely paid ad staff with no benefits. The Ban deodorant brand, bought by KAO Brands Company in 2005, recently invited consumers to submit their own custom ads on what they would like to *ban,* the best of which ran on a site with the winners featured in *Us Weekly.* Ban's assistant marketing director, P. J. Katien, told the *Wall Street Journal* that in the past the formula for marketing to young female consumers was "you explained the benefit and explained the product and they would buy it. Now it's about getting her to feel she is involved. No more one-way messaging."

---

* Started in 1968 by the New York American Marketing Assoc. (www.effie.org).

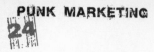

Detergent Identity Crisis (Out, Out, Damn Stain)

Ever wish you could find a laundry detergent you can really identify with? One cleaning buddy you bring home to your family? No, neither have we. So why have two popular brand-name laundry detergents adopted an Internet campaign with as much cool factor as a Coke ad from the Doris Day era? We have no idea.

Gain and Borax are trying something ~~desperate~~ new. They've each launched promotions online with a twist that would never have worked in traditional media, mostly because the ideas are so antiquated.

Borax is giving away, via kickslikeamule.com, $2,000 toward a new washer and dryer. The Kicks Like a Mule contest is a promotional campaign for their 20 Mule Team Borax, a cleaning and freshening additive for your normal detergent. In its silly game, the participant tries to get an animated mule to kick an old washing machine over a clothesline. It's all kind of boring—an annoying twist on finding information from prospects, which then enters you in a sweepstakes for the two grand. The game and the sad-looking mule are ploys to attract an online audience who, according to the people at Borax, apparently need sleep-inducing entertainment to become customers.

For giggles, www.ilovegain.com is the next stop. The launch of the new type of Gain is really titled Gain: Joyful Expressions and is now accompanied by a badly produced site, which asserts that the company ran out of mail samples to promote how fantastic the new product is. With scents like Apple Mango Tango and Gardenia Delight, the people at Gain are hoping we can have an entirely new experience with our laundry.

Here's where the laughing stops. We're not exactly sure what they mean by new experience with laundry. They encourage consumer participation with a comments section so that those of us nearest to a coma can fill out catchy Joyful Expressions, such as "Nothing makes life stress-free more than fresh Apple Mango Tango bedsheets!" and "The sassy scent of Gain brightens your day like your mother's warm smile." Creepy, but they didn't ask us for our advice.

We imagine all the high fives at Gain's corporate marketing office because they're so darn clever. But, alas, they will rue the day they used joyful expressions to make us feel that Gain folks are fresh.

Will the type of detergent we use ever change our opinion about doing laundry? We hate doing it but we do it, it's an accepted norm like flushing the toilet, so give us a product that works. We do not need to love the detergent the way we love our cars, nor do we need to identify with it the way we do our chocolate milk brand. No matter how fancy the site is or how much money you might give us, we're still going to see you as laundry detergent. So for the sake of consumers everywhere, stop trying so hard and spend money on R & D.

They're behaving like the unpopular kid at school we want to beat up when they should be like the science teacher we respect because he knows his shit.

SIDEBAR

The promotion resulted in over four thousand entries and a truly wild 13 percent jump in sales.[2]

Government Employees Insurance Company, or GEICO, an insurance company managed by a lizard and a wholly-owned subsidiary of Warren E. Buffet's Berkshire Hathaway Inc., wished for a way to reach the eighteen to thirty-four-year-old young-adult audience who had previously ignored those too adorable commercials that run every six seconds. So they invited the younger types to create short films they could run online and allotted such prizes as a trip to Hawaii, cash, portable DVD players, and LCD televisions as the bait.

And the Cadillac division of General Motors had an "Under 5" promotion where consumers created films that were five seconds long to communicate the impressive 0–60 mph acceleration—in five seconds, right?—of their V Series. It was part of a copromotion for another Travolta fiasco, *Be Cool*, and the five-second entries were judged by the director and cast, including Mr. Greased Lightning himself. The winning film was aired as part of a national campaign. According to Cadillac, the promotion resulted in a 358 percent increase in Web traffic and over forty thousand "incremental requests" for information on the car.

Mozilla Corp., distributors of open-source browser Firefox, is to some extent the epitome of a world without middlemen. Like the operating system Linux, the Firefox software was created, they say, for the people and by the people. So what better way to promote the Firefox launch than for Mozilla to create a site for donations so "they could all" place an ad in the *New York Times*. Strange but germane—and the plea worked. After 10 days the deluge of small donations flooding in from ten thou-

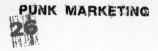

sand self-appointed helpers was enough for a two-page ad in the paper of record, which is no cheap feat.*

And there's more. In early 2006, Mozilla launched a contest for users to create their own thirty-second spots for the browser, which it dubbed Firefox Flicks video contest, with a grand prize of $5,000. The winner, *Daredevil,* was a well-produced short by Pete Macomber about a young woman's passion for surfing and for the Firefox browser. Pete used the original tagline "My other browser is a surfboard."

These are initiatives where consumers are invited to be integral in branding. If they hadn't been asked to, they would have been tempted to take matters into their own hands, simply because they don't appreciate the marketers doing it themselves! (Ask the people who've created an antibrand ad or the SprintStillSucks.com site and they'll shrug and say the marketers didn't understand them!)

Soon after the Coca-Cola Company's CEO, E. Neville Isdell, vowed to improve its marketing, a group of outsiders did it for him. A guy called Harry Webber, together with folks from within and outside the ad industry, sent Coke an unsolicited "A Cool American" campaign. Webber founded Smart Communications to do what he thought Madison Avenue was no longer doing: being evangelists for creative thinking in America. The bad part—his ads were hackneyed. The copy consisted of such lines as "Loves Deals. Hates Games. Drinks Coke. Runs Late. Thinks,"—and images were Photoshopped businessmen walking daintily on a sidewalk. But nonetheless his philosophy was right.

One Toronto agency went further by running an unsolicited commercial on TV (they *paid* for the time). Vaughn Whelan & Partners created a spot for Canadian national treasure Molson beer as a way to showcase the group's creative skills and told Molson Breweries of their intentions before running it twice. Molson requested them to cease, please.

The ruse, done to get in on a closed agency review, didn't work, since Molson

---

* A two-page mono ad in the paper would cost about $80,000. The campaign was described in the ad column of the *New York Times* under the heading "Unauthorized campaigns used by unauthorized creators to show their creativity become a trend" on December 23, 2004, thus granting Firefox more exposure in their paper of choice!

did not invite them to the closed party. Vaughn got coverage and expensively raised the agency's profile.

Of course sometimes consumer-created content can go where marketers are unwilling to traverse. Volkswagen threatened to sue the makers of an unsolicited commercial for the German-made Polo when the ad began getting *too much* attention on the Web in 2005. The badly timed "suicide bomber" spot, as it came to be known, displayed a man of Middle Eastern appearance driving in his Polo to a restaurant and detonating the bomb wrapped around himself. After a muffled explosion the car itself remained intact. This was followed by VW's existing tagline, "Small but tough." The spot, done by prospective admen Dan Brooks and Lee Ford as a self-promotion, was meant to be anonymous, but after a London newspaper revealed their identities, they had to apologize to the carmaker and insist this had not been meant for public viewing. Sounds vague to us.

Taking the Gate off Its Hinges

It's not just agencies or advertisers being caught in the cross fire between consumers and middlemen. The mainstream media are finding that consumer-made content is having an effect on their role as the traditional middlemen. The rise of these never-ending blogs and podcasts as respected forms of "citizen journalism" means that the media are no longer the sole gatekeepers to news, information, and opinion.

The blog was merely a form of Web journal that had been around nearly nine years when it came of age during the '04 presidential race; the influence that blogs had to sway opinion was recognized, and amazingly bloggers got invited to attend national political convention events along with the fourth estate members (traditional newspaper and wire-service writers, broadcasters and pundits). The bloggers' presence among the *real* journalists became the story itself for the traditional media, who had nothing but dull political nothingness going on around them.

Bloggers also jumped into a happy spotlight when they unmasked CBS Broadcasting and Dan Rather for covering a fake memo about President George W. Bush's Army Reserve records. It was all blog all the time in 2004. Katie Couric, she who has taken over for Rather, has been thanking these pajama-wearing opinion makers ever since.

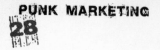
According to data compiled by blog-search biggie Technorati, in August 2006 there were over fifty million blogs with the number doubling every six quick months. At that rate according to their calculations, there'll be over one hundred million by the time you are sitting with us.* With the way the world can't stop crowing about bloggers, companies are finding what's written about their products and corporate images in blogs can have a quickly felt effect on their businesses.

As is often the case, companies find after a crisis that rather than pretend that negative opinions expressed in blogs do not exist, they are better used as tools for learning what consumers think. (For the DVD firm Netflix, discovering a way to give information to the guy behind HackingNetflix.com was not only handy, but decisive. According to those close to the situation, Hacking was felt to be a pain in the ass until Netflix realized that playing nice with him made the bloger a fan, friend, and admirer†. And, for years movie studios have been looking at what blogs say about pending releases to see which are generating buzz (er . . . *Snakes on a Plane*,‡ anyone?) and which are going to have their remaining marketing budgets shit-canned and the money shifted to buzz-y projects!

Technologies are available to track what's being said in blogs as well as in chat rooms, and even in proprietary services such as AOL, on message boards, and on so-called product-review sites. An article in the *Washington Post* discussed how ConAgra Foods Inc., by monitoring online chatter, saw low-carb dieting was on the way out.[3] This led them to promote its popular Healthy Choice brand soups, entrées, and lunchmeats more than previously planned. Real-time software devices give companies such as ConAgra an edge and ability to search and tabulate postings made on the Net and react according to the buzz.

Nielsen BuzzMetrics, a company trying to create a global measurement standard for consumer-generated content, boasts it can determine incidence and tone of online opinions expressed in blogs and elsewhere. Some human-touch companies (or, consultants) also advise companies on how to respond if bloggers attack their products,

---

* There have been criticisms about Technorati's research methodology, and it's probable that the actual number of active blogs is way smaller. But it's still a lot!

† The DVD supplier runs ads on HN now. Not so oddly, so does Blockbuster.

‡ When the movie bombed, this proved that people putting up sites are showing off—they aren't fans.

"You've Got—Uh, Er, Nothing to Say"

America Online announced in April of 2006 that it would officially change its corporate name to the shorter and more easily identified by largely senile subscribers to AOL. It's a moment for marketers to ponder. Who has time for lengthy company names when fighting past the pop-up ads one is bombarded with when logging on? Yes, AOL subscriptions are free, but somehow its management still thinks AOL is a brand worth writing press releases about. You want a better Internet, as they used to say.

Jonathan F. Miller, at the time chief executive of AOL LLC, made this statement while springing this really exciting and now neutered news on the masses: "Our new cor-  porate identity better reflects our expanded mission—to make everyone's online experience better." How exactly does the changing of their name from two words to three letters reflect anything different about the company other than their disdain for big words? Will they feel freer to behave differently with this new identity, much like a stripper who in her professional life goes by the name Anastasia? Or perhaps this would better be compared to the aging father letting his son call him by his first name instead of the respectful title of Dad.

This isn't news. Nor was it news when Game Show Network became GSN or The Learning Channel became TLC or American Movie Classics became AMC, etc., etc. And even Outdoor became OLN, which we think takes time to figure out (and thus less time spent outdoors), and has now changed its name to Versus—to which we respond, "versus what?"

AOL LLC is two clinging fists slowly losing their grip on a consumer base with growing intelligence. It's a sly maneuver to get a company into the news and make everyone think they've got some tricks up their sleeves. The doves likely died a long time ago for good old America O . . . Sorry, AOL.

Rant over.

by identifying the powerful and pointing out the jokers. These firms duly establish a constructive relationship with bloggers—it's often done by holding their hands.

We recommend getting in front of the blogosphere and having blogs written about a firm's products with a free hand by a trusted source within the company. It's an informal and honest way of connecting with consumers.

Generals Motors vice-chairman Bob Lutz has his own blog, FastLane, which

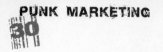

seems as if he authors it. This regularly updated journal is well received by outsiders because it has thoughts from a senior executive whom people are intrigued by. The old days of "From the Desk Of" memos by intermediaries, and stodgy official public statements, are gone for good. Lutz even cheerfully includes negative remarks he receives from consumers. Similarly, Robert Scoble, a highly respected technology blogger who tells it pretty straightforwardly, was at one time employed by Microsoft to write about all of their existing, new, and forthcoming products, including warts. The self-described "technical evangelist" Scobleizer stated for years that all opinions were his own and weren't read or edited before posting by anyone paying him.

If blogs from the POV of official spokespeople such as Lutz and Scoble (who left Microsoft in June 2006 to "vlog" or video-blog full-time at media company PodTech) can gently push products with honesty, then an unofficial blog from a runaway company employee can get the firm into hot water, especially when the company's known for secrecy—like Google Inc.

Soon after joining G, new employee Mark Jen, an associate product manager in the company's AdSense advertising unit, used his Ninetyninezeros blog to chronicle his experiences in the company. In it he criticized the health-care plan and the free-meal offering, which he claimed were an enticement for employees to stay late. Google simply fired him for his troubles.[4]

Yet it didn't end there. The blogging community went haywire on Google for its actions, and Jen soon found work elsewhere—helping Internet contact service Plaxo Inc. coordinate its blogging efforts in their own marketing strategy.

BMOC Google didn't want or need the attention, but struggling Plaxo saw a positive in Jen's abilities—and the PR that followed him there.

There's money to be made for enterprising bloggers, and there are opportunities for marketers to reach those who read and interact with them. Someone with a blog can make a few bucks, for instance, by letting in ads from Google on their pages (strange, but there aren't any on Jen's blog).

Yahoo! Inc. and Microsoft Corp. have also been busy catching up to Google and are now selling space to advertisers who wish to reach niche audiences; it doesn't get much more specific than this.

The Punk knows it's always better to connect in small numbers than irritate in large. The New York Times Company is also building up its offering to advertisers in this area and in February 2005 agreed to buy About Inc. (About.com) from publisher PriMedia Inc. for $410 million. The veteran Net company About, a series of five hundred and counting specialized sites by every type of expert you can imagine, seemed like a good fit for the Web-moving Times Company. Now, along with journalism, so-called experts are available to give you "other knowledge" that is hardly journalistic.

Well-established blogs that generate tons of traffic have been known to do lucrative sponsorship deals directly with advertisers; it's a grassroots way of doing business where the bloggers themselves call companies and say, "Let's play."

Nick Denton's always-newsy Gawker Media, for instance, which is host to many Web logs based around the world, has inked deals with Nike and Absolut vodka and many of the big gaming sites that are called illegal by U.S. legislatures; as far as Gawker is concerned, anyone with a cleared check can play on Gawker's blogs.

In 2005 Sony's sponsorship of Gawker Media's Lifehacker blog—which includes recommendations on software downloads and other sites that save time—included ad placements on the Gizmodo blog (all about gadgets and devices) and reportedly reaps the Gawker folks a sweet $25,000 per month from the electronics conglomerate.

Citizen journalists sometimes act as reporters in the field, delivering news and images ahead of the regular media. During the 2004 Asian tsunami disaster, thousands of people caught up in the horrors of the day posted digital pictures and film footage long before professional photojournalists were on the scene. Japanese news organizations made quick use of the images, and MSNBC threw them up on its site. That's how it began its page devoted to news stories posted by outside contributors, a standard practice now.

Then in 2005, during the terrible bomb attacks on London underground trains and buses, many people present sent digital pictures and film footage from their cell phones of the aftermath, many of which were immediately posted on BBC and Sky News sites as "news."

In the end, the blogs are places people love to visit, so that makes them a serious business that no one can ignore. The days of writing on your personal site as a hobby . . . well, people still do that, but, gosh, look at all the opportunities for both writer and marketer!

A company specializing in connecting marketers with bloggers is BlogAds, a

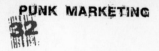
network of blogging enthusiasts who write on subjects ranging from music to politics. CEO Henry Copeland says the best ads are the ones that are appropriate to the spirit of the medium. An effective blog placement does not interrupt. It might look like a blog *within* the blog itself and link to other sites that have previously given "props" about the product being advertised.

To make effective use of this undefined medium, marketers must recognize that a huge reason why blogs are so popular is their unobtrusive and stripped-down-bare way of delivering information or opinion or both. A marketer worth his spit should maintain this style rather than attempt to change the flow with brash or jarring sales and PR pitches. A shrewd one will identify the most influential blogs, period, and treat these as they would a reporter from a respected off-line venue.

Just feed them information and exclusives; make the bloggers feel they have the edge and are "in on" what's happening. Marketing pros can empower these citizen journalists and in doing so let them build the brand, thus becoming an unofficial, yet hugely influential, sales force. Anytime you "present" as if your target is captured prey . . . you lost him/her.

Recognizing the value that consumer content adds, Korean online media service called OhmyNews, founded by a Mr. Oh (for real!), augments articles from fifty or so staff with reports from thousands of popular "reporters" around the country. It now gets over 750,000 visitors each day (oh my!).

Regular joes are creating content for everyone to consume at any time, day or night, and not necessarily while staring at their monitors. Podcasting means people have every imaginable kind of audio or video automatically delivered to them via feed, which is downloaded onto their iPods or other MP3s for listening to at leisure. Podcasts are already becoming a tried and tested way for sponsorships and advertising of all kinds.

One of the pioneers of podcasting, former MTV VJ Adam Curry of OnRamp and ModemMedia fame* runs a network called PodShow, with over fifty of the

---

* Curry, who owned "MTV.com" before Viacom asked for it back, was famous for usurping the Coke and McDonald's URLs in the early days of the Web before companies realized their value; he eventually made a fortune in creating Web-based brand initiatives for companies he had originally pissed off. Very can't live with/out scenario.

most-listened-to podcasts, including his own *Daily Source Code* (a show about him and the world of podcasting) and *The Dawn and Drew Show* (a show about nothing much, recorded by husband-and-wife team Dawn Miceli and Drew Domkus).*

The Internet-access company EarthLink Inc. advertises on *Daily Source Code* and has been persuaded to let consumers create the ads that it runs. This came about after listeners loudly criticized the dull EarthLink spots on his show, so Curry and company urged them to let listeners try it themselves.

In this experiment people voted on their favorites and the winners got cash. One notch in the belt of the middlemen-murderers!

While content created by consumers has mostly been confined to the Web, as the Converse and Cadillac film contests demonstrate, it has also spilled over into the traditional. Environmentalist Gore's cable network, Current TV, encourages consumers to submit their own stories on video. Anyone can upload a video to the Current site, and online voters decide what ought to run on the TV channel. Current TV pays a nominal fee ($500 to $1,000) to license the short pieces that it features on air, and it ostensibly becomes an audition process for fledgling artists. Current also invited viewers to create its commercial spots. A sponsor such as Sony Electronics will review and decide whether to run them but promises to pay those whose productions are in heavy rotation. The first spot to run on this V-CAM system (that's Viewer-Created Ad Message) was the one by precocious student Tyson Ibele, mentioned at the chapter's long-ago start.

In mid-'06 regular folks' mobile-phone video got programmed on various shows and was later featured at currentTV.com/mobile.

For the 2007 Super Bowl, a host of marketers asked consumers to submit ads to run in the super-hyped commercial breaks. A Harvard Business School professor was quoted in *USA Today* as saying, "It's a great way to build buzz, but a debatable way to build a brand."[5]

Of course, consumer content is not necessarily good content. If it doesn't engage others and translate into sales, the consumer-driven content will evaporate. It's a process of elimination; only the best will remain on this island.

---

* In February 2006, PodShow announced it would provide the professional-grade tools to let consumers distribute their podcasts and to monetize through advertising.

Brand Me, Me, Me!

If what teenagers are doing is any indication of where the media are headed, then online social networks are going to be the Viacoms and Time Warners of the future. For what some observers have described as the generation of young people that are constantly connected through cyberspace, places like upstarts LiveDigital, FriendWise, Tagged and veterans Flickr (photo-sharing) and FaceBook (a network for students), all grant them one hell of a social identity.[6] Often their likes and dislikes, interests, photographs, music tastes, and even sexual orientations are made available for all to see like a store displaying shiny wares. In fact the Web pages on sites like these are an individual Brand Me for the people who have created them.

Here in the cyber village, *real* brands—the ones you can actually buy—exist alongside the human selections. Check out a profile on MySpace, and among the photos posted you might also find ads that blend into the overall look of the page and, if clicked, link to other sites that have paid to be featured alongside the nut you're viewing now.

MySpace started as a place for budding, unsigned musicians to showcase their music, but today even the proven commodity rock stars, Depeche Mode and Prince included, must have their own page to be considered part of the music scene. And it's not just about music now; as of this writing there are fast approaching 100 million registered users, making it one of the most popular destinations online period,[7] where an entire generation uses it as a place to hang out. Shopping malls, thy will be empty.*

Marketers have been experimenting with social networks like MySpace—now the property of Rupert Murdoch's News Corporation, which bought it for $580 million in July 2005—as a way to launch brands and reach a consumer group that will be swayed by more traditional media. Murdoch went so far as to name a group of leftover TV stations that weren't invited to the WB/UPN merger dance in 2006 "MyNetworkTV," and it's been jokingly suggested he rename News Corp. "MyCorp" to signify his evangelical belief in the power of the social Internet.

---

* Although the number of active users is far smaller. Many people register, try it once, think "nah," and try something else instead.

MySpace attracts hordes of sixteen-to-thirty-four-year-old consumers and is a feeding ground for marketers (and sexual predators*) desperate to reach this elusive group who don't care as much about TV . . . and are likely to be found playing computer games, surfing the Net, or instant-messaging (IM-ing) their pals and dates . . . all at the same time. Even the mighty Google recognized the power of Rupert's MySpace as their number one source of traffic and in August 2006 inked a deal that would guarantee $900 million to MySpace in exchange for exclusive rights to provide search and ads on the site.

NBC's *The Office* had its official premiere on MySpace, while new releases from bands Nine Inch Nails and Queens of the Stone Age got launched on the site and then sold more in the first week than any of their other CDs had.[8]

Some marketers get more out of this than others. The Coca-Cola Company sponsored a CD of samples of music from local bands released and distributed for free by a social network of music fans called Buzz-Oven. The fans were given free music and the corporate giant was seen as an enabler, helping teens acquire what they actually wanted. Not so cool was Procter and Gamble's attempt to create its own independent social network around its Sparkle body spray, a product aimed at tween-age girls. After its own social experiment failed, it found more success with Sparkle on, yes, MySpace.

In fact brands such as Tiffany and Starbucks have created areas for fans and foes alike on MySpace. Wendy's, home of "old-fashioned hamburgers," has been seeking to "youthify" their brand for years; recently they managed to make one hundred thousand friends on the site after it posted its own profile, proving it *can* be hip to be square.

But beware friendly marketers! Don't take yourselves too seriously—be prepared to be mocked too—if you want to play this game. A casual browse through the pages of these sites will turn up as many mock brand sites as the real deals.

FaceBook connects students at colleges around America—eight out of ten of them, they claim—and so "premier brands like Apple, Electronic Arts, Paramount

---

* In June 2006 a Texas teenager filed suit against MySpace for $30 million in damages after, it's claimed, she was sexually assaulted by another MySpace member.

Pictures, and Victoria's Secret . . . interact with the most engaged online community today." Advertisers sponsor informal consumer groups at FaceBook and encourage open dialogue about shared common interests in a product or brand of theirs.

Apple Computers Inc., for one, is the paid provider of a session of college kids over the moon about the Mac. Because users create profiles based upon legitimate college e-mail addresses, advertisers can target them individually based upon discovering what they want, where they live, what classes they take, when they'll graduate, whom they voted for, what sex they are, how much they have, whether they wear boxers or briefs, and anything else the student *wants* to share. Need we proclaim how exciting this is?

While the ads posted by commercial enterprises support these free services, some are always grumbling that these are detrimental to their experience. Over twenty thousand MySpace users have signed up in a movement aiming for one hundred thousand signatures to force cofounder Tom Anderson to change the type of ads and avoid those that this group finds to be "seductive and violent . . . out of respect for our morals and beliefs."

This is the first time we've heard of young people requesting ads that respect morals and beliefs. What would Pat Robertson have to say? Even if the morals don't win, technology might: MySpace Ad Skipper is now available from developers who claim it blocks the ads that appear on social networking's big daddy.

It's clear that power does lie with the people, and as quickly as they flock to one MySpace, they will run to another if their needs are being neglected. Friendster, you may recall, was the first big social-networking site but is hovering near death now because something came along that better respected and sought out the needs of its users.

Chapter 4, "Who's Eating Your Lunch," might be a good place to find out how to stay ahead of competitors ready to pounce on your customers when you yawn.

Use This at Cocktail Parties

1. With the easy availability of all sorts of whiz-bang technology, consumers are finding they can create their own content and marketing that competes with the content created by professionals. We marketers can encourage consumers to

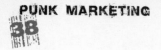
jump in and be actively involved in shaping brands, since the days when they can be thought of as passive recipients of marketing messages are over.

2. Consumers are using such tools as camera phones, blogs, video blogs, and podcasts to become citizen journalists, thus changing the role of the traditional media. Smart marketing means giving consumers whatever they want to make loud voices heard rather than simply placing ads that jar with existing content. In an August 4, 2006, *New Yorker* article, citizen reporters are numbered to be 34 percent of the 12 million bloggers (you do the math, we're already exhausted).*

3. Social networks grant younger consumers online social identities or, better put, their own individual brands. Marketers that share these same values without lying about it (hire a kid) will reach them through highly focused campaigns—which for the most part are acceptable, as everyone gets this is part of having a free service. Beware. Push the tolerance of consumers too far and there could be a backlash against these sites and/or the brand marketers that screw with them.

4. Finally, what you learned most of all: cut the middleperson out and save your ass. They are not as viable as the need to get your customers to love the new flexible *you*.

---

* Said Glenn Reynolds, a University of Tennessee law professor and the guy behind Instapundit: "Millions of Americans who were once in awe of the punditocracy now realize that anyone can do this stuff and . . . better than the lords of the profession."

Punk is . . .

Bringing in an expert from a completely
different field—a cabinetmaker, a tree surgeon,
or sushi chef—to talk to your team and learn
from the experience.

Hiring people not just based on the amount
of relevant experience they have in your
industry but on how some unique skills they
have will help the organization to grow.

[to be continued]

Tasty Morsels

- Apple and Samsung are among those using excellence in design to break out of the pack and rise above the clutter in ways that are quite novel.

- Motorola's drive to make design a priority (and stop their G-d-awful streak of nonsales) resulted in the Razr and made it again the leading handset maker, almost miraculously, after being called for dead.

- A Bathing Ape T-shirt made artificially scarce can be priced at $400 or more (more like, "There's a sucker born . . . ").

- A less rare-than-believed pair of Nikes will fetch thousands at auction.

- The scarcity Ty Warner created for Beanie Babies was made from thin air—and made him one of the richest men on any list.

Three

Brand Not Bland
How to Stand Out so You Are "The Chosen"

Which do you want to hear first?

Start with the bad: it's becoming increasingly difficult to cut through the white noise of me-too products and the incessant marketing that appears as something new. The good stuff is that the rewards for being among those few that make it through all that clutter are huge and worthwhile.

The power consumers now hold to choose among competing products should not be a cue to make marketers try to follow these folks wherever they go with "please, just try one." Consumers' all-knowing power should encourage brand holders to attempt some sense of "how to be different." The me-too products are everywhere.

We think the placement of ads where consumers least expect them, such as finding a message on a urinal, is both adorable and passé.* While the ad over that cake gives the male consumer something to aim for, there's no way he will buy after zipping up. Marketing that takes a step backward from all the fuss and gives our consumer something to entice them *in*, works.

---

* EarthLink, the Internet service provider, placed ads in restrooms to tell people how it protects their privacy on the Internet, using the line "EarthLink Protects Your Privates." Hilarious. To some. To others, just a case of pissing on the brand.

In an interview with *USA Today,* Gary Ruskin, executive director of Commercial Alert, a nonprofit group whose goal is to protect communities from commercialism, complained to anyone reading, "There's an effort to turn every square inch of this country into a billboard. When you have so much cognitive pollution, it's hard for people to get some peace and quiet."[1] We love the phrase "cognitive pollution" to describe this stuff!

"What's wrong with taking every opportunity to, uh, inform consumers about the one thing they might not even know they want until they cannot help themselves and just have to have one?," you were going to plead anyway, so why not make it better for everyone's blood pressure?

Beauty Sells

Design is the excellent differentiator we often take for granted. It takes a product that would otherwise be a mere commodity and gives it a shot at becoming an icon that transcends and even redefines the category it slides into. Apple's iPod was beautifully designed, not only in its sleek, elegant look, but in its simple user interface, packaging, and advertising push. All elements work seamlessly as one, sending an unwavering, unstoppable message of cool-as-all-get-out design that makes you want to hold one, touch one, hear one—oh, and buy one.

Design seeps out of every pore at Apple, and it's not surprising its products do damn well in prestigious international awards such as Design and Art Directors (D&AD) or Industrial Design Excellence Awards (IDEA, from the Industrial Designers Society of America). For those of you who think we are award worshippers, please visit AwardsAwards.com and we will tell you what we really think. It's our "open 23 hours"* online destination entirely devoted to awarding everyone in as many industries as we can muster for their masterful placing of lip-locks on their own.

Design is the new black. Firms from all around the world are cutting through.

---

* A reference to 1983 yuckster *Easy Money* with Rodney Dangerfield and Joe Pesci. The stars, desperate for an all-night diner after an evening bender, find one after much consternation. Rodney gets to the front, and as he reaches for the door, all the lights go out. He looks at the sign and it says, "Open 23 Hours." Class over.

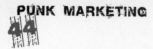

Nike Inc's Considered shoe from the United States demonstrates design innovation through a combination of styling and environmental benefits, while another brand, Solemates, makes a shoe in India from recycled paper and at fifty cents a pair is both cheap and crazy disposable.

Design works in even mundane categories to develop product must-haves.

Originality Matters

In 2006 the state of Wal-Mart launched an ad campaign with a striking similarity to another campaign dating back to 1993. The original, from Sears Roebuck & Company sporting the tagline "Come see the softer side of Sears," emphasized the company's diversity. The discovery of a woman shopping for a refrigerator and finding a leather coat helped the store prove it was more than most believed it to be.

Wal-Mart's parallel campaign in 2006 used the exact same concept and the tagline, "Look beyond the basics." Even the execution of the campaign was remarkably similar, especially in print ads. Each used two-page layouts with a household item on the left and the surprise item on the right.

Gurasich, Spence, Darilek & McClure (the chunkily configured GSD&M) is the agency behind Wal-Mart's cam-  paign and swore it wasn't even aware of the Sears campaign. To not be aware of such an effective ad campaign for one of America's most beloved consumer institutions does not bode well for any agency. Being informed about the industry you toil in is the only way to make it.*

Ah, what occurred when it was pointed out! The excuses flew and at one point a representative of GSD&M said this was a classic advertising method. This is where the authors got a good chuckle. Take note: this is everything Punk Marketing is not ever. Going with the tried-and-true, being safe, disregarding your instinct for what's already been proven, is *not* what we're talking about here. To get someone's attention and money takes attention-getting and money-deserving. You're constantly taking a chance with something that's been done before. Give your customers credit.

---

* No one pays attention! Three recent ads said "like nothing else" on TV—at the same exact time™! Hummer, Sony Electronics, and a Roche drug called Boniva all were the one and only. Sony's period-lacking Like.No.Other ™ (sic) is seeking a proofreader.

There is, for instance, the Spring Roll fetch toy for puppies from WETNoZ International, ultraknown makers of designer pet toys, which honestly looks like a big spring roll! Or the stylish and overpriced BYO Lunch Bag from design-focused accessories company Built NY Inc., that keeps your food cool while making you look cool too as you schlep it.

One toilet design has made its designers flush from a run of success! The Purist Hatbox Toilet includes an electric pump within its minimalist casing so it doesn't need to be plumbed into the water pipes and can be placed anywhere in the potty area or perhaps in the living room as a conversation piece (or stopper).

Another award-winning bathroom fixture is the Revolution showerhead by Moen Inc. Moen's team of designers, engineers, anthropologists, marketers, and managers found that people wanted distinctive shower experiences whether in the morning, the evening, or after sports, and so they included a dial that gives the user a choice of shower sensations. For their all wet research, dudes spent hours watching people showering (in swimsuits, they said).

A major winner in those 2005 IDEAs was the coveted Motorola Razr V3 mobile phone. It *is* as thin as a razor and has the keypad etched onto its metal casing, which is made from "aircraft grade" aluminum and magnesium. The antenna is incorporated into the mouthpiece, and a built-in camera uses a chemically hardened lens. This tremendous design helped the Illinois-based Motorola out of a really horrible slump to smash Nokia into second place and make it the number one handset seller in the United States in 2005.* Cingular—the cell service provider that carried the first Razrs—introduced the exclusive piece and rose above the din to pull in customers who had stuck with their competitors (it helped that their own lobby efforts to get "porting" succeeded just then).†

---

* However, in 2006, the Nokia 8801 gave us pause to reconsider when ring tones in the new model were created by the severe but gorgeous Asian classical composer Ryuichi Sakamoto. *That's* connecting people to some classy music. We are severely impressed.

† Porting is filing to get your mobile phone number switched to a competing carrier. As you can imagine, companies like Sprint, Nextel, and the defunct AT&T Wireless, who kept customers prisoner when they couldn't dream of giving up their number, fought this act tooth plus nail. They lost—but not until a fairly public fight.

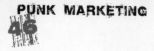
Razr's success at Cingular led competing provider Sprint (and soon Sprint Nextel, then surely Sprint Nextel T Mobile Bell South Crosby Stills Nash & Young) to rush out a vastly inferior copycat called Samsung A900, which ended up as appealing to customers as its devilishly awful customer service.

The Razr firmly established Motorola as the last stop for design in phones. They became accessories—not just something to keep in your pocket that tickles you every now and then. A public statement, perhaps!

Motorola sure had the background for this as innovators in technology. In 1928 they were responsible for the first car radio, then the first walkie-talkie, and that huge clunky first cell phone in 1983.* Design had always taken second place for Motorola. Until they realized it was make a statement with the phones—or change businesses.

How this came about is a metaphor for design's now-ensconced place in the hearts of corporate executives. Early in the millennium, the chief of Motorola's cell phone division, Mike Zafirovski, boosted the in-house arts team and hired as chief of all designers Jim Wicks from Sony Corporation, who had been head of their Innovation and Design Center in San Francisco. As part of the investment in design capabilities Jim and his team conducted more consumer research than ever before and opened a new design center in chic Chicago overlooking the Lake Michigan shoreline in an effort to recruit the hottest design talent. We mean, after all, Schaumburg, Illinois doesn't have quite the same cachet.

Wicks now headed up a division of about two hundred folks worldwide that included among its designer crew a bunch of psychologists, sociologists, musicologists—and a bunch of other ologists—that still today ensure that all phone designs meet consumer needs and win awards. Wicks said, "Back then we were saying, 'Here's the features and the technology,' then put a wrapper around it. Now the starting point is 'What does the consumer want?' and then apply the technology to that." Music to a Punk's ears.

So, yes, it is desirable to attempt to understand what the consumer wants before designing products that break through the brand clutter. But breaking through is

---

* The Motorola DynaTAC 8000X weighed two pounds, had half an hour of talk time, cost $3,995, and was butt ugly. It was called The Brick.

also about breaking rules and taking risks. Without a gamble, a true innovation in design is—damn it—hard to achieve. Highly respected New York design firm OXO International routinely takes risks and happily makes mistakes while creating beautiful *and* functional consumer products.[2]

Such boo-boos have led to the best learning and most outstanding successes; that's why OXO has thirty regular ole home products inside the permanent collection at the Cooper-Hewitt, National Design Museum, of the Smithsonian Institution New York. That museum with the unwieldy name is the one U.S. collection devoted to historic *and* contemporary design, so to have a potato masher in there is quite an honor.

OXO's humble masher was in fact born through their own mistaken assumption that traditional design would do fine. According to lore, they received a letter from a customer who asked why the original handle was vertical rather than in a more natural horizontal positional, so the company saw it as a Thing That Makes You Go Hmm and created a new device that lets users mash down on a cooked potato by pushing the palm on the more sturdy and soft Santoprene masher rather than a normal vertical handle that seemed to give poor mashers serious blisters.[3]

OXO also made an error attempting to solve a consumer problem when there was none. Take the cheese slicer. (No—please—take it.) This crucial element for any Scandinavian smorgasbord possesses a thin metal wire with which to prod through the Jarlsberg for wafer-thin slices; the cheesy eater can drop them on an open sandwich. Yet in slicing the wire often snaps, sometimes in midcreation! OXO's crack designers thought it through—maybe even too much. They felt it made sense to create a wireless slicer, and the engineers replaced the wire with a more durable metal blade. But remember that those who slice have for years treasured the wire-based doodad, so it was tantamount to treason and customers revolted.

Not a pretty sight.

OXO went back to the wire and used a stronger variant. They almost screwed up by being too damn innovative.

Dull product categories are often overlooked in design standards. Yet Eric Ryan, cofounder of Method Home, the San Francisco maker of home-cleaning products, proclaims with pride, "There is no such thing as dull product categories, only dull brands." With cofounder Adam Lowry, Method Home chose to invigorate a dull category full

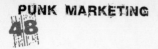
of yawn-inducing home-cleaning products. Procter and Gamble, SC Johnson: A Family Company, Clorox, and Colgate-Palmolive Company had dominated the market for decades, and all products looked pretty much the way they'd looked for half a century or more.

In a clever burst of imagination, Method made the leap for home-cleaning products from toxic substances hidden beneath the sink to all-natural, biodegradable, lovely countertop accessories! Design was a key part of their strategy to make consumers "think different" about the products that Lowry, a chemistry graduate from Stanford University, developed to be safe around people yet stubborn in removing dirt. Beginning with a line of spray cleaners whose unusual teardrop design and bright-colored liquids got distributed in supermarkets such as Vons, a large division of grocery chain Safeway Inc., they were suddenly on their way.

They persuaded Egyptian-English design guru Karim Rashid—whose designs for furniture and housewares are in collections of museums such as the Philadelphia Museum of Art and Museum of Modern Art in New York—to come aboard as chief creative officer to create a "dish-soap bottle" you'd be proud to show your concubine and/or mistress. This piece had to be elegant and functional, so Rashid devised an inverted-bowling-pin-like design dispensing soap upright when its base is twisted. It took brain-busting thought and strange engineering, but, boy, does that dispenser stop traffic in the kitchen!

Make Yourself Scarce

In a rare Duh moment for us authors, we inform you that design is what high fashion is built upon. Clothing creators have at their disposal a useful tool for creating desire, one used to sell more of their products than any other: it is called scarcity.

High-end handbags, scarves and *shmattes* from labels such as Hermès, creators of "timeless, darling" Birkins, are awfully scarce as a result of the practical difficulties of producing high-quality items from raw materials shipped finished from faraway lands. But that's only half of it. Some labels—Chanel is loved *and* hated for it—purposefully restrict supply so as to keep demand strong, and long-term profitability up.

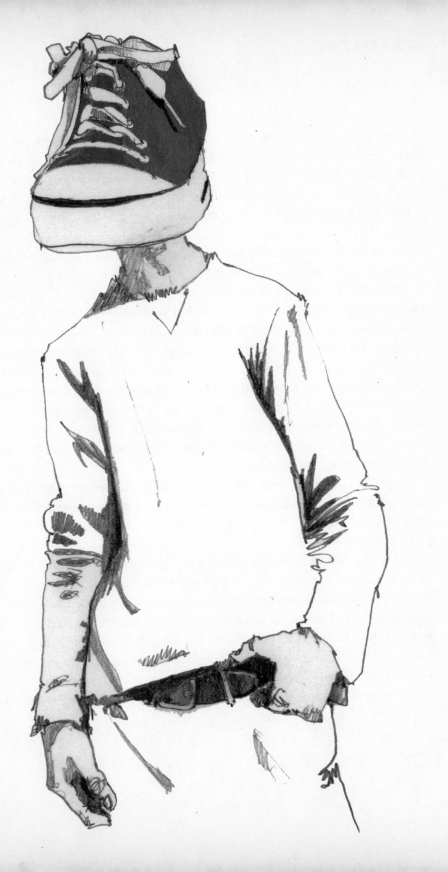

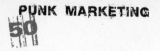
Over in Japan, creating scarcity has been a marketing strategy for street-fashion labels. Street is the clothing invented and worn by young people rather than that of established designers, and in the Tokyo store of British skateboard label Silas & Maria, customers are let through the doors only in groups of twenty, with others kept waiting in line outside by a guy behind a rope. After the current group of shoppers leaves, products are replaced on the shelves and the new gawkers are allowed in.[4] This gives the store a rarefied atmosphere akin to what you might expect to find in a gallery rather than in a run-of-the-mill clothing store.

Crucial to the success of Japanese streetwear A Bathing Ape (or more cutely, Bape) is how one T-shirt would be priced at $400 and sell like hot sake. See, only a few hundred of a particular design are made and can be found in only a few stores around the world. Bape's founder, Nigo, is a real Punk Marketer, whom we admire; formerly the drummer with the Tokyo Sex Pistols, he found inspiration from Charlton Heston's *Planet of the Apes*. He says the moniker is a comment on Japanese youth who—like "an ape bathing in lukewarm water"*—take everything for granted and blindly follow one another to the next trend. Isn't this ironic given that young people buy the outrageously priced Bathing Ape products to be like each other? Nothing says irony like high fashion.

Nigo-san's skills at creating desire for what might be commoditized products have received a nod from UK sneaker maker Reebok. Together with high-profile rapper Pharrell Williams of the rap group N*E*R*D, Nigo created for Reebok a brand of limited-edition sneakers called the Billionaire Boys Club. The shoes are the centerpiece of Reebok's RBK line of shoes from rap stars like Jay-Z and Fitty Cent so as to appeal to "sneakerheads," who collect and sell limited-edition sneakers for profit. Typically a RBK line of sneakers is sold exclusively in high-end malls like L.A.'s Fred Segal and stocked for only a few months to keep the demand high. The theory is that if the sneakerheads endorse the shoes, urban kids will in turn be ur-motivated to buy them, and then so will the youth of America and finally the world. It's the sneakers-as-dominoes theory.

If being scarce works and absence makes the heart grow fonder (except for

---

* Literal translation of the very brand.

Madonna), Nike has used the pseudo-limited-edition strategy to the widest effect. In March '05 it released but a few Air Jordan XIII Retro Lows, and hundreds of sneaker-heads snaked around the Niketown store in Manhattan to snag a pair! Fights broke out, madness ensued.

Weeks earlier police were called to break up a brawl at a Lower East Side authorized Nike dealer between dozens of 'heads all trying to grab a rare pair of Pigeon Dunks—allegedly there were 150 in the world like them. Shoes like Pigeons will cost a couple of dollars to make and fetch hundreds or thousands of dollars on collectors' Web sites.

Taking the Mass out of the Market

Using the fashion industry tactic of creating scarcity to pump up demand of a sneaker is okay, but try doing it with soda. The Coca-Cola Company produced a limited edition as a way of making the sugar-free Coke Zero brand more *special,* or just as an antidote to the brand's ubiquity. Its specially designed kits included six numbered, contour glass bottles of twenty-four total put up for sale on eBay as a publicity stunt; the $2,750 winning bid went to charity, the publicity going to Coke.

On the other more successful side, Jones Soda, a teeny soft-drink maker without the everywhere-ness problem Coke moans about, produces limited runs of monthly designs on labels that feature photographs of its actual customers. You submit a snapshot and get the chance to be one of twenty images distributed each month. You can even go onto the My Jones section of their site (jonessoda.com) to order your own personalized case to Jones on.

So there's Coke, who realized long ago that being everywhere it wants to be has advantages (i.e., products within arm's reach of consumers in every port) and a downside when the competition goes nuts. For teenagers, soda labels brand the person as much as jeans do, so the youngsters are often motivated to seek out a beverage that has less mass appeal.

Starbucks Corporation is the master of ubiquity, but as Punks we tip our hats to anyone who gets away with anything. In their case we add a codicil: so far. In towns across many continents you find three or four stores within inches of each other; it appears customers enjoy the familiarity and are allegedly reassured by the fact that the java *and* the atmosphere will be the same no matter where they go—even if it's just steps!

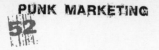

But in being so uniform Starbucks runs the serious risk of letting its brand become so single-dimensional that it will begin to lack the special something that made it alluring when coffee was bland. Remember that coffee at $3 a cup is a special treat that we hardworking people duly deserve.

Customers still talk about the Starbucks they frequent as "my Starbucks," but the company does hardly anything to promote uniqueness of individual stores, which we cannot condone in the Punk world.* There are *some* variations in decor, but the shop in Morristown has the same feel as the one in Malibu. Why not reflect the local surroundings and the baristas who toil there?

Krispy Kreme, at one time the most blabbed-about take-out treat, fell hard once it expanded nationwide and sold its soul to franchisees. Those delightfully indulgent doughnuts had been in heavy demand because they were pretty gosh darn hard to locate. People would drive twenty miles in wee hours to scarf a twelve-pack from the little bakery down in Atlanta, bless their souls, and only for the experience of seeing the doughnuts being made H O T through the window.

But, alas, once the stores started popping up like, we guess, doughnuts, and without a bakery attached, the little hole-free wonders could be found in supermarkets everywhere, and the jig was up. Krispy Kreme corporate did a deal with the devil and soon no one cared; the thought of a dried-up KK confection made you sick to your stomach. What a waste.

One of us had the pleasure of running the advertising for a chain of restaurants while it expanded and tried to retain a sense of the uniqueness that had made it truly popular on day one. Buca di Beppo ("Joe's basement" in *italiano*) is a casual-dining chain for customers who believe their branch is the only one in existence. How could it not be, with kitschy decor, framed photographs, and garish figurines all fighting for wall space? There were pictures of the restaurant's kindly proprietor, Joe, and his darling family of immigrants stuck in the time warp of cheesy 1950s Americana. As a devoted Catholic, you see, "Joe" left religious imagery and artifacts

---

* We note they sell special and seasonal coffee beans, or Black Apron Exclusives, available for limited times, blah dee blah. This tactic should be used more to include beans or drinks that pop up only in a single venue. Then you can mean it when you say *your* Starbucks.

Do Ya *Think?*

Have you ever dined out or gone to a bar with someone and come back from the bathroom to see the person you've been immersed in conversation with totally zoned on his pager or phone? Giving the impression that—whew—he got the chance to do something when you were gone!

We only remember one time when one guy was just sitting there in his own thoughts. When we asked—a producer for *Ellen DeGeneres*, no less—he remarked, "Time to think is important."

We dropped our spoons.

See, people do not think thinking is important. It's bet-ter to be busy and moving on. But how bad would it be if we

just all looked up one day and said, "Time for a change."? What would that look like? Messy, for sure. It might make us more apt to question everything around us.

What happened to reading too? Any true media junkie obsessively keeps up with the daily newspaper and weekly magazine world, particularly since so many of them are endan-gered species. As Jefferson remarked sometime, a long way back: "Were it left to me to decide whether we should have a government without newspapers, or newspapers without a govern-ment, I should not hesitate a moment to choose the latter." Choose one day to read up on all the crap you've been sent—keep it simple and do it. Read Letters to the Editor like mad. Pour through that stack of *New Yorker*s that are a fire hazard and get them inside you. Fundamen-tal, and obvious, but these days being interesting is better than being interested.

throughout the restaurant, including a Pope's Table with a central bust of the Poppa. And each Buca restaurant is blessed by a priest during its opening ceremony!

Obviously, there was no Joe—at least not a Joe that the decor, loud atmosphere, and fare of huge Italian dishes suggested.* There were, however, more than a hun-dred restaurants in a chain of Bucas. So for us, the goal of its ads was to retain the

---

* The CEO of the chain *was* Joe Micatrotto, a larger-than-life guy who included his own name in the restaurants when he took control of BdB.

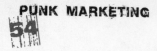

uniqueness of brand and perpetuate a local feel of each BdB while helping build sales and grow the chain to perpetuity.

Did it matter that customers knew there was another Buca di Beppo somewhere else? Who cared? Each should still feel as if theirs was the only one ever.

Strategy was to create local ads for each, the down-and-dirty sort that a mom-and-pop would put out, not the ones bought and paid for by a national chain. Our agency produced branded dry-cleaner bags taking potshots at the big messy portions found at the (individual) restaurants, along with flyers and a smattering of tiny print ads that ran in local papers. All of which had a consummate homemade feel. The print ads were individually created using rubber stamps to make the type look amateurish.

Our idea was to keep it real, and in line with the decor and sentiment of the restaurants, some of the print ads were truly outrageous! One boasted a headline "To Johnny, sorry about the vasectomy. But welcome home from the hospital! From Joe at Buca." And underneath an innocent mention of a menu item that could come across as a taunt to poor Johnny: "Our meatballs come three to a plate!"[5]

Mommy, I Want One!

Creating scarcity to build a following of consumers who stay firmly attached to the brand has been a favorite of the toy industry for eons. The bane of many parents' lives is the notion of not being able to find the "hot" toy of the season, and it's usually a deliberate tactic that manufacturers use to create a feeding frenzy around a new-product launch. In 1998 it was the time for Furbies—those lovable furry creatures made by Hasbro Inc. subsidiary Tiger Electronics—to be the must-have toy for American kids.

Tiger's launch strategy included a carefully orchestrated and much-whispered-over PR campaign with events at F. A. O. Schwarz stores in New York and Chicago. Though fiercely denied by the company even today, skeptics suggested parent company Hasbro deliberately limited distribution to drive up demand. Regardless, it was too clever for words. It was hilarious: Furbies spoke their own language—Furbish—and only learned English after spending quality time with their new owners. Put two Furbies together and they spoke only to each other. Our guess is that they were saying, "Ha! We hooked a couple more."

But for toy aficionados, the grand boo-bah of scarcity = demand was good old Ty Warner, who somehow came up with that crazy Beanie Babies notion in 1996.* The successful tactics he used to sell those cuddly bags of stuffing helped make him one of the richest men in the world (number sixty-five according to the *Forbes* list in 1999), beating out Amazonian Bezos, among many other billionaire stuffed shirts.

Warner's strategy of creating scarcity resulted in Beanie Babies becoming collector's items for adult toy-mongers as well as kids and may have been serendipitous rather than planned. That is, at first. The reason Warner kept introducing new Beanie characters and suddenly changing lines (thus creating a cry of "Huh?" and mad rushes to stores) was because he just wasn't satisfied with a single line's design or color, leading people to pay hugely inflated prices for the original version—the *scarcer* Ty Warner first draft!

He found, much to his amazement, that abruptly and capriciously ceasing production of a model—a "retirement of the model," said each press release—had the same effect as the artistic reasoning. Bingo!

Warner also understood value without apology and sued anyone who was even sort of infringing his trademark and/or selling Beanie knockoffs.

Remember, this was way before social networking, so there was little official information available about Beanie Babies collectors—a group whose gatherings we'd like to be far from. But nobody ever knew how many of any single design existed, and Ty Warner never did any advertising for the obnoxious creatures.

Crazed collector collectives cavorted through the corridors of Kohl's to catch clues. They used a price guide from former IBM engineer Mary Beth Sobolewski, an avid collector, who had an inkling of how much the Beanies were fetching, *Mary Beth's Beanie World*, the magazine, had at its peak in 1998 a circulation of 650,000 copies *per month* at a price of $5.99. MB Sobolewski is our hero.

This story ends in 1999, when, perhaps to pump up flagging corporate sales, Warner announced he was ceasing production on all Beanie Babies. Early the following year, as with The Who's or Barbra Streisand's many final tours, he reversed the

---

* Punks rarely come up with ideas at the office, which is code for getoutmore. In a survey by *Prevention* magazine, British researchers asked 254 businesspeople where they got "your best, most creative ideas." The most popular answers were hardly the places you expect: bed, car, socializing. Shower did not make the top five. . . .

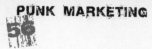

Harry Potter's Marketing Magic

Bloomsbury Books, the original publishers of the Harry Potter book series, and author J. K. Rowling have used scarcity of sorts to great effect to pump up interest in the launch of each new title in the series. For instance, when *Harry Potter and the Goblet of Fire,* the fourth of the nonstop collection, was launched on the same day in July 2000 in the United States and the UK—unusual in itself—little information was made available beforehand to media, booksellers, the public, even devilish Harry himself.

Famously, nothing about the book's storyline was ever released; cover design was kept tight-lipped; Rowling gave no interviews prior to publication; and even the title was closely held for a time. Retailers were under stricter-than-death orders to keep copies under wraps till launch, and many of them decided to open doors at midnight to be able to push out when the embargo was lifted. Very *Star Wars* of them!

Subsequent launches of the series followed the same pattern, with added twists, such as the "Oh, my, sorry!" release of fourteen copies of *Harry Potter and the Half-Blood Prince* at a Canadian independent bookseller days before its official date stamp. The Harry Potter brand is worth over a billion dollars and has made a shy, disarming Rowling one of the richest women in the UK and someone whom the media cannot get enough of, if they would ever try.

retirements, but it was too late.* The mourning period was over, and despite this ploy, sales continued to decline, and although today you can buy Beanie Babies at ty.com, the market is light-years from what it was. Punks everywhere applaud the Beanie Babies nuttiness because it was the longest, most lucrative scarcity folly in history. We have gained much knowledge from Ty Warner's antics, not the least of which is not to push your luck and ruin a good fad.

---

* Stephen Sondheim once wrote the lyric: "Being great is knowing when to get off."

Use This During Elevator Moments

1. Breaking away from the clutter of too many products and too much marketing does not mean you have to use dated stealth-marketing tactics to catch consumers in places where they were least expecting you.* What this clearly demands is finding ways to make the brand stand out.

2. Excellent design will add an emotional appeal and, when combined with fantastic functionality, can make a product in even the most boring market desirable.

3. Marketers must take risks and make a few damning errors when attempting to create something distinctive to chuck into the marketplace. Bombing is only a true failure if we don't gain from it.

4. Clothing industries have used the tactic of creating scarcity to drive up demand for such products as a T-shirt or pair of ultimately disposable sneakers. Giving something that *could* have been mass-produced an element of uniqueness can have the same effect, whether it's a can of soda, a diner, or a chain of flower shops. Marketers can add individual flavor to what they are selling to make consumers want it with abandon.

---

* Stealth marketing is also known as undercover marketing. This is when consumers do not know they are being marketed to. We call it underhanded marketing.

Tasty Morsels

- To stay competitive you have to be nimble: act small while thinking big.

- The Virgin Group companies traditionally act as if they're the underdog even though their thirty-five thousand employees earn them yearly revenues of over $8 billion.

- Nimble Dyson sells 50 percent of all vacuum cleaners in the UK, while once giant rival Hoover now has only a 10 percent market share (after just a few years ago having more than a quarter of the market).

- Consumer giants like Procter and Gamble now steer away from mass-market approaches to concentrate on niche audiences.

- Smart small brands remain fierce by appealing to small groups of consumers who remain loyal to them.

Four

Who's Eating Your Lunch?
Make Them Spit It Out

A true capitalist will tell you the definition of business is someone out there waiting to steal your customers. If you're a big company, it may be the little guy you go "feh" to who seems content picking up scraps from your table but really has a far bigger appetite. And if you're the small guy, you may be thinking your lunch doesn't have appeal to the biggies until the day you wake up starving to death.

A Punk Marketer learns to keep looking over his shoulder for the competitor who wants to eat his meal and is constantly seeking ways to do things better, so the customer's eventual choice is his brand over the monster's.

Regardless of whether a company is gigantic or puny, it pays to act small while continuing to think in the biggest possible way. That may sound obvious, but people forget that image matters most. When someone says to us, "I'm not big enough for that," we think, *Go away, fool.*

Who's to say who's ready for what?

Consumers want to feel the company they buy from has their, and only their, absolute best interests at heart; so for them that means being treated respectfully as sole beings and not units in some amorphous lump.

In the past, mass production was appealing to consumers because they knew the product they bought was identical to all others from a factory. A brand name represented consistency and predictable quality assurance.

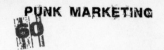

Some quality was known to be "better" than others, and *better* remained a differentiator among brands for a while. But better came to be taken for granted and eventually became an issue only when something went wrong.

Today we live in postquality America. Consumers no longer choose based on qualifications—they assume that competing products will perform flawlessly and they're right; they expect swift action if somehow a manufacturer or a distributor screws up.

Mass production has lost its competitive edge and being big for being big's sake got tossed away.

Big Certainly Is

Hugeness has advantages.

When it comes to food and beverage brands, consumers often want the same experience wherever they go around the world, and in a networked age where we carry our load with us, this counts for a lot. We know that a Big Mac bought in a Boise, Idaho McDonald's will taste exactly like Le Big Mac in Biarritz.

But *big* has a bad connotation that most companies should wish to run from. *Big* means "big business." Big business is bad because it is faceless. Big business is in it to make money at any cost, even sickness or in some cases death to the consumer. Big, big, big: greedy and selfish and uncaring. Big is all about you taking advantage of us. Big means using labor forces in harsh conditions in faraway factories to get the prices down a penny. Big is a giant box store demonstrating in sweaty auditoriums how seamstresses cutting fabrics cannot leave a scrap behind because that means a few cents could be wasted! Big means globalization and treating all cultures as one and so ignoring local differences. Big means you are looking for cash from all Americans no matter what.

In 1999, Seattle's mayor imposed a curfew after protesters clashed with police during a rowdy demonstration held during World Trade Organization (WTO) meetings. Starbucks locations throughout the city were trashed by protesters angry at the way they felt the WTO was writing the rules for global trade while ignoring the varying needs of the vast majority of the world itself. To the many in attendance, Starbucks represented the quintessence of American imperialism, and protesters demanded it introduce new responsibility rules to ensure that fair prices were paid to the impoverished coffee growers supplying its beans.*

At the same time, the McDonald's Corporation's "restaurants" have suffered at the hands of antiglobalization protesters around the world who view the number of billions served—fast approaching 100 billion—as proof that McDonald's is just a big bad empire that needs to be slowed, if not stopped. French farmer and folk hero José Bové, who was jailed after vandalizing a French McDonald's, emerged from imprisonment to shouts, in French of course, of "We are all Bovés!" A sucky PR day for Le Mickey D.†

The most put-upon of all, Coca-Cola, has had its share of problems simply because it is the market leader in most countries around the world; in many of them Coke is the number one English word (besides Beyoncé). Naturally, no one

---

* Under pressure, Starbucks started selling Fair Trade coffee that protected the coffee farmers, although the Global Exchange is asking the conglomerate to go further by making Fair Trade coffee its "recommended brew" just once per week. So far, no.

† Bové is considering a run for French President in 2007.

can dispute that Coke represents all things American. Ergo, they are an easy target for worldwide antitrust suits. In Europe for instance the EU Commission took issue with Coke's rebate policy that pushed retailers to stock its whole range of products, making it difficult for competitor brands to get a foothold.

For most of the last century the bottle king rode high on the wave of positive sentiment toward American brands around the world. Shit, in those days countries were happy to have the best of the United States. Today U.S. citizens pretend to be Canadian when traveling abroad.

In 2002, a French Punk entrepreneur launched a company—perhaps in retaliation for the "freedom fry"—to take advantage of negative sentiment in Muslim countries toward American bigness. Tawfik Mathlouthi, an ex–radio journalist, had high hopes to make Mecca Cola the soft-drink brand of choice for Muslims. What goes better with Mecca (Cola) than the slogan "No more drinking stupid. Drink with commitment."

Another Coca-Cola killer-in-waiting is Peruvian soft-drink maker Ajegroup (formerly Grupo Kola Real). They began to threaten the giant's hold in the eighties by selling their own soft drinks in recycled beer bottles to meet local demand as the Shining Path rebels in Peru began hijacking Coca-Cola trucks. That's a different tone than those ads with P. Dud driving around a Pepsi truck. . . .

In a usual moment of seriousness, we must point out that Ajegroup holds a stunning 20 percent share of the Peruvian market. They recently arrived in Mexico's towns and are slowly eating away at Coca-Cola's business in what is the second-largest per capita soft-drink market in the world—by selling large quantities of soda at way low prices in the poorest of neighborhoods.

Gee. They are eating a Coke lunch!

Acting Tiny

Richard Branson of the Virgin Group is a master at playing off against the established to get noticed; even when it's not true, he wishes to be seen as the underdog who merits a chance. He says, "We like to use the brand to take on some very large companies that we believe exert too much power." Surprise! Virgin is an enormous business, comprising hundreds of companies as diverse as airlines, wedding planning, mobile phones, condom manufacture, and publishing, with over thirty-five thousand employees that pull in combined revenue of over $8 billion. No matter. Branson's tactic has been to position himself as the teensy guy entering a market as a fresh alternative to the humdrum behemoth. Many have heard of his long-standing rivalry with the nameless heads of British Airways PLC;* this goes back to the late eighties when the much larger airline used "dirty tricks" (Branson's words) to discredit the fledgling airline. Branson was right: in 1993 BA was found guilty by the High Court in the UK of libel against Branson and the airline and forced to pay over three million British sterling to the Virgins.†

Recently Branson has continued to use publicity stunts to take shots at BA and the way of doing things that they still represent. To promote a Virgin Trains route from London to Manchester, Virgin staff boarded a BA London-to-Manchester flight wearing T-shirts in the Virgin shade of red. The statement GET YOUR SICK BAGS READY stood out. Virgin Trains claimed the team got "threatened with arrest" if they continued to be "walking billboards." BA denied it, publicly stating how pleased it was that the Virgin crew decided to travel via airline. All in all, a good publicity ploy for Sir Richard. When Branson launched Virgin Cola in the United States in the late 1990s he was already quite adept at declaring "war" on the big guys‡ and wheeled a vintage World War II tank through Times Square, something that would be a no-no today.

We Punk boys look forward to two new Virgins and the attitudes they disperse: the low-cost domestic JetBlue–style airline and Branson's constantly bandied-about flights to space.

---

* Although BA chairman Lord King was his main adversary.

† BA paid £500,000 to Virgin boss Richard Branson and £110,000 to his airline, as well as incurring legal costs of up to £3 million.

‡ As in Coke—and Diet Rite. Just kidding.

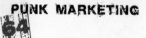

Still another British entrepreneur has fought industry giants like a real David, in the guise of vacuum-cleaner salesman James Dyson, the guy on TV always telling Americans, "Fact: Vacuums don't work effectively." Dyson's story is an inspirational tale and ought to be a textbook lesson to all those who think their shit don't *stank* (ref. OutKast).

Hoover was synonymous with vacuuming and is still a verb used by an elder generation (how long before it's "to Dyson"?); it was an icon in the days when corporations got to the top and stayed there with arms folded. At the start of the nineties the famed Hoover factory manufactured a quarter of all vacuum cleaners sold in the UK and had the audacity to turn down designer Dyson's idea for a bagless vacuum cleaner.

Hoover was too obvious when it turned down the concept: Why lose the income from bags, even though it would *help* consumers? Lo, ten small years later more than half the vacuum cleaners sold in the UK were made by Dyson Ltd. and the market share for Hoover had fallen to *10 percent.*

Now the joke. Seeing the success of Dyson's invention—the bag-free Dual Cyclone—Hoover, never one for subtlety, copied his patented design with its own and called it Triple Vortex (it sucked up the company's money!).

After Dyson sued, in 2001 a UK judge ruled that the Triple Vortex was a copy of Dyson's Dual Cyclone, and it was banned from sale. James Dyson, shaking his head, remarked, "Why on earth don't they think of their own ideas instead of copying ours?"*

A decade earlier Hoover gained notoriety for thinking up a novel idea of their own, but it's one Hoover would prefer be forgotten forever. A true Punk will never forget how, in 1992, Hoover had a sudden desire to clear its showrooms of unsold vacuums and washing machines and so launched a marketing campaign where consumers won round-trip flights throughout Europe if they spent a mere £100 on a Hoover product.

---

* Hoover hasn't quite caught on. Today they are pushing the world's first "sport utility vacuum," titled the Z700, in a time when gassy SUV sales are dropping every month.

Too good to be true has never been proven to be more right. Travel agents tried to cope with demand from people trying to redeem freebies, and wouldn't you know it? Hoover launched a second phase of the promotion with flights to the United States! Soon more and more customers found that flights were unavailable on dates they wished to travel, because blackout dates (and leftover tickets) were behind the promotion.

Then the unexpected revolt began. One consumer became a UK hero when he kidnapped a Hoover truck. Numerous disgruntled customers took the company to

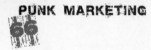
court, but a not unimpressive 220,000 people did eventually fly on Hoover's dime.* The biggest laugh was that every local classified was replete with "still in the box" Hoover products. This campaign has gone down in history as among the biggest European marketing mistakes of all time.

By now you're possibly tired of British stories, so off to America for one on blatant ignorance of product innovation and the use of desperate marketing ploys to prop up sales. The giant trio of car manufacturers has suffered a sad fate in the last few years as their complacency has led them to be attacked from every direction, most notably in the sensitive purse area. So we thought we'd pile on.

In *The End of Detroit: How the Big Three Lost Their Grip on the American Market*, author and *New York Times* Detroit bureau chief Micheline Maynard gave an indication of how Toyota, Nissan, Honda, BMW, and Hyundai began little by little to eat the lunches of Ford, GM, and Chrysler in the nineties. How? They concentrated on those much smaller markets ignored by El Mayor Tres.

Maynard has suggested that while importers had a laser focus on many distinct market sizes and scopes across the nation, Detroit's focus had been on being biggest and not particularly the best at anything. The domestic automakers relied on the patriotism of Americans and so resorted to what gets people excited (they thought): deep discounts, incentives, cash-back offers, and undifferentiated flag-waving marketing. This left the biggies fighting among themselves for that segment of buyers who cared less about cars and more about bargains. And while reliance on constant discounting has continued there are signs that the Big Three are starting to act smaller (just in time for Chapter 11!) and have finally created distinctive products to appeal to niche audiences.

Even Procter and Gamble, the biggest brand conglomerate on planet Earth, has started acting small. At the turn of the millennium it tried to buy the Gillette Company, partly out of desperation, to boost revenues in that vertical.[1] The one-size-fits-all approach that both corporate monsters had built their houses upon was suffering at the hands of new and hardly moved buyers who didn't care how long

---

* Hoover Europe's corporate parent eventually spent $72 million to fly the over two hundred thousand consumers who demanded they make good.

they had been around. They just wanted to be treated like individuals rather than as a market of masses.

Then to add fire to the forest, retailers like Wal-Mart (see sidebar "Meet Ol' Roy," page 68) were offering their renditions of P&G brands at lower prices.

This market fragmentation has extended to the media as well. Marketers can no longer reach large numbers of consumers in a single fell swoop. In the 1960s an advertiser like P&G could reach 80 percent of U.S. women with a spot aired at the same time on three major TV networks (CBS, ABC, and NBC). Today it would need to air on hundreds of TV channels to get anywhere close to that reach. That math is astounding, and not for the obvious reasons. Forget that broadcasters are nowhere near as powerful as they once were; more urgently it means a marketer needs to focus on where a target audience is at every moment of the day—and what different segments of the target audience want.

P&G has changed its spots (even Tide has them!) and has become one of the most vocal advocates of niche branding and marketing, thanks to a focus on acting small. A *Wall Street Journal* front pager from 2005 remarked how P&G—the biggest advertiser on earth with a budget of $6 billion plus a year—would be cutting up to 25 percent of its spending on cable TV and 5 percent of its network advertising.*

The previous year they had announced a reduction in their reliance on commercials in favor of new methods such as the Net and product placements on TV shows—the oxymoronic "branded entertainment." Jim Stengel, P&G's beleaguered head of marketing, told the American Association of Advertising Agencies (AAAA)† during a landmark speech how the existing marketing model was "obsolete."

He closed with "We must accept the fact that there is no *mass* in *mass media* anymore." Nice sentiment. His approach for P&G has been to be more up close and personal and treat people as . . . er . . . people; Stengel's overlooked concept is to

---

* Many in the PR industry felt P&G would never keep it up; called it a PR stunt and were probably right. P&G received more positive press for "cutting back" than any other corporation for a marketing release that year. Spending did go back up by a few percentage points. P&G claimed they were being smarter about how they spent in traditional arenas.

† They're fairly drunk with A's if you ask us.

Meet Ol' Roy

Come and listen to the story about a dog named Roy . . .

See, back in the day, if you saw people putting cans of store-brand dog food into their shopping cart, you immediately thought one thing—they hate their dog. (Or, secondly, those people are poor.) Times are changing rapidly in this area, so the story of Wal-Mart's Ol' Roy dog food is a good way to monitor this change.

Named for Wal-Mart granddaddy Sam Walton's favorite hunting companion, the private-label dog food Ol' Roy was introduced to his stores in 1982 as a low-price alternative to the national brands. Ol' Roy eventually became the biggest seller of all dog-food brands in the country, surpassing even Purina. It was so successful that Wal-Mart used this case study to expand its line of original-brand products, which today are outselling many national brands sitting on the shelves beside them. These aren't the less tasty, no-frills packed string beans of yesteryear. We're talking quality household necessities, baby!

Big chains everywhere have discovered that they can offer their customers quality, even with their store name on the label, and make some serious bills in the process. Look at Trader Joe's. They keep costs low by stocking the shelves with their own brand-name products. The Charles Shaw wine they sell is huge and so cheap it's affectionately nicknamed Two Buck Chuck. Like many supermarkets, Joe's consistently offers free samples to its shoppers to promote its line of goods—and prove their value and goodness. The popularity of Joe's brands grew not from expensive advertisements and promotional campaigns but because of awesome word of mouth.

Someone calculated that one in five items sold in the United States is now a store brand. This is scaring the hell out of the old big brands and may for once actually be something positive that a heretofore corporate culture is doing for the consumer. The gamble of Sam Walton's day has worked because it was good for the customer. Give people something they actually want, such as quality at a low price. What a concept!

offer advice and counsel that consumers cannot get elsewhere rather than tell folks how a product will help them!

Some of P&G's innovative marketing initiatives have involved reaching niche audiences through deeds rather than words. Take its campaign for Biomat detergent in Israel, where a target audience of Orthodox Jews for the most part shuns television. P&G got smart and placed posters on street locations asking people to donate secondhand clothes to distribute to poorer families during Passover week. Clothing donations were collected by trucks that actually contained washing machines; while the trucks drove around the religious communities, donations were washed and contributed in full view of the people. This unique, hardly corporate campaign was honored at the 2005 Cannes Lions International advertising festival and resulted in a 50 percent increase in market share for Biomat—focused, niche, successful.

To that we say, *Zei gezunt.*

However, even the smaller companies can get a place at the big-boy table and eat a good lunch so long as they stay nimble, fresh, and creative. Dating to 1910, Saucony Inc., a legendary supplier of athletic shoes, casual footwear, and clothing, based in Massachusetts, is loved by us for their bowling shoe. But Saucony has a thin 1 percent of the $13 billion U.S. sportswear market and would not even dream of competing with the marketing muscle of estranged siblings Nike, Adidas, or Reebok.

Unlike Saucony, those giants can sign multimillion-dollar sponsorship deals with sports stars and rappers and could make a nobody into a superstar if they chose.

Who the hell can compete with that?

So in 2002, acting on a hardly comparable scale, the Boston boys created the ultimate Punk production: the Saucony 26 campaign is an absolutely fabulous example of grassroots marketing. Here, Saucony shared inspirational stories of twenty-six people running in L.A., Boston, Chicago, and New York marathons—each measuring a distance of 26.2 miles. In this brave initiative Saucony went public with its deep care for runners. Those heralded in the Saucony 26 were from central casting's best diverse-background list, and each was individual enough to gain attention via local media and on a popular Web site.

The Saucony participants in the '04 L.A. Marathon included Brian Gillespie and

The Little Brand That Could

It's the third-largest clothing company in Cardigan Bay! Huh? The small seaside town in Wales, that tiny nation on the left side of the United Kingdom. Okay, it's tiny, but Howies has always had big ideas.* Dave and Clare Hieatt are constantly on a mission to make people think about the world we live in through a range of sports clothing whose every fiber has a social conscience. Not in a hectoring way, mind you, but through great design, intelligence, and irreverent humor.

One of its early T-shirt designs was a favorite of skateboarders, who always got suspicious looks because the young 'uns looked scruffy. It was titled Shoplifter because, as you might guess, an electronic tag sewn into it would set off shop alarms. You have to admit—that's Punk.

It was banned for causing a public nuisance, which gave the company some fab publicity. And in typical underdog fashion, Dave Hieatt leveraged a legal threat from Levi's over just where the Howies tag sat on the back pocket of jeans. An article in the UK *Guardian* titled "David v. Goliath Battle as Welsh Jeans Company Tells Levi's to Butt Out" was priceless and profit-making.

While Howies uses—and we're serious here—organic cotton for much of their clothes, to them creating products that last as long as possible is the way to conserve resources and preserve the environment. Here's the tag: "That which has the greatest use possesses the greatest beauty."

It is worth it.

Its designs for clothing, the packaging, a Web site, and even unusual displays (e.g., abandoned freestanding closets painted to present a Howies POV) are consistently recognized by the worldwide design industry. Even with a good vibe, Howies is considered to be one of the UK's most influential sports companies.

Howie's marketing is low-key and on purpose. They don't run many ads and instead rely on the biannual gorgeously produced catalog to get a message out to their base. In the book are details about the products, images, and musings, all of which are bent on conveying the beliefs they wish to share. It makes customers think—and, yes, thinking makes customers want more! Oh what a world our parents gave us.

For instructions on how to make customers think, go to howies.co.uk.

---

* Coauthor Mark helped manage Howies from 1999 to 2001 and is still beaming.

Maureen Kennedy, who, as their story goes, met at Mile Marker 6 during Marathon '98 and returned four years later to marry just in time for the Saucony 26!

Another honoree was ninety-one-year-old Ernie Van Leeuwen, the Boston Marathon's oldest participant, who had recently set a U.S. record for his age group.

The shoemakers gave their carefully selected runners a cash bonus for each mile they completed in the name of proud Saucony. Naturally, most donated winnings to charity, which, too, was a big PR moment for the underdog.

In the UK, a smoothie maker named Innocent Ltd. fought to survive among dominant competitors such as Jamba Juice that ruled the day. The personality Innocent created was of a straightforward, humorous, and irreverent bunch that delivered its wares in "cow vans"—seen in cities and on roadways with horns, eyelashes, udders, and tails and each with a name, personality, and bio.[3]

Among the fruity ingredients they would list "a few small pebbles." Farther down it was: "We lied about the pebbles." We love Innocent for its unerring sense of humor and the push to be unusual. They produced their own book, *Stay Healthy. Be Lazy*, and gained raves through the media.

The company decided to do TV commercials, but recognizing a slick commercial might destroy the brand's hard-earned homegrown sensibility, the Innocent founders shot it themselves at local Gunnersbury Park in West London, around the corner from their corporate home (Fruit Towers, naturally).

This clever and notable ad concerns the amount of fruit that goes into a large carton of Innocent smoothies, which, as you may imagine, is "so much" that there's just no room for "additives, concentrate . . . or chickens." Yes, chickens.

For a glimpse, go to innocentdrinks.co.uk/bored/screensaver.

Growing Pains

Small companies like Innocent and Saucony turn profits by keeping up strong appeal for their products from what is really a small group of loyal consumers. But the world keeps turning and nothing stays the same—or some other cliché—and as a result one of these scenarios is set:

First: A bigger company gets wind of how handy it is to appeal to a heretofore unnoticed niche audience, so it goes after the same group and uses its experience,

The Attention Economy

This was the theme behind the 2006 San Diego Emerging Technology Conference. At its core was something part ridiculous, part hysterical: Continuous Partial Attention (CPA). So in an era when we finally identified "Restless Legs Syndrome" (RLS) as a dysfunction we can't live with, we are glad to see there is finally a term to refer to our way of not really paying attention to anything.

Linda Stone, a former Apple and Microsoft executive, was at the conference to discuss this modern phenomenon. She spoke to an audience of people with their heads stuck in their laptops and BlackBerrys. Not a great audience, but an ideal illustration of CPA.

Open communication channels, nonstop e-mails, interruptive instant messages, and ever-updating Web feeds have caused us all to fade our attention in and out. Continuously. A fine coping mechanism, but surely it's a problem in the workplace when the inter-ruptions intrude on tasks that require someone (anyone) to concentrate. Constantly checking your mobile for new mes-sages or Web updates on news.google.com signifies a dis-interest in a situation you are not committing to.

Everyone seems to have forgotten 90 percent of success is just showing up.

People are more and more interested in what else is going on rather than what is hap-pening in front of them. It is making the person who finally does capture the concentration of a CPA-infected individual feel as though each moment is a struggle to keep that person listening. Take you for instance. You've already tuned out in this sidebar while we are trying to help you tune in. Pay attention!

"Constantly being accessible makes you *in*accessible," explained Stone.

A notable resource for the CPA-afflicted is our friends at getmoredone.com. The Web site was created by the company Pace Productivity, whose business is helping others improve pro-ductivity through time studies, consulting, and training programs. Pace vows, "Once we know how your time is spent, we can show you how to be more effective in meeting your objectives and competing better." Mark Ellwood, its president, relies on a scientific method to help us get our respective shits together. His company even offers an electronic time-tracking device to help us manage how much time we spend on specific tasks.*

---

* Here we get sheepish and admit that one of us (Richard) used the time tracker once and failed miserably when he kept forgetting to set it. Who has the time?!

Ellwood actually follows a minimalist approach to peace of mind by not using a cell phone, Palm plumber pager, fax machine, IM, BlackBerry, iPod, or even laptop. No he did not travel here in a time machine from 1965. He simply believes that "every new technology comes with wonderful benefits, but it also comes with unanticipated side effects, glitches, and maintenance issues. We seem to keep inventing more and more ways to be out of touch with each other." Of course Mark is Canadian, so he can get away with that.

Yet he does make a good point. Technology has created new ways of communicating that help pass information quickly over serious distances. What it hasn't succeeded in is making communication any easier between human beings. How many times have you sent an e-mail that got misinterpreted? When we are not face-to-face and talking to or touching each other, communicating a message is a difficult navigation.

So what can we marketers take from this dissertation? Well, we're fighting harder than ever to get the attention of *anyone.* Fast, focused, and easily absorbed ideas are dominant. Finding seamless ways to insert your company's message into our daily tasks will be a true necessity. Diverting someone's attention *away* from something and *toward* your message is going to be the challenge.

SIDEBAR

Don't you wish to go back to the time when *CPA* made you gulp and think, "Tax time"?

resources, and spending power to enter and conquer. UK grocery chain Tesco PLC is opening dozens of small convenience stores on the U.S. West Coast to take business from mom-and-pops lacking Tesco's global strength.

In a moment of you-can't-make-this-up, in order to find out how the M&P's operated, Tesco executives posed as Hollywood producers on the quest to film a story about grocery stores. How they sleep at night is beside the point!*[4]

Second possibility: A bigger company will decide to buy the bugger that marketed to a niche audience in the first place. Nike, for example, had been trying to break into the growing skate, surf, and snow ware market for years and so bought southern Californian cult surfer dudes Hurley International in 2002, after recognizing they weren't going to do it from scratch. (It's also probable Nike knew that

---

* We wonder if *Clerks* started this way.

this big-is-bad audience would see anything branded "Just Do It" as crap.) Still, even today, Nike has been trying without success to go it alone in the skateboard shoe field with its own Dunk Low Pro SB shoes, first out in the 1980s. Retailers are allowed to order twenty-four pairs per color of shoe in each shipment, thus keeping supply scarce to feed demand, but since it's a skater crowd who detest all things mainstream, the notice of Nike's *sih-woosh* has not made for success here.

Third reality: boredom. People just get sick of you.

Final reality: A brand may grow beyond a core of loyal buyers. Once reaching beyond the first movers, a company loses its distinctive positioning as it attempts to appeal to a group that is far outside its original company values. So what do you do? Stay where you are and forgo potential market share or grow and alienate those early adopters?

In-N-Out Burger is a cult burger-chain restaurant in So Cal that currently appeals to an audience who refuses to live without them, including Britney Spears. . . . Anyone who has ever stepped inside an In-N-Out knows a national push will mean customers will no longer feel as if they are part of a secret club.

Remember Woody Allen's line stolen from Groucho that went, "I refuse to join any club that would have me as a member!"? In the case of In-N-Out, the club's members *created* the place and want to keep it exclusive. It has its own language that while never written down has been passed from loyal customer to new recruit via media coverage. Say you prefer that burger wrapped in lettuce and no bun? Ask the counter associate for "a Protein." Oh, now you want everything—bun, lettuce, tomato, cheese, sauce, onion—*but* the burger? How about an "Air Burger"? One of In's signatures is the "Double-Double Animal Style." That's two burgers, two slices of AC (American cheese), fried onions, sauce, lettuce, and tomato. Scrumptious, true, and great food is what people flock to In-N-Out for. The menu consists of four items. No salad tongs found.

Can anyone say simple? Take it to the masses, and it just becomes another burger joint, only this one will, for its puny offerings, get laughed out of Boise!

Use This with Two Aspirin

1. Being a macho mass-produced product was a positive attribute when it reassured consumers they would get quality and consistency. Now quality is no longer a differentiator (you don't have it, you're the weakest link, good-bye). Being big is now seen as a negative. It connotes arrogance and selfishness. All marketers need to act small. That means you, up there.

2. The inroads made by small companies such as soft-drink maker Ajegroup demonstrate to anyone paying heed that a big idea can steal share from larger competitors. Be audacious and daring, darling.

3. Even monoliths such as Virgin Group can portray themselves as an underdog if they go all out comparing themselves with a big bad enemy ("BBE") that does business as usual. Those who think they are invincible because they have cash should worry a lot about the little competitor with biggish ideas. Real innovation rules!

4. The age of mass-media marketing is *fin*. P&G has an ad budget in the billions and it is shifting focus to concentrate on niche consumer groups, proclaiming in much well-placed PR that they wish to have deep and meaningful connections with customers without even taking them to dinner!

5. Brands like sports-enthusiast outfitters Howies (see sidebar, page 70) and Saucony can carve profitable niches by being wholly terrific and using full-on marketing tactics that focus on building loyalty and keeping it.

Tasty Morsels

- The cell phone industry is worth north of $115 billion globally.[1]

- There are over 2 billion users worldwide and 200 million in the United States.

- Wireless data services are predicted to be worth $14 billion by 2008.[2]

- Sixty-nine percent of U.S. teens own a mobile device (plus a few whose parents are clueless about it).[3]

Five

The Sell Phone
Use and Abuse of the Cell Phone for Marketing

Most of us have a love-hate relationship with our cell phone. Love that we're always in touch, hate that we are constantly in reach, you know the moan.* So it's not surprising that an annual MIT study found the mobile is the device we hate most but cannot live without.† Even those few quiet moments without a phone signal—on the subway for instance—are starting to slip away as wireless networks are extended to pretty much everywhere we can hold a phone.

Almost everyone now has a cell—two-thirds of the people in the United States for instance—creating an industry worth over $115 billion globally. No wonder businesses across different industries are hungrily eyeing the mobile device as the conduit to our other portable companion, our wallet.‡ On top of the cost of a handset, many U.S. consumers will readily spend $600 a year or more on a cellular service,

---

* Funny sign of the times: In the eighties Cliff Robertson appeared above the slogan, "Reach out and touch someone," in an ad for AT&T—made us feel good. Today if a mobile company said that, we'd run for a competitor.

† Lemelson-MIT Invention Index, 2004, has 30 percent of people nominating the cell phone as the device they hate but would not even dream of living without.

‡ In "Wireless Works: Exploring New Brand Connections," a weird 2005 survey, agency BBDO and Proximity—a direct mail group—revealed 26 percent would go back home more for their mobiles than for their wallets if they left both at home.

and some will add another $200 or so on top for the entertainment now available through most carriers. That's a lot of cash being spent on something we didn't really need a few years ago.

And because we rely on our cells so much (our true life partners) that it goes with us wherever, there is growing interest in its potential role in marketing—especially to younger people. The mobile device is becoming the ultimate in "sell" phones.

While most cite rational factors for their umbilical mobile dependence, such as convenience and safety, or basic help when in danger, there seems to be a strong emotional component at play. We need to feel connected with others in stressful situations or ones where we feel alone or anonymous. Why else would so many people reach out as soon as the plane has touched down and we are "permitted" to do so?

We aren't kidding ourselves. Any smarty knows it's less a need to be in touch and more fear of having silence anywhere. Thinking is so passé. (See sidebar, "Do Ya *Think*?," page 53.)

So, using a mobile device in front of strangers is a shout-out. As we become more connected with those around us we can now be assured: "I am not alone, ever. See? I have people who need and love me. So there."

More than with TV or the PC, the relationship we have with the Third Screen makes it a potentially powerful means for marketers to get to us, as anybody born after 1990 knows. Oh, but it is fraught with danger. Annoy the cell phone user with unwanted advertising messages, and you've ruined a beautiful relationship with your brand before it begins.

So marketers beware: Use this portal into personal space with great caution. Tread lightly or risk losing out on *billions*.

Luckily, help is at hand. While the United States is often the groundbreaker in many forms of marketing innovation, in the case of cell-phone marketing Americans learn from others. The Finns and South Koreans are so ahead in matters of mobile technology it hurts. Finland makes sense since it is home of Nokia, the biggest handset manufacturer in the world, and the South Koreans because their government badly wants the country to become a world leader in all forms of connectivity.*

---

* Apartment buildings are obliged to post their speed of Internet access on a sign out front!

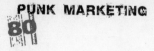

Message Across without Being Cross

Texting through the Short Messaging System (SMS) has been a big deal in most European countries since the early part of this decade, for it is the communication method of choice for teens and young adults. In the United States it's still pretty new—as shown by the fact that when AT&T invited viewers of *American Idol* to vote by text message, half said they were SMS virgins! (Probably it's because lazy U.S. citizens aren't yet keen on the ABC to DEF format of SMSing.) But SMS is catching on; thanks to know-it-all PDAs that have an SMS THIS button and a QWERTY keyboard.*

In the UK a typical marketing campaign using text messaging might involve codes being printed inside the packaging of a snack food: if you message a special phone number, you can win a prize, such as free airtime. As in all lead generation, contests work because in exchange for giving presents, the marketer compiles a valuable and rich database to be used to send info and offers. And, oh, yeah, thanks for playing, here's a brand message back at you!

Key to mobile marketing campaigns is—as in anything decent—to make them permission-based. Text-message spam has been a problem for years in Europe (and soon to be one in the U.S.), where 80 percent of cell phone users polled said they had received it.[4] It can be particularly irritating for consumers whose plans dictate they pay for inbound text messages, so at ten cents or more a shot you are asking people to pay for your nuisance. No, Virginia, there is no such thing as a paid-for ad, yet.

Still a number of successful SMS campaigns have won our hearts as certifiably Punk. For instance, ipsh!,[†] a San Francisco mobile marketing firm part of the Omnicom Group Inc. family of marketing and PR companies, has created campaigns for the Kellogg Company, Anheuser-Busch's Budweiser brand, and Reebok USA with claims that only 1 percent of subscribers demand their numbers be removed.[5]

According to ipsh! CEO Nihal Mehta, about a quarter of the alerts that movie-

---

* The authors think someone will make a bundle in the next few years with $100 accessory keyboards that can be connected to phones; type away with ease. We wonder why the ten-cent-per-SMS phone companies don't *give* these to customers. Make it on the back end.

† "Why ipsh!?" we hear you ask. "Instant power single-handed." Or the first syllable of a cool new curse word.

ticket seller (and ipsh! customer) Fandango.com sends subscribers about new releases result in a ticket sale. Mehta recommends that no advertiser should send a text message more than once a week, no matter how special.*

Enpocket, a mobile marketing consultancy with headquarters in Boston, says response rates to a typical text message campaign—15 percent—are infinitely more than those of direct mail advertising. Start your engines, people.

The phone companies are wary of opt-in campaigns, mostly for fear of miffed subscribers blaming and dumping them. For a national promotion in which consumers are asked to send in a "special code" to a retailer's phone number—say, five digits—a marketer needs to get clearance from the carriers to have them recognize the code over their networks. This can be difficult because carriers are wary of consumer backlash. There is a better way. Marketers can capture details for use in the future by holding events during which a crowd sends up flares of texts during a trivia quiz. How much more user-friendly than forcing people to punch in a code, right? You tell the crowd, "Now's your chance to enter that sweepstakes posted on big screens above your heads; and please watch the ads."

One of your authors, a professional futurist/show-off, once envisioned a time when you or we would walk by a shop and a special discount or a menu would pop onto our teeny screens. Since now our phones include government-enforced Global Positioning System (GPS) and Radio Frequency Identification (RFID) technology, this is certainly possible. An obvious scenario—when we got a whiff of a nail salon, we'd be sent a message saying free pedicure with that manicure—hasn't found a way into our lives. But wait a bit.

Time will tell if GPS-located messages to consumers' mobiles will be a terrific panacea for marketers or just piss everyone off, making us feel hounded more than usual.

Beyond the generation of cell phones with SMS capabilities are those tiny handsets with Wireless Application Protocol (WAP) and other browsers allotting us content richer than text, but which hardly a multitude have used (fewer than 20 million). Marketers, sometimes those that sponsor free ringtones and other boring

---

* This is advice everyone needs to take. It's as if marketing people discovered how easy it is to push SEND and do so as if they were five years old.

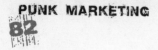
products, have already created campaigns that use banner ads on WAP phones, but the small screen size is not conducive to sophisticated advertising, and no matter how clever the ad is, it always seems like spam.

For some core users—eighteen-to-twenty-fours—exposure to banner ads as barter for a service or product is acceptable, but for others it just gets in the way of expediting needs.

In a 2005 survey by market researchers In-Stat, four out of five users oppose the idea of cell phone advertising and would scream to high heaven if any variation started up.[6] Where is high heaven?

Entertainment, Go!

Our mobile devices are far more than a mere communication device; these handy handhelds are becoming an entertainment center for games, music, video, porn, and anything else we need to stimulate us. On some available handsets, users e-mail, text message, browse the Internet, take and view photos or video, listen to music, record anything aural, watch short movies, play games, shoot pool, throw dice—oh, the list is endless. . . . Now you can even watch boring live TV. The optometrists must be lovin' it.

In the end a Punk realizes that before long this third screen will be our only friend and the only thing we need for happiness.

We all know a tiny screen, no matter how brilliant the image or sound quality, will not be able to compete with a fifty-inch plasma when it comes to viewing *Spider-Man 7*, nor a Bose system for tune appeal, nor an Xbox 360 for game playing, no matter how much the manufacturers might hype the newest version on the street. But, as we spend more of our lives as pseudo-road-warriors, sheer convenience is what we seek.*

The iPod is surely not optimal for music—gosh, the thing compresses sound—but with tens of millions using them as their only way to get a fix, the appeal of

---

* In Americans' nonstop need for another new category, *road warrior* became the nom d'hype for busy executives in the nineties; now everyone who takes a short hop to Miami considers himself "so busy, always on the go." Thus we are all tough, harried street fighters, making our way. . . .

something that's easy to use, cool to look at, and fits in your pocket (as Dirk Diggler might boast) is large and all charged up.

Marketers who see the potential of the cell as a way to get to consumers wherever and whenever have already started to experiment. Some have created innovative campaigns using features on the modern mobile device. As part of the launch of the big-marketing-budget Pontiac G6, General Motors held a sweepstakes that invited its remaining consumers to take pictures of the G6 with their camera phones to win a million bucks (and let GM create a pretty sizable database). To wit we respond, congratulations, GM, for being Punk for once.

Utah's largest phone company, Qwest Communications, also used the device to engage teens and introduce them to miracles of cell technology. In 2004, Qwest organized a scavenger hunt for high school students throughout the state. Students took pictures via phone of semacodes (similar to info-filled bar codes), after which they received clues by text. The proudest school with the most points, Layton's Northridge High School, received a cash grand prize, and other schools that took part each got $2,000. The winners naturally donated prizes to the Christmas Box house, which provides services to abused children.* The winners are hereby applauded. When we were teens, that'd never have happened!

Perhaps some of you remember the Coq Roq campaign, named for a rock band with tons of attitude, and brought to you by Burger King Brands Inc. This was the King's way of introducing a music-recognition service for cell users. To play, you'd send in fifteen seconds of a favorite song via mobile device, after which you would receive a permitted text message telling you the name of the artist and the song. You got it only after CR's lead, Fowl Mouth (geddit?) shouted, "I've heard enough! My ears are bleeding!"

Clever stuff. Yet most marketers do not yet consider the mobile to be a serious medium. This is partly because, except for young adults, relatively few U.S. blabbers use their cells for more than calls despite the complex array of features you *could* learn about if you bothered to read the manual and felt like shelling out to use.

But let's talk about South Korea, where 75 percent possess a mobile; this little nation is considered to be at the absolute forefront of cell phone technology. Many

---

* Not the abused victims of marketing campaigns, however. These poor souls are left to fend for themselves.

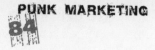

businesses use the people in Korea as guinea pigs to iron out cell phone service sna-fus before the services are launched elsewhere.* Both Samsung and Microsoft's MSN Mobile division often launch products in the United States after six months of testing in South Korea to ensure all is copacetic.

Our advice is to book a trip to Korea—www.fly2Korea.com—to glimpse future possibilities and be a trend-spotter. Koreans can currently conduct financial trans-actions on their cells using built-in payment apps and will soon have the ability to receive wide-range Radio Frequency Identification (RFID) tags on products to get "the goods" about any product or, of course, to get special offers.

Expect them to use RFID so passersby can receive signals from a movie poster and download a trailer, so it's not beyond the realm of possibility of one day downloading a product demonstration or commercial from an RFID tag on a prod-uct right there in the store. Then there are retail displays containing Near Field Communication (NFC) tags that "talk" to mobile phones in the vicinity that have Bluetooth radio technology and deliver text graphics and videos to them in a flash. Most phones don't currently have the ability to read NFC tags, and in trials by the UK's Channel 4 TV network, many users left the area before the content was fully downloaded, but, hey, it's the early days.[7] The plan is that before too long people will be able to buy the things they see on their tiny screens by paying for them there and then. Stores? Who needs them?

Coming to a Teensy Screen near You . . .

In Korea, live TV for cell phones has launched in a big way, even if Western consumers seem skeptical about the idea of watching video entertainment on theirs. The majority of consumers surveyed in a recent poll in the UK, for instance, said they had no interest in that kind of eyestrain.† There are 3 to 4 million video-

---

* This is hardly new. Circa the early 1900s, Alexander Graham Bell's phone company went to Cuba to try out his phone service on the island before wiring the States. Until the nineties, it was Cuba's hilariously antiquated system of phones. When it rained, no one was able to talk on the phone.

† According to the survey released by RBC Capital Markets in March 2006, only about 23 percent of roughly one thousand people polled said they had an interest in watching TV on their mobile phone.

enabled handsets in the States compared with almost 25 million in Korea[8]—and in the States the number of those subscribing to services for downloading video is a fraction of the 200 million that have phones.

But a potential market trumps all fears. Huge service* and content providers are hell-bent on having TV catch on since televised entertainment is what we live for au naturel. A subscription plan that charges $15 to $25 a month on top of voice/data services could net billions per year. That saying again? Follow the *what*?

If it needed a kick start to make mobile video a mass-market phenomenon, the industry needed to look no further than Steve Jobs. Apple's 2005 launch of its video iPod and its arrangement with the Walt Disney Company's ABC Television to let users download episodes of a few of its popular programs, such as *Desperate Housewives* and *Lost* (followed by nearly every other smart-to-act broadcaster and popular cable outlet), pushed the medium to new limits.†

Given the incredible success of the iPod since its '01 launch, the cell phone industry is sure that the next step is all of us chickens staring at videos on our cell phones walking down the street, crashing into each other all along the way. Maybe we will watch so much out-of-home TV that full-scale zombie hood will finally set in.

And you know small-screen video has become legitimatized when the Academy of Television Arts & Sciences unleashes a new and much covered Emmy in honor of "nontraditional viewing platforms"—such as cell phones and iPods. Nominees for the 2006 awards—the very first for the category—included *It's JerryTime!,* a series of mobisodes created by Jerry Zucker (producer of the classic *Airplane!*) and his brother Orrin Zucker, based on the former's life, and *24 Conspiracy*, a series for mobiles based on Fox's hourly *24* series.

---

* We use the term *service* loosely here. But you know that.

† *Lost*, meanwhile, is a mystery/suspense/sci-fi mixed tape, so it released much content from within the show—fictitious books of actual works "written by characters on the show." Then ABC released news that the characters' fiction was that of famed adventure novelist Laurence Shames, who denied it but said "everyone should read it" to the media. Subsequently, ABC got wise and has premiered programs with nonforwardable commercials on its abc.com portal, in addition to iTunes. The games have begun.

Many broadcasters and cablers strike deals with cell service providers for content in exchange for a revenue share. Sprint PCS Vision customers receive content from Cartoon Network, CNN, and E! Entertainment, and Verizon Wireless's V CAST offers hundreds of video clips with content from Comedy Central's *Daily Show with Jon Stewart,* but mostly castoffs from CNBC and other aforementioned "content sources." Most is reconstituted from network TV, but it is important to note that limitations of the small screen—plus legal hurdles of content rights beyond regular platforms—has led to more original content for cell phones.

In April 2006, Disney Mobile was launched as the first service targeted at "the networked family,"* and in doing so granted Mickey and pals a piece of the contract pie wherein a third of all contracts are family plans. Disney is firmly in control of every aspect of the service including product development, marketing, customer service, and even cute bills. Features include a parental handset so guardians can directly manage how their kids use their phones, and a GPS enabling parents to locate their stray offspring. Uh-oh. The Mouse is watching.

Service providers are desperate to avoid being bypassed in the content race just as they were wrong when cynical providers passed off ringtones as a passing phase (d'oh!). Disney wireless service is contracted through Sprint Nextel, so a carrier is still part of the equation, but services like the one launched by Sling Media are another thing altogether, and one in which Sprint Nextel, Verizon, AT&T, and T-Mobile play no part.

The initial Slingbox device gave users a chance to divert signals from a TV cable box, satellite receiver, or DVR directly onto a computer-connected online—anywhere. And a newer SlingPlayer Mobile extends its reach to include Windows Mobile—enabled cell PDAs.[9] Are you wondering when spiteful carriers will block signals from entering their phones? Wish to be part of our Revolution? *Then don't stand in the way of the Revolution.*

---

* Another category to mention. One of our authors launched the first "networked family" service for the Children's Television Workshop when *Sesame Street* hit the Web in 1997. To this day it is felt that a family tied via the Net will grow and remain happily connected.

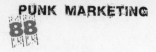

Want My "M" TV

U.S. and European consumers experienced the wonders of live TV on their cells while getting up-to-date with the "luge action" during the 2006 Turin Olympics, and then again cheering a soccer game during the hugely popular 2006 FIFA World Cup (the USA team looked good for a while, but Americans were busy watching Howie Mandel).*

Whether it's good for marketers to irritate consumers during a sporting event is a whole different ball game, though. As with thirty-second TV spots, the ten-second commercials found on mobile units had better be wholly engaging and relevant to the content and not just tossed in because "we can." Remember, marketers, this is the ultimate personal device and not a TV sitting pretty in a house.

How long before ad skipping devices for mobiles, we wonder?†

Games and Beyond

When the founder of gaming giant Electronic Arts (EA), Trip Hawkins, says, "The next big thing is games on cell phones," let's pay attention. His company Digital Chocolate Inc. (named because Hawkins wants the same desire for games that people have for cocoa beans but no messy fingers)‡ competes in the mobile gaming market with EA Mobile—once JAMDAT Mobile—to tap into a growing market for mobile gaming.

Those 3-G phones have been commonplace in Asia for many years, and they hold some pretty sophisticated animation and video-based games that give a sense of the future of mobile gaming on our shores. Hong Kong provider of mobile games Artificial Life Inc. launched "virtual girlfriend" Vivienne that appears as an animated

---

* Mobile TV is not video on demand (VOD) and uses different technology—Digital Video Broadcast-Handheld (DVB-H) or MediaFLO—for broadcasting TV this way.

† Of course, as satellite radio has found, the danger is in too many monthly subscription services—when will the camel's back break! XM is now offering free service to DirecTV customers with radio playing on their TV because in some places they just wanted the numbers (damn the subscriptions!).

‡ We made up the messy fingers bit.

character on subscribers' cell screens. She's a real needy girl, that Viv, and demands constant attention and gifts you pay to provide via the monthly subscription fee; mostly to keep her on your good side. If she is neglected, Vivienne refuses to speak. We're tempted to say "just like a woman" here, and we hold back.

The *New York Times* explains how Viv won't ever be naked but will wear skimpy outfits to the gym if you beg.[10] You can marry her and end up with a mother-in-law who will even phone in the middle of the night to ask how you've been treating her daughter. It's a virtual headache.

Crazy, right, but we're so bored with the old tech that anything smacking of the new drags us in. The cell's role is far more important than that of just talking away on something that matches our outfit! As the Internet proves daily, with societal boundaries breaking down we are no longer bound by a shared geography, and something mobile helps us feel we are still part of a bigger world, one where we can interact and spend some money!

The key to marketers is ensuring that customers feel they are in control. This is clearly demonstrated by the emergence of the phenomenon called "flash mobbing," in which groups drawn together by a common purpose use communication networks—cell or the Internet or carrier pigeons—to coordinate large-scale actions at the same time in distinct locations. The civil unrest in France in late 2005 was largely coordinated through texts sent to one another by the young Muslims who felt alienated from French society.

Happily there isn't always such a serious issue at stake—or such unfortunate repercussions—for flash mobs. In the first reported FM in the UK, five hundred people gathered in a central London store and began speaking without using the letter O. (This is definitely a subplot for a smart sitcom writer—call us for more.) And in both the UK and in the United States there have been numerous instances of mass pillow fights that start seemingly spontaneously but have again been coordinated through text messages. That's a lot of feathers.

Some ahead-of-their-time marketers have even started experimenting with using flash mobs to draw attention to their products. In India in 2003, Sony orchestrated a flash mob outside a mall in Mumbai to begin chanting a TV title it was promoting.

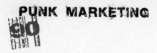

Use This for Pillow Talk

1. The cell or mobile phone is something consumers rely on not just for communication but as a means of staying connected with the rest of the world, thus meeting deep psychological needs unfulfilled since the crib.* It offers a world of possibilities for marketers, and more than any other medium represents a massive risk: consumers rejecting unwelcome marketing, and the brands they are associated with, forever more.

2. Campaigns that use texting to engage consumers and reward them with prizes or offers are effective only if strictly permission-based. Give the participants something relevant to them that attaches them to the brand completely. The people have to recall it was you who gave it up.

3. In the United States, despite that new handsets host endless new features, people just don't care. (We often wonder whether each menu slide has too much text on it.) Consumers mostly want fewer dropped calls and clearer voice communication. But the mobile is fast becoming the entryway to entertainment that includes video, live television, music, and games; innovative marketers are experimenting to bolster their campaigns. Imagine the porn apps that will pop up in your lap. . . .†

4. With nonstop further advances in cell technology *and* quality content *and* user experiences, features such as live TV on cell phones and cool-as-shit mini-commercials are sure to follow. But just as with commercials on regular TV, marketers have got to take a deep breath and start with step one: if these ads are

---

* Let's be clear. We mean *baby crib*, not the place you take an unknowing sex partner to.

† In 2000, we worked with two women who attempted (key word attempted) to launch the Erotigo service so you'd have had all that Web-sought sex in the palm of your slick hand. Our meetings with them were sure fun.

not both fun and totally "something that matters to me," consumers will avoid them—and subsequently wonder why you are bugging them, again.*

5. Before long cell phones with RFID reading abilities will enable consumers to find out a ton of new information about the products by scanning codes or print ads and downloading short videos onto their phones, giving new opportunities to engage consumers through compelling content. Can you see us now?

---

* We Punks got a charge out of Robert Iger, Disney chief, telling the *Wall Street Journal* in June 2006 that tested ads were *watched and recalled* when abc.com streamed free episodic dramas; but of course! The viewer was informed each ad break would be no more than thirty seconds. Hmm.

Tasty Morsels

- The mobile networks have been concentrating on new customers and totally writing off existing ones; as a result the industry receives more complaints than any other.

- Forty-two percent of consumers call "customer service" the element businesses need to improve upon most. And they had better.

- Half of all customers would change to another cell carrier if it weren't for early termination fees or good old American laziness.

- Developments such as cheaper mobiles and Wi-Fi handsets are sure to mean consumers will no longer have to enter into lengthy contracts. That, and death threats to companies who insist on merging.

- Someone who experiences a crappy interaction with an employee leaves with a bad taste about the manager and even his company. Customer service should not be an oxymoron.

The Captive Consumer
Callous Corporations Con Customers

Marketing should not stop when a consumer has taken out his wallet. That should be the beginning of one hell of a friendship. A business needs to ensure that its customers never want to leave and have a strong emotional attachment toward the brand and the brand's attributes! As marketers we will never have as much opportunity to connect with people as when they land in our lap. An old adage in business says that you ask for everything during the initial period because the love is new and you can do no wrong. In the case of marketers, this becomes a missed opportunity or an abuse of trust the consumer has placed in us by saying, "You are the man!"

The absolute biggest abuse of consumer trust comes from those industries in which the accepted practice is to entice customers through promises of a wonderful life if only they would sign up for a service. Those persons are non grata once they do, however, because so many businesses make it famously tough for consumers to leave when they realize it was a crock of lies they purchased.

In that list of repeat offenders are credit card companies, health clubs, banks, Internet service providers, and clueless mobile phone networks hanging off a cliff as we type. Many of these businesses make stupendous profits by tying customers up without thinking where such behavior leads. Such short-term gain at the expense of long-term *anything* needs to be rethought.

These folks don't seem to have taken on-board lessons from their friends at the airline industry.

Beware of Low-Flying Airlines

For years, larger-than-life airlines thought they needn't worry about keeping customers happy because frequent-flier programs handcuffed them into flying their unfriendly skies. Travelers put up with being treated like burping pigs because they rightly felt they had zero choice. Until those wily smaller discount airlines came along and dazzled them with cheap fares, amazing service, and strong branding.

Then it was all over.

JetBlue Airways and Southwest Airlines started consistently getting high "flies" in customer satisfaction via surveys like the J.D. Power & Associates Airline Satisfaction Index Study and made profits as a result, while other carriers struggled to breathe! JetBlue even used to have a section on their Web site about *how they make a profit* titled JetBlue 101.*

In announcing results of the J.D. Power 2005 study, Linda Hirneise, partner and executive director, tossed the biggest smack: "Dissatisfaction with a lack of amenities is an area the industry needs to keep a close eye on as more carriers reduce their offerings in favor of lower operating costs. However, what we're seeing in low-cost carriers like JetBlue and Southwest is that airlines offering a consistent travel experience and that listen to what's most important to passengers are proving to be very successful."

When managing an office of ad legends Crispin Porter + Bogusky, author Mark helped create a marketing campaign for Aeromexico in the United States that dove headfirst at how folks felt about those monolithic airlines. We're Flying in a Different Direction was the theme that provocatively displayed smaller Aeromexico as a real alternative with fabulous service and a one-to-one caring attitude as opposed to cattle-oriented treatment of its competitors.

With little budget with which to play, the program needed to focus in and around those key airports the airline flew into, using media that demonstrated Aeromexico's refreshing distinction in attitude.

---

* Somehow they felt it did not fit the brand anymore. A spokesperson sweetly e-mailed: "We found [the Learn More page] worked best as we continue to evolve JetBlue.com to meet our customers' needs and . . . more people become familiar with the airline." We obviously disagree and *wanted* to include it for your perusal but were advised against it by legions of well-shod lawyers.

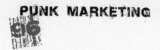

Pretty Sneaky, Sis

As airlines continue to struggle with just about everything, including in some serious cases taking flight, they're seeking new formats in which to make money. Since they can't possibly raise ticket prices, many turn their attention to advertising. Think about it. They've got us locked in our seats with little to stare at for hours and nothing to say to our seat mate (who usually is wary of us anyway). It's an advertiser's dream!

Some airlines are putting full-blown ads on tops of tray tables. The smart ones are more subtly using corporate-sponsored headsets, snacks, and games. MasterCard International provided complimentary snacks, movie headphones, and puzzles and games aboard nearly six hundred American Airlines flights during the 2005 holiday travel season. Just about anything on a plane is available for corporate pushing. "This meal brought to you by the new Lincoln Zephyr!" "This life vest brought to you by Target!" While we *think* we made up the latter, why not? It seems no surface is sacred these days. No *place* is sacred. They took away our freedom from advertisements at the movies—and now even at live theater. Next they're going to get us in the air. This is more junk than Punk.

The more ads on a plane, the less clear is the airline's message ("More legroom in coach!" becomes "Stretch your legs in Danskin!"), and that equals less connection to their passengers.

Take JetBlue and Southwest. They've honestly managed to stir up customer loyalty and word-of-mouth buzz. People don't loathe flight travel quite as much because of airlines like these. They're the envy of the jumbo airlines, bringing in heaps of cash without beating their passengers over the head with irritating ads. But in the end, money is money and airlines are eager for the revenue. The challenge will be in the artful ways they incorporate advertising of products alongside advertising themselves. People do not like to feel an advertiser has them *too* captive. Soon a backlash will rise up and the airlines listening to customers will survive it.

To illustrate Aeromexico's impressive on-time performance, CP+B placed one guy among the limo drivers waiting patiently at baggage claim with a marked sign stating cheekily to the *other* passengers, "If you were flying Aeromexico, I wouldn't have had to wait this long." And to stress that Aeromexico still served proper meals aboard, CP+B placed dioramas at airports with real sachets of beef jerky attached to them and the line "A complimentary snack for our friends flying other airlines."*

Surely it isn't just airlines whose committed customers announced that they want to see other people. According to a recent study of the banking field, a scant two out of seven customers say they are "highly committed" to their bank.[1] As you can imagine, feeling committed makes a big difference in the number of a bank's services a customer will use (3.3 on average compared with 2.5 for those with low or little commitment) and the likelihood they will recommend the financial institution to a friend (87 percent for the committed versus a why-bother-opening-the-doors 5 percent for the lowest echelon).

Health clubs are often criticized for making it gorgeously attractive to join but, as in the classic episode of *Friends*, so unbearably difficult to cancel.† We all know we start the year with good intentions but kill them off once we realize how bad we are at showing up. Health clubs get a whopping increase in new memberships after the holidays as people resolve to get fit, and then at the start of beach season as well, but most new members end up not using their membership at all. It takes less than a moment to sign up for a membership at the counter, but cancellation needs to be in writing and requires reasons and a visit to a dark chamber.

Then there are those gaudy Internet service providers (ISPs) who market heavily to get people to sign up and pay a monthly fee yet are far from yielding once the relationship runs its course. After growing dissatisfaction with the service, in 2002 Time Warner Inc.'s AOL started losing subscriptions hand over fist;‡ competitors such as NetZero and Juno Online Services zeroed in, offering cheap, bare-bones services, and a year later AOL had lost over a million subscribers.[2]

---

* Continental seized the idea and now advertises boldly, "Other airlines feed you promises. We feed you."

† Chandler and Ross go to cancel and are beset upon by a hot woman who sultrily talks them out of it.

‡ A May 2002 survey by ChangeWave Research revealed that 40 percent of respondents were dissatisfied by the AOL service, the most negative and overwhelming results the research and investment firm had found in over one hundred similar surveys on other companies.

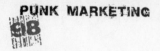
Unwilling to take defections lying down, AOL needed to find ways to keep their customers from going elsewhere. Not through better service or "that better Internet," but through unscrupulous means. New New York Governor Eliot "Ness" Spitzer accused the company of making it unduly difficult for folks to leave its service, and in the resulting settlement in August 2005 they agreed to pay $1.25 million in penalties and refunds.*

And it's time to say to AOL, "WTF?" They finally went free in mid-2006 after years of losing customers who thought, "I don't need you, bitch." We Punk boys used to watch the spots for "AOL broadband" and think, "Well, wait a minute. I already have broadband, why do I need to add AOL?" Their chieftains finally figured that one out and made the access to their content—which was made free on AOL.com earlier in the year—advertised as gratis. It only took them six years.† Now they're focusing their business model on ad revenue. When you move slowly you have more than a little catching up to do.

Can You Hear Us, Dammit?

The number of mobile/PDA users has grown to an astounding 200 million annoying people in the United States alone and more than two billion chatter bugs worldwide. What do you do with such a robust installed base? Why you ignore it as you focus on the acquisition of new customers. Sales growth looks good but masks the growing dissatisfaction most customers feel about the way they are treated by providers. A number of studies proclaim that in terms of customer dissatisfaction the cell phone industry is in pole position. Read these sorry stats weeping:

■ The industry achieved second-to-last place in the American Consumer

---

* We would be remiss not to point out to keen readers that the math is in AOL's favor. They must have made more than $1.25 million in keeping people "in."

† In the year 1999 of our Lord, AOL.com was announced as a place you could go to "access your AOL mail" if you hadn't received a clunky AOL disc. Smart analysts would ask the giantess why she wasn't using that site for a greater use, like maybe to make money.

Satisfaction Index survey taken during the first quarter of 2005, barely scraping above hated cable TV (blurry bastids!).[3]

■ A study by Consumer Union's *Consumer Reports* from February 2005 found that only 45 percent of respondents were completely or very satisfied with the service from their cell company, among the bottom few of the services measured.

■ Worse yet, a 2004 consumer study by Milwaukee's American Society for Quality—whose members include managers and technical employees who are responsible for establishing quality control—placed the cell phone industry dead last.

■ Also in 2004, the U.S. Council of Better Business Bureaus received twenty-eight thousand complaints about mobiles and PDAs, more than new car dealers (not used, naturally), credit card companies, collection agencies, or even marketers! Now *that's* a cry of disdain.

The cell phone industry may be heavily criticized for the way they treat customers, but there are signs these mega-faceless entities are improving. They still have a long, long road ahead. Most dissatisfaction stems from consumers feeling they are prison stooges. Pushing phone users to sign up for two-year contacts to prevent switching, except for a hefty fee, has become standard practice for carriers.

An investigation of Cingular Wireless by the California Public Utilities Commission (CPUC) in response to tens of thousands of complaints from consumers concluded that Cingular had been "fundamentally unfair to consumers" by locking them into contracts and failing to provide the services promised. Despite glossy brochures and bold, kooky ads suggesting unbroken coverage in major cities across the state, subscribers found poor or no coverage. Investigators posed as potential customers traipsing into Cingular dealers and were told coverage was "good" or "had no problem," despite numerous dead spots known to the company. And it forgot to mention the network overload (dropped calls) customers experienced frequently. Try our new phone, which we call the Luzr!

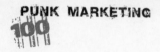
Headlocking consumers into two-year death grips has become even more the norm since Independence Day, November 25, 2003, when for the first time mobile users were allowed to *port* their number if they chose a different service provider. In theory this freed consumers from staying shackled to the same carrier forever. Consumer advocate groups applauded the change, assuming it would force this group of money-grubbers to finally compete on prices, features, and coverage.

Not so fast.

What they didn't count on was that customer service would *not* improve. Instead of going all out to make it better, some carriers spent cash on new, inventive manners to stop what Woody Allen once called "major fleeing." During the summer

of 2004, consumer watchdog Foundation for Taxpayer and Consumer Rights went ahead and sued AT&T Wireless, T-Mobile, and Cingular Wireless for locking their handsets—thus making it impossible for consumers to whisk them away to a new love. Whatever happened to making customers actually like you instead of finding devious ways to make it difficult for them to leave you?

Then to make it worse, these companies defended themselves by claiming they subsidize the cost of the handsets and would lose money if said set went on a competitor's carrier. Recognize the justification—it was used for lengthy contract terms! Public Interest Research Groups (PIRGs)—a nonprofit, nonpartisan advocacy org—reported that that early-termination fees (ETF) ranged from $150 to $240 depending on the mobile freak show you strived to escape, and that nearly half of customers would switch carriers if it weren't for those egregious fees.[4]

The cell phone industry has long faced legal challenges in many states that questioning the fairness of such fees, and in response, an industry trade group oddly named CTIA—The Wireless Association has argued that the early-termination fees are not a penalty, but an "integral part of the customer's rate plan." They say that it's expensive to acquire new customers, but their members have magnanimously chosen to spread these costs over term of contract rather than charge them an up-front fee. Tilting customers toward you is expensive—on the average $392 per new customer.[5]

Two points in response. First, all businesses have costs of acquiring (we like to call it "winning over") a new customer. Aren't these really the costs of doing business recouped through honestly won sales during a budding relationship with the customers? Be real, cellies.

The first few thousand cups of coffee a virgin Starbucks store sells surely don't make enough to cover the costs of leasing the space and fitting out, stocking, and marketing the shop. Yet Starbucks doesn't send a bill to those who go to the local diner after tasting their wares.

And second: Do we believe for a split second that cell service providers pay to the handset manufacturers the full retail price quoted to the surly masses? We would think they should be getting a discount for the millions in orders.

After a deep breath, ponder: If buyers do not like one's offering once they've tried it, don't they have a G-d-given right to go elsewhere? It is the duty of any concern to make a customer want to—not feel obliged to—stay.

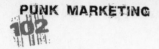
Mobile companies could improve by investing in infrastructure that services its citizen talkers. Good customer service is training folks who are not only informed but are motivated to solve problems rather than make them. The Sprint Nextel store is a shitty experience that everyone copes with, whereas if you call the Customer Service Center you can go bald talking to careless cretins on the other end—assuming, of course, you get through the automated system.

The next step on Recovery Road is to be honest about weaknesses as well as strengths. Punk Marketing means avoiding empty promises. Consumers have an uncanny knack of finding out the truth today: people talk, despite repeat dropped calls.

The addiction to contracts is not only killing the veterans, it has driven new companies to copycat crappiness. No matter how clever newbie Alltel's advertising is, they still make you sign a contract, so it's all for naught. Reasoning from all those guys is that they know we would leave them in a heartbeat (if an alternative to cell service flew into town), and that we think *they* think, "We're just as bad as the other, so why does it matter how awful we are?"

Today all mobile companies are secure in their own *mishegos*. And when an industry gets complacent, it's ripe for an innovation from an outsider to shake it to its core.

Two obvious contenders are the arrival of the cheap-cheap handset that you can nearly dispose of, and the Wi-Fi phone, both of which will make it more difficult for cell companies to keep customers at their whim.

Philips Electronics has already announced plans to develop handsets by 2008 that will cost less than $15.[6] And the GSM Association—a trade group for mobile operators using GSM—is developing a cheap phone for those in emerging markets (e.g., Asia and the Far East). While such phones will not be on sale in the overdeveloped world anytime soon, having cheap phones that service providers will not have to "subsidize" would reduce the need for consumers to sign any sort of service contracts.

In 2005, Vonage Holdings Corp., one of the top Voice over Internet Protocol (VoIP) phone services for making cheap (though below standard quality) calls over the Net, unveiled a wireless phone for calls at Wi-Fi hot spots, thus bypassing the cell providers. The handy Vonage Wi-Fi phone made by UTStarcom automatically sniffs out a signal so it can be used anywhere in the Wi-Fi universe. For a Vonage customer who pays around $25 a month for unlimited usage, calls can be made without limits on minutes and times of the day.*

Wi-Fi isn't everywhere yet, so a phone like Vonage's is perfect at home, in hotels† and in Starbucks and airports, but not so much in the car where we all gab endlessly. But Motorola wants to help the captive by introducing a hybrid usable on a traditional cell network that switches seamlessly to the cheaper Wi-Fi.

Please Don't Squeeze Us for All We're Worth, Mr. Whipple

An inordinate number of businesses make a mistake of saying to themselves that what they offer is so appealing that *they*—people who pay their salaries by buying from them—wouldn't dare go elsewhere.

Let's talk about Wal-Mart Stores Inc., the one that consistently offers the lowest prices by being the biggest and having the most buying power, by forcing its "lucky" suppliers to cut margins and by paying shamefully low wages to its cultish workers. Despite legal problems about employment practices‡ and accusations that they destroy local economies wherever they open a store, Wal-Mart has forged on in the belief that all people care about is that they're cheaper than anyone else on earth. Right, nothing matters besides what I'm paying, so their sentiment goes. Cheap, cheap, cheap.

Birds do it so why shouldn't we.

---

* You cannot dial 911. Vonage has solved that problem with its own emergency call center for you to call.

† If you have ever wondered why mobile phones do not work inside some hotel chains, it's because they allegedly deploy *jammers* that stop the signal. This way you pay for calls. Sleazy.

‡ Let's get recent: It paid a fine to settle federal charges that underage workers were operating dangerous machinery; it agreed to pay $11 million to settle charges that its cleaning contractors hired illegal immigrants; and it has been involved in a class action lawsuit by female employees who claimed that Wal-Mart discriminated against them because they were ladies.

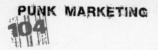
Cracks have started to appear, and in August 2006 Wal-Mart reported its first quarterly profit decline in a decade. Gas prices and the cost of closing its German stores were blamed, but perhaps it also has something to do with its customers finding themselves dealing with poorly or cheaply designed stores cluttered up with merchandise piled to the rafters and less of that down-home stellar customer service. Archrival Target Corporation, in stark contrast, offers a striking combination of appealing stores, stylishly produced or commissioned lines, really top-grade customer service, and surprising prices that have won the hearts of consumers in all parts of America. Oh, and let's not forget a snazzy ad campaign and a dippy chocolate called Choxie that makes people feel good—and full—when shopping at Tar-jay!

Plus, the Target PR sounds good to the more discerning shoppers, namely those who would cry before shopping at K- or Wal-. The key differentiator is that this chain hires talented buyers who stock shelves with "only those products we think you'll appreciate" (a paraphrase), rather than one of everything. The message is, we select so you don't have to. Neat, subtle, and the quintessence of Punk Marketing.

Why can't companies understand the damage the treatment of a single customer can cause? People like Dave Thomas of Wendy's wagged their fingers at young'uns and said: "Each customer has to be the only one." Still, people rarely remember.

According to a survey of seven thousand by BIGresearch, someone who experiences a less-than-friendly employee interaction is left with a bad impression of not only that guy but his manager and the whole company.[7] This enlightening survey claims more than 85 percent of customers say *service* is staying the same or getting worse, and 42 percent feel it's the one aspect businesses needed to improve most. In a similarly alarming vein, consultancy firm Accenture reported poor customer service was the reason customers switched to another technology service provider, with almost half of Brit and U.S. consumers surveyed saying it made them change to another provider of at least one industry during the prior year.[8]

Good customer service can't be a Band-Aid brand bandage for poor products or dishonest words. The whole package, man! Give an integrated engaging experience that makes people love you all over. That's not as difficult as it sounds. Businesses need to stop all that legalese with contracts and small print and captivate, not capture, buyers through use of creativity from product design to marketing. (See chapter 13, "It's More Than Just Us," and sidebar, "A Real Live Conversation," page 182.)

Postscript (Just Because You Made It This Far)

Every cloud has silver, and the same Wal-Mart that forced mom-and-pops out of business in a never-ceasing quest to provide the *lowest everything* in the unchained world has been trying to give consumers an alternative within the perpetrator of the worst service ever: the banking industry. Wal-Mart has continually been knocked out of the field by lawmakers.

Banco Walla-Marti* would provide a service banking industry heavies will not, such as *really* free checking without a catch in sight, and interest payments on any account balances. This is not unlike Commerce Bank,† which rolls your pennies and is open Sunday. Read our lips: no minimums whatsoever! It would be banking privileges for those without privileges—the typical Wal-Mart customer. While we find it hard to believe our government would allow Wal-Mart to sink the cash cows that are the banking corporations that pay election bills, it would be fantastic if someone with such a large customer base and the buying power of kings could shake up an industry that has long been oh-so-complacent about how it treats the customer.

Use This When You Can't Think of Anything to Say to Your "Lovah"

1. Industries that rely on contracts to tie customers in have not learned from the woes of the airline industry, which has seen competitors that offer a better experience rake it in.

---

* Our name—for sale.

† And whose ads decry "stupid" banking fees.

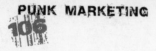
2. Marketing that overpromises combined with a product that over*sucks* forgoes customer loyalty for a profit. This is the view of economics where St. Peter clucks when you enter the Pearly Gates. Marketers have a duty to be honest about products so consumers don't ever feel conned.

3. A smart marketer takes advantage of a complacent industry's assumption that consumers are stuck by using fresh thinking and outlandish positioning against the main players in the industry (see that chapter we love so: "Who's Eating Your Lunch?").

4. The mobile networks have charged unnecessary, immoral ETFs riding a ludicrous excuse that they must cover the cost of customer acquisition. But other businesses aren't penalizing paying clients who use competing products or services (though they give it thought!). Those who market need to make the people who buy their stuff *want to buy from them.* There is always a bright, shiny object to zigzag our attention away from you. Do we have your attention now!

Punk is . . .

Saying something in a meeting at work that jars groupthink away from the safe, tried-and-trusted routes—need we say more?

Putting yourself in others' shoes to see in a more objective way if what you're doing makes sense to the outside world or whether you're just talking crap to yourself.

[to be continued]

Tasty Morsels

- Storytelling as a marketing technique has been around for decades in all kinds of forms. It's all about a damn good anecdote, so your mission is to become the best raconteur you can be!

- The *Halo 2* computer-game launch had elements of creative storytelling throughout its entire marketing campaign. Its prerelease sales of over $120 million means it became *the* most successful entertainment launch ever.*

- *The Art of the H3ist* told a great story that got stolen by the audience. Now that's putting your customer behind the wheel.

_____

* It held this position for many months until pipped by another sequel, *Pirates of the Caribbean: Dead Man's Chest,* in the summer of 2006.

Seven

Now It's Story Time
The Art of Making a Case through Storytelling

Once Upon, Yeah Yeah

Tom Cotton, cofounder of Los Angeles ad agency Conductor, believes that every brand has a story to tell. Conductor is that new breed of agency that feels one-on-one connection with consumers is the way to stretch beyond the blasé TV-spot format and so mixes Hollywood storytelling techniques with marketing expertise. They did a series of thirty-second spots for the NHL and eventually turned out a five-minute short that played at cinemas, on United Airlines flights, and even monitors at Best Buy stores. This beautifully produced film feels like a trailer for a Hollywood drama. It's the *story* of an NHL player who in the guise of a samurai warrior prepares for an epic battle—one on the ice, ice baby.

Normally staid Ford Motor Company reached to the Web as storytelling medium for its innovative launch of Mercury Mariner, a small SUV that Ford felt was right for a new generation of female consumers who wouldn't test-drive the Mercury if they saw it as their forefather's favorite.*

Over a series of short Web flicks we are told intertwining stories of a group of ten odd people and their pet frog. Starting in late 2004, once a week *Meet the Lucky*

---

* Stories did not last; eventually Mercury just talked about how it has fancy-named backseats and SIRIUS Satellite Radio. The car—that's there too.

Ones offered a new chapter in the story of each character. These were parables about mundane activities such as cutting grass or washing clothes, albeit in a *Twin Peaks/ Six Feet Under* surreal sort of way.

Uncannily, Mercury is hardly featured except in one or two meandering shots. And yet, the car company says 75 percent of site visitors clicked onto pages about the Mariner product. More than 50 percent of the half million clickers attracted to the *Meet* opera over six months were under forty-five-years old (as compared to the felt typical sixty-year-old Mariner buyer).

Mercury attributed five hundred car sales directly to the campaign, which industry talker-up *AdWeek* called one of the best ad showings of '04. Seems to have done the—truck!

One advantage of stories as marketing strategy, often called narrative marketing, is the media buzz it will generate if you make it interesting enough. A recent

European marketing campaign for the Volvo S40 was designed to get nothing but media attention. The ads were kinda beside the point.

The Mystery of Dalarö is the story of a small Swedish village of no more than a thousand inhabitants where some thirty-two of them crazily bought a new Volvo S40 on the exact same day. Much like the darling of all things viral—*The Blair Witch Project*—*Dalarö* is told as a documentary with the viewers left to wonder how real.

A series of movie-trailer ads on TV encouraged viewers to go online to see what happened at Dalarö. Through interviews with village inhabitants and myriad S40 owners, plus the perplexed scientists who are trying to figure how this happened, filmmaker Carlos Soto explores various theories for this phenomenon, including what he terms the "collective subconscious." Mystery, suspense, intrigue, and, oh yeah, bullshit!

On another Web place, supposedly unrelated to Volvo, Soto questioned the authenticity of the story Volvo had told him; he now wonders if he may have been an unwilling stooge in an advertising stunt created by those crafty Swedes. The plot thickened then as consumers had to decide what part of this was real.

Who was Carlos Soto?

It turned out to be Spike Jonze, legendary director of the movies *Being John Malkovich* and *adaptation.,* and the man behind that unforgetable music video featuring scary Chris Walken. Layering the story in a delightfully obtuse way kept momentum alive, and as Tim Ellis, global director of Advertising at Volvo cars, said, "Once you think you've got it, we offered one more layer to the communication to question that assumption."[1]

It is the way TV megahit *Lost* gains viewers as it unveils itself. Give people more to talk about and they will talk about it.

A spokesperson at MVBMS Fuel Europe, the agency that created Volvo's complicated campaign, proclaimed, "People are absolutely saturated with advertising these days and we need to find new ways to capture their imagination."[2]

These days the car companies and games studios have taken this approach to a new level by creating marketable tales that play out on both the Net and in real life, and where customers actually *are* characters in the stories. This new branch of marketing is called alternative-reality branding (ARB) and derives from something that uses similar techniques called alternative-reality games.

A respectable example of a hard ARB is to be found at the launch of video game

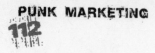
Take Our Tops Off!

The yogurt brands Yoplait, Stonyfield Farm, and Dannon found an interesting way of standing out from the crowd recently, which involves removing tops. We're talking about the tops of yogurt containers, unfortunately. We liked those plastic lids because they meant we could drag them in our knapsacks all day, without having one of our many pens rip into it and mess up our pajamas.

All three claim to have the environment and our health in mind, but are using different stories to get to our hearts. Yoplait is using guilt as a tactic. Their "Save Lids to Save Lives" campaign is a fight against breast cancer. It's simple. Buy Yoplait yogurt, mail them back the clean lid, and they'll donate ten cents to the Susan G. Komen Breast Cancer Foundation. With the accompanying slogan "If you held the cure in your hand, would you throw it away?" it says to women everywhere: Buy us or . . .

We find the message alarming: Don't buy Yoplait yogurt and apparently we'll never find a cure for breast cancer. How could you reach for anything else in the supermarket?

On another hand, Stonyfield Farm is focusing on creating less garbage. As an environmentally conscious company, or so they say, Stonyfield has put a lot of time and effort into creating the environmentally friendly packaging for yogurt that *also* is lid-free. Apparently, the container is not the best they had hoped for: Stonyfield asks that if you cannot recycle its containers locally, then send back the clean cups and lids and they will recycle them for you. What do we derive here? Recycling is still a lot of work.

Dannon, in a bid to appeal to consumers who are buying Stonyfield, has also stopped using the plastic lid on their containers, The lone foil cover, they say, will eliminate the production of 1,620 metric tons of wasted plastic and likely drop their packaging cost significantly. Win plus win! As part of the new campaign they've asked us, "What would you do with 3.6 million pounds of plastic?"

So, like Yoplait, this firm has asked us to dig deep inside for some moral fiber. Dannon's answer is toys for needy children. They're donating $100,000 to Toys for Tots saying plastic is better off used on toys for needy children.

It's a tactic for getting at consumers' heartfelt wallets. Similar to right-wing Republicans claiming, "If you don't support the war in Iraq, you don't support our troops," someone is now saying, "If you don't buy Yoplait yogurt, you're in favor of people dying of cancer."

Is this logical? No. One of the above has worked. Democrats, take special notice.

Halo 2 by Microsoft Corporation in a time when the M-ster was stringently attempting to establish itself as a major games maker. The pressured marketing team knew that they had to think uniquely to make it work.

Chris Di Cesare, director of Xbox marketing at Microsoft, told us he thought of it more like launching a slice of entertainment than a game, and so he began to study the campaigns created for blockbuster releases such as *Spidey, LOTR* trilogy, and the many sequels of *Harry* (Potter, not Dirty). Di Cesare knew the budget would be tiny and he'd have to work harder with *his* money.

While the world of movies is all about box office numbers on opening weekend, to the gamers it's all about preorders. Together with 42 Entertainment (Microsoft's agency), Di Cesare concentrated his limited resources on driving those much watched numbers skyward.

The storytelling approach went nuts in bringing consumers into a secretive, enveloping, and strange plotline that combined elements of online and real world.

Di Cesare wanted tons of buzz and naturally developed a site called I Love Bees! It started as a trailer for *Halo 2* that ran in theaters months prior to the game's release.

Bzzzzz.

Di Cesare was confident even six months before the November 2004 release that his was going to be the biggest *anything* weekend in U.S. history. (*Spider-Man 2* had sold $115 million on its first weekend, so that's saying something.) Di Cesare's team's strategy was one of "polarizing the core [of gamers] and feeding the masses."

The story of the game that was showing on ILoveBees.com fed directly into the storyline of the game itself (created by Bungie Studios), and that drew in the gamers. Then the novelty of the campaign was ballyhooed in the media, and the game reached a broader audience of people who were not gamers.*

---

* PR plays a role, but so does careful planning within segments. Jackson's *Thriller* was monumental because Jackson and CBS Records released one song for each marketplace: a rocker, a pop ditty, a kid's song, a novelty number, a McCartney track, and one bitching dance tune. Say what you will about El Jacko, but no one had mastered anything close to this phenom back in 1982.

Some fans went to extraordinary lengths to be part of the game. One dude from Florida stood hanging onto a pay phone to receive clues during Hurricane Ivan until the actor on the other end demanded that he put the freaking thing down and run!

The campaign was compelling entertainment, and it didn't matter to most of the players that they had immersed themselves in a giant marketing scheme.

Yet the marketer doesn't always have full control of the game board in these sorts of campaigns! Sometimes those invited to participate in a reality campaign influence the plot more than the creators had intended. For the new Audi A3 launch in 2005, agency McKinney created *The Art of the H3ist*, a complex story that lasted three long months.* Toward the end, some shrewd attention-payers took it upon themselves to change the carefully scripted story.

H3ist involved six new Audis containing encrypted codes for an in progress "art theft" where one car contained the keys to all. This car was, ahem, "stolen" from a Park Avenue dealership and surveillance footage was somehow posted on the Internet. Each progressive fragment seemed more real. On a series of sites people tracked the action through e-mails, video, and blogs.

At the Coachella music festival outside Indio, California where part of the story was taking place, knowing gamers turned up earlier than expected and dodged security and forced Chelsea Pictures, the production company for the online video, to change the script on the spot and even incorporate some of their staff into the story line.[3]

The next day, the gaming community was in an uproar. Everyone was buzzing with news of the infiltration, and now more people were caught up in the story. In fact McKinney's research said that throughout the campaign over half a million people were searching for the missing Audis!

The level of detail the advertising agency included to make the story so real

---

* Web stories, like movies, are visual beasts. The name is THE ART OF THE H3IST, which when placed strategically spells within the red letters T H E A 3 (see graphic).

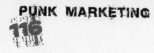

iNeed to Get Over It

The iPod has unleashed a ridiculous amount of so-called competition. Big names and no names are in a race to offer an alternative—any alternative. Not one has had comparative success, although corporate execs are frustrated and desperate and hating the beloved white carryall.

SanDisk, an "internationally recognized authority on nonvolatile memory technology," wins the gold medal for being the biggest iPod hater we know. They're responsible for www.idont.com. This fabulous site is attempting to appeal to the nonconformist who takes one look at masses with their iPods and wants to puke. SanDisk offers an alternative for sale, naturally: their own MP3 player with similar features to the device they love to hate.

Usually this approach will lead to failure. Tell people the other guy sucks and we are great. Not so much.

Idont is a mite different and yet still doesn't work. It preaches why we should all leave the church of iPod and try their "better" piece and goes so far as to offer merchandise "denouncing the white God." Somewhere out there a geek is pulling out his credit card to buy an anti-iPod shirt from idont.com.

This plea to consumers is not Punk. It's more of a really intricate whine and enforces how sour SanDisk is for being a runner-up, an also-ran, a wannabe, a battle-weary seller of words that are not telling us anything.

We bring this message to you in hopes you will think twice before becoming sour. Oh, and if you're reading this far, note: Creative Zen's machine is way better than iPod. (Although that hasn't stopped the mighty white machine, and so the Zen is boiling mad and has resorted to suing Apple for patent infringement.)

caught the imagination of the young adults whom they needed to interest in the car; they were willing participants in a winding plot. The sites created for the art-recovery business featured in the story included archives of e-mails among all the main characters, as well as phone recordings, videoconferences, conversation transcripts, and text chats going back months before the campaign started.

Interested parties in the *millions* perused blueprints, maps, crime photos, suspect lists, surveillance videos, security-camera footage, and audio files that were filled with content that you could not get on television.* Although a great many of those who got immersed in the story might have been younger than the target buyer for Audi, the data collected suggested it led to a large number of leads and test-drives.†

All the meticulous planning paid off handsomely. But the real lesson is, a bunch of Punk-as-all-get-out marketers were willing to try—and stick with—something innovative to get consumers engaged in the idea of the car.

One of our favorite stories concerns the Beta-7 campaign agency Wieden + Kennedy put forth on behalf of client Sega Games. It began months before the launch of Sega's ESPN NFL football release and was the story of a battle between Sega and a geek who said he was Beta-7, hired by Sega as a "tester." On his own site, visitors learned that since testing the new *crash cam* feature on the game, he'd had an uncontrollable urge to tackle people; he included amateur footage of him tackling strangers.

Beta-7 used his own site to release a plea to other testers who may have suffered the same to claim beaucoup medical damages against Sega.

Beta-7 poured water on another site he said was created by Sega to refute the testers' accusations of any side effects of the new NFL football game. He showed several cease-and-desist letters from Sega, and swore they'd hacked his site and even ransacked his apartment. To add to the *Is it real, is it fake?* nature of the campaign, a commercial about the cam feature included a wild-ass statement: "Excessive playing of the game will not lead to violent or erratic behavior," neatly adding fuel to an outlandish fire.

Campaigns that map out the many twists and turns that may/can/will unfold draw consumers into them in a way no one will forget, not the least of which is the marketer, and represent a refreshing antidote to dull, old linear marketing.

Storytelling keeps interested parties on their tippy toes; immerses them in what we do for a living. See? They want to be a part of your day job. These people are anxious for more—are looking everywhere for it.

And that is the best ending we can have. The End.

---

* Keep up. Damn it!

† See the site, it's still up: http://McKinney-Silver.com/A3_H3ist/.

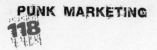

Use This While Waiting for the Light to Change

1. A story doesn't have to demo a product front and center so long as its meaning and its principles are conveyed to the target audience.

2. Narratives with many layers create buzz with those first-at-bat and leverage money spent on paid media with gobs of earned free media.

3. ARB, or alternative-reality branding, is a mouthful that succeeds in using online and real-life components to tell a story whereby consumers become part of the action. This can be incredibly effective especially for young-adult consumers who are used to being challenged by marketers—and expect it.

4. Take liberally from other industries—film or music or porn—to set different goals for how you market. Use their techniques to create impact-filled marketing campaigns that make you feel good about the job you do daily.

5. When consumers are asked to participate in The Story, a marketer needs to accept you will lose some control in order for it to be wholly interactive.

Then—as a coda—remember not to tell a narrative when you don't have the goods. Only do stories you believe in. It's what every first novelist is told by his forewriters: Create what you know. Nothing but.

Punk is . . .

Being a greedy consumer of knowledge from
every single source on earth and discovering ways
to apply that info to your own business at times
when you least expect it to come through.

Finding ways to be happy in your work,
knowing that happiness is good for creativity
and creativity is good for more creativity,
which is good for business, which makes you
happy, which gets you more sex.

[to be continued]

Tasty Morsels

- Consumers are hit over the head by so many choices they end up with a quizzical look on their faces. Not a happy look.

- The average U.S. consumer is bombarded by three thousand marketing messages a day, representing over $2,000 spent to attract the attention of each man, woman, and child a year. Did you know what you were worth, and have you asked for your money back?

- Sixty one percent of Americans feel the amount of marketing and advertising they are subjected to is out of control, and 65 percent say they are constantly bombarded. They want a divorce.

- Sixty percent of the programs watched by DVR users are recorded; 92 percent of the ads on those programs are skipped over with gleeful abandon.

- In any three hours of evening programming on four major TV broadcasters in the United States, there was (in 2003) an average of fifty-two minutes of promotional messages, up an astronomical, unforgivable 36 percent (from 1991). Who's the desperate housewife now?

Eight

Leave Me Alone, Will Ya!
Too Much Stuff, Too Little Time

Walk into a typical grocery store and find a dizzying array of choices of any type of product, whether toothpaste, jam, or detergent. Or in the authors' dairy case, we bemoan the fate of our beloved Pop-Tarts!*

Welcome to the wonderful world of consumerism in which unlimited choice is available and spending power means freedom from having to pick just one. Is Colgate-Palmolive ashamed or bewildered that it offers us adults more than twenty-five varieties of toothpaste (there are countless for kids), and all under the Colgate brand, each coming in astoundingly different pack sizes for quantity and tube size/style?

Ah, yes, these include gels and pastes and several able to remove plaque and gingivitis, plus a couple for teeth whitening and others for those with sensitive teeth. (We're convinced the toothpaste people made up the last descriptor.) The types have names like Total, Max Fresh, Simply White, and Sparkling White. The shopper will definitely know that their every tooth-cleaning whim has been considered and catered to. Minty fresh!

---

* We looked for yummy chocolate P-Ts at the grocery store because they made us feel young and careless. We found lots of types, some with frosting—still others consisted largely of different varieties of "fudge." We ended up grabbing No Brand in disgust.

And if shoppers are unable to read through all of the product information on the packs while standing on one foot—perhaps because the eggs in their carts have started to hatch already—they can postpone their buying decision until they get back home and log on to the dandy Colgate site. Though slightly disorganized and hype-y, Colgate.com offers the shopper a plethora of helpful decision-making processes based on what might be most crucial to a toothpaste aficionado.

Most people haven't got time to stand at the supermarket shelves staring at hundreds of different choices, undecided what to sacrifice, and certainly don't have

the will to seek out the information on a corporate site (and if they do, we want to avoid them at a party). We would personally rather use twigs to clean our teeth and spend the time saved rearranging the sock drawer.

We cannot blame Colgate. One of us brushes with Colgate (the other uses twigs), and we get it: they are pressured to try to fill every conceivable market gap—or cavity—lest a fickle tooth lover amble over to Crest with Tartar Control or that teeth-enabling Aquafresh with a hint of wild berry. That's a big fear for these teeth fairies, and there, there, we understand.

It's a dilemma begun by giant-making committees inside conglomerates where the proclamation was made at one of 3 billion meetings: "As G-d is my whiteness, er, witness, we at Colgate-Palmolive had better have covered every single base, or darn it, we will lose to them." Then they debate who this "them" are that will no doubt win. We imagine Colgate then whips out oodles of research that proves a plethora of products is more likely to encourage consumers to worship at the Colgate altar.

But we have other research that says too much of a good thing is killing consumers' desire to shop! Once shopping was the only therapy that could cure a blue day; now it's producing anxiety!

Too much choice anesthetizes or paralyzes the consumer. In the case of over-choice, we're standing there with our thumb up our ass when, if we could find *our favorite brand in its natural state,* we would be home in our pj's already.

Trend-spotter emeritus Alvin Toffler predicted in his 1970 classic, *Future Shock,* the following scenario: "Ironically, the people of the future may suffer not from an absence of choice, but from a paralyzing surfeit of it. They may turn out to be the victims of that peculiar super-industrial dilemma: over-choice."

The future is now, Al.

A study by researchers in a California supermarket duly illustrates overchoice.[1] They set up a tasting booth offering lots of varieties of jam. When twenty-four varieties were displayed, 60 percent of passersby stopped by to check it out; when six types were put out, a lesser 40 percent stopped.

It appears that the more choice they got, the more likely it was that people stopped to peek. Allow us to get uppity. Just 3 percent of the jammers made a purchase when twenty-four were thrust out, while *ten times that*—or 30 percent for the math-impaired—with a mere six at the booth.

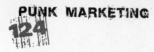

Cute to Push Stupid

Amazon thinks we're idiots. They e-mail to tell us that based on what we've already bought, their statistics show we should be willing to buy this, that, or the other!

Selling to the masses as if the masses are schmucks hasn't once worked, but it is still a tactic used by the largest Net retailer. It's true; we are more than just a number to these folks. We're also the losers who like being told what we should buy because they—like Mom—know so much better. We're their stooges!

Situations like this forced our hand. The Revolution begins. Lazy-ass prodding of smart consumers is so obviously not the way to get things done—at last we see it clearly. Don't be telling us what you think you know about us; don't be saying you will use synergy as the way to get us to buy. And whatever you do, don't be so public about how you're reaping the sale.

Bottom line: let us tell *you* what we want.

One of us stopped rolling our eyes for a sec and went to the annual Milken guru convention, where the bigwigs get together to clap each other on the back for being so good at manipulating marketplaces. The year was 2003, the beginning of the end of a good time for marketers.

At the convention, the big guys of the industry, including a freshly minted AOL CEO, talked an unerring blue streak about how they "captured" customers, how they "got them," "hooked them," "manipulated them," "procured them," "reeled them in," "took 'em from one part of their business and swayed them to another." This went on for about forty-five minutes until our red-faced author spoke up:

"Okay. You got them. You hooked them. You've treated them like prey. And they're going to hate you for it. With all due respect, Mr. AOL, you aren't wooing customers via creativity."

They were shocked. They knew better, their eyes told me. Corporations stopped loving the customers because the bottom-line mentality says that's too expensive. You just got to *get them now*. Think spam.

SIDEBAR

The lesson continued: "I'm not prey. When I go shopping, I'm *hunting* for the right thing, *searching* it out, *fishing* for a bargain. Does that sound like prey to you, Mr. A?"

Marketers! Get this through your heads: Our brands are the prey; our customers the hunters. So stop trying to stalk and start doing what you're supposed to do—look enticing.

And while we're at it, the next time we go on iTunes and a little mini store goes up telling us *related* (Apple's term for "we know you better than you know yourself") songs and videos, we're immediately switching to Rhapsody, or, even, Zune. We'd rather have less of a selection than you telling *us* what *we* like. Same goes for TiVo. As we said earlier, stop suggesting you know me. So what if we watched two episodes of *Leave It to Beaver* when we were feeling nostalgic for our days as a kid? Don't give us a Season Pass to *F Troop*.

This, therefore, is not a book of theory. It's a practitioner's guide for those who understand that endless creative choices are available (if we get off our behinds and figure out how to use them), and why we're on a new (we mean that word *new*) track that's going to make us a lot of bank.

Marketing bigwigs like Amazon have got to know: the free ride is over and you guys are precariously perched on the edge of a cliff. That jolt of reality will throw you so far from where you think you are sitting comfortably you'll wonder (a) how it happened and (b) where do we go from here.

Let's go.

SIDEBAR

A big selection indeed stops shoppers. They go "Ah!"—right before they head to What Now?Ville.

In another experiment, someone said pick from two groups: thirty Godiva chocolates or six Godiva chocolates. The big group was, said the participants, more enjoyable—size matters—until after scrutiny, when they claimed to have "felt more dissatisfied" with their choice and less likely to purchase again! A smart grocery chain ought to add a shrink next to the pharmacy, dry-cleaner, bank, and prophylactics sections. Put him or her near the toothpaste.

The wonderful world of consumerism and the unlimited choice it brings has a dark side for the consumer as well. In a 2004 paper with a title that makes us giggle, "Choose, Choose, Choose, Choose, Choose, Choose, Choose: Emerging and Prospective Research on the Deleterious Effects of Living in Consumer Hyperchoice," authors Mick, Broniarczyk, and Haidt start off with words of choice:

"The ideology of consumption and the imperative of consumer choice have washed across the globe. In today's developed economies there is an ever-

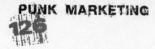

increasing amount of buying, amidst an ever-increasing amount of purchase options, amidst an ever-increasing amount of stress, amidst an ever-decreasing amount of discretionary time."[2]

This has implications for marketing pros trying to manage a portfolio of brands. Or as an associate professor of marketing at Stanford Graduate School of Business, Michaela Draganska, puts it, "It's a widely held belief that unless you constantly introduce new products, you cannot stay in the game."

While products with new flavors or scents—what's with all that vanilla nowadays?—produce a short-term spike in sales that may look good in a résumé*/annual

---

* A strong CV is important to product managers who act shiftily; they typically have only about a year to deliver results. CMOs, less.

More Stupid (Nipples Optional)

Our svelte agent told us this after the '06 Super Bowl fetish-fest:

"So, I'm watching the Stupid Bowl with my family: easily outraged wife and brilliant, high-strung six-year-old boy. Sports, feh. We tune in to one game a year—this one—and only because we like the damn ads.

"This year, we turned the TV off during every commercial break.

"Why?

"The clever ads, of which there were few, were flanked by scary/violent previews for movies and prime-time TV shows that had one thing in common: high-energy violence and palpable menace. I realize that ABC views this as an opportunity to sell its lineup, and the movies buy these spots to capture a male demo, but a whole bunch of sets were turned off because ad programmers forgot that viewers are parents first, customers second."

Really now? Advertisers are losing touch with the people they're trying to sell to? How novel. Not. Consumers are not stupid, as we say on every single page. They know well when they've been hit over the head—and a repeated message is just that. Customers-to-be are sick of being scared into watching something or buying something that's promoted over and over. And parental customers are over advertisements that are as detrimental to their child's development as most TV shows are! Despite the ridiculous fine CBS had to pay for Janet Jackson's booby mishap, maybe some light was actually shed on what advertisers and those hiring them needed to be reminded of. There is a time and a place for everything, turn turn turn.

Lesson learnt: choose wisely where you place certain ads that will duly be appreciated by consumers. Think before signing off. Take responsibility. Some things are still sacred to American families, so stop messing with them.

That's our civics lesson for today. You may go.

SIDEBAR

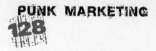

report/memo to Mom, the line extensions often have negative consequences. Her research, conducted with Dipak Jain, dean of Kellogg School of Management at Northwestern University, suggested that while local and store brands might benefit from longer product lines, biggies like Colgate-Palmolive or P&G are absolutely better off with *less* variety.

Let's do the math. Of thirteen yogurt brands observed by Dippy and Micka, using a proprietary mathematical model that no, we don't care about understanding either, only three benefited from having a line extension, and these three were all low-price or no-frill products that truly suffered from lack of variety. They concluded that "a longer product line might be a signal of higher quality and boost their image in comparison to the other lower-priced alternatives," while nationally known companies Dannon and Yoplait already had a large variety at premium prices and would benefit from reducing their product lines. In other words, less was more (and more was less).

And, hey, some really smart professors from Columbia University found the same thing is true of 401(k) plans too. So, don't tell us choice overload is confined only to jam, chocolate, and yogurt.[3]

More research—bored yet?—we uncovered proved how happiness with a decision plummets when the number of options rises.[4]

It's not that people don't like *some* choice—it's a bummer being told that's all there is—but we do have a problem making decisions we feel good about after being thrown too many possibilities.

As Punk Marketers we will do something about choice overload by making our individual offerings distinctive and stopping the tyranny of choice for its own sake. Our products will be just as good, and honestly different, from everything else *we* sell (and the junk our so-called competitors toss out).

You make more money with fewer offerings. Many of us are learning this now.

Starbucks offers a lot of ways to consume caffeine, yet customers don't seem paralyzed by choice, and neither of us has seen anyone take a look at the menu and say, "Oh, forget it" (except when they were mocked in *The Sopranos*, but that was fiction—we think).

The way Starbucks presents a menu is manageable, and choosing ends up being fun. Despite the seemingly endless variety, a newly minted coffee connoisseur easily understands how the counter person prepares his favorite legal addiction. Even if we said simply, "A small latte, uh, please," no one laughed at us because we didn't say *tall*. We felt unintimidated. Actually, we felt knowledgeable and empowered.

If Starbucks is an example of a brand for which choice is used to terrific effect, General Motors is surely an example of choice turning to ruin. While we don't wish to kick a dog when down, GM needs to make sense of the lack of differentiation among its product lines. Please. Today.

More products to choose from = more messages with which to contend. Every one of these bastards fights for our attention every day, screaming, "Me, please! Me! Choose me! No, not him! Me!" Marketing spending has steadily increased over the past few years to astronomical figures: in 2005, $620 billion in the United States, more than double the figure from a decade ago.[5] This works out to more than $2,000 per every human being in America. We, well 61 percent of us, would rather it stop.[6]

So, okay, it is difficult to avoid marketing messages. No kidding. Even if we have a DVR like TiVo/Replay and we can fast-forward over ad breaks or even possess some kind of computer software to block pop-ups, marketing has sleepily crept into every part of our lives, and even show-offs like us are sometimes caught unawares.

There is product placement in movies and television shows, ads running on gas pumps and on public restroom urinals! (When you flushed, a voice spoke to you. A new low.) And sponsorships have turned innocent entertainment into "brand experiences." The average consumer, exposed to three thousand or more marketing messages per day, makes no connection to anything, and the consumer is left bereft of your message.

The assumption by marketers is that as long as you break through a consumer's consciousness, you've won the battle. But to be made aware of something—whether a new or existing product or an ad or a shouting toilet—is not enough anymore. In fact, when humans are bombarded with competing possibilities for our limited attention, time, and money, we feel overwhelmed and do nothing. And we Punk authors are so easily bored. Both of us majored in Milk & Cookies.

Let's turn to Mark Ritson, who was assistant professor of marketing at the London Business School when he said marketers tend to do whatever it takes to grab attention: "As an industry, our prime goal is to discover ever more annoying, repetitive, and unwelcome ways to immerse our unfortunate target segment and the rest of the population on the brand. Our response to clutter is more clutter."[7]

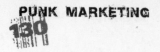
Clutter, clutter, everywhere. The Federal Communications Commission makes no limitations on how much TV advertising time a broadcaster can subject adults to.* Wouldn't you know it—the four big networks take advantage. A 2003 study explained how they air an average of fifty-two minutes of noncontent during prime time from 8 to 11 p.m.—130 commercials, programming promos, and public service announcements (PSAs). That's a shameful increase of 36 percent since 1991![8]

Golly, TV is more of a time-waster than ever before. A Forrester Research report informs us that 60 percent of programs watched by DVR users are recorded and 92 percent of ads are skipped over.[9] So that's new math! A consumer now gets nearly an hour to do laundry or have sex—or prime-time viewing pleasure of three hours with frustration.

Where consumers go, marketers will follow. Everywhere. Some marketing executives will stop at nothing to annoy prospective customers. You cannot avoid our attempts to reach you! (Insert evil laugh.) A patent application filed by Philips Electronics in March 2006, but not quite approved, could force viewers to watch commercials on TV through technology that ostensibly prevents us from switching channels during pee breaks. It was comical watching the media furor this brought about.

Grasp one thing if you grasp anything from us: Stop! The people at home are not the problem; it's your ads that are so bad that people would rather force the dog on another walk than watch.†

De Cluttering: De Lovely

Some brilliant businesses have recognized consumers' need to simplify by removing clutter and obstacles so they can make choices that are undoubtedly *good* for them. We respect Time Inc.'s *Real Simple* magazine, which is "dedicated to helping

---

* For children twelve and younger, the limit is 10.5 minutes an hour of advertising on weekends and 12 minutes an hour on weekdays.

† We have a dream campaign for one network with balls: "Feel free to take a break whenever! This is Must Pee TV!"

you simplify every aspect of your life, saving and creating time for the things that really matter," as one of their most successful new titles, which at the start of 2006 spun off several hardcovers and a series on grand poobah PBS!

Same week the show debuted, Dutch, orange-themed banking firm ING launched its campaign with the umbrella slogan "Your future. Made easier."* ING told anyone listening how they discovered consumers said navigating choice in financial services sure was difficult.†

Citibank found time to understand consumers' needs to cut through financial complexity by introducing a much advertised credit card called Simplicity. The card allowed you to call and *speak to a live person*. The joke to us is that those still straddled with Citi's more complicated cards now saw themselves treated like bad rats.

Marketers can control the number of selections tossed out and slow the release of new products to help customers out. Yet no one can control their competitors going all out with overchoice, which can give an entire field a bad name.

New technology helps consumers make decisions. With the risk of sounding like their overly monotone advertising, today Microsoft Corporation is developing software that will help people search for the things that their past behavior suggests they may find useful. As Marc Smith, a research sociologist at the giant whose job is to make sifting through our e-mails easier and speedier, notes, "We're close to carrying capacity—we're close to the limit of human attention to messaging content"[10] The software they launched at the end of 2005 is known as Snarf‡—bless you—and analyzes prior e-mail behavior to decide how to prioritize your incoming.

There are also technologies to make fine use of data aggregated from numbers of us to guide individual choice. Collaborative filtering was begun by those dotcom deadbeats in the nineties and now waltzes into our inbox regularly through Amazon and everybody else. We customers are given "suggestions" for products we "may" like based on choices made by others with similar buying problems—habits. (See sidebar titled "Cute to Push Stupid," page 124) You ordered a book on poker

---

* Note the cruddy use of periods. Full sentences are much too difficult for almost all copywriters.

† According to an interview with ING, "ING Retires Fresh Thinking to Focus on the Simpler Life," in the *New York Times* on January 12, 2006, three out of four people wished financial services were easier to deal with.

‡ Social Network and Relationship Finder.

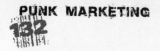

and someone who bought that book also has a thing for flower arranging, so you got to buy that too. This happens on most devices now too—even the cooler-than-thou iTunes.*

Another way is via tagging systems on sites like Yahoo!-owned darlings del.icio.us and Flickr—the latter's PR launched by Richard & Co. when Flickr was a video game!—where members label sites, pictures, or whatever they think is interesting and let their preferences be sorted into databases that are then searched by other people, even horrible ones.

Online social hangouts like MySpace and Orkut and Bebo use this principle of connecting folks through what turns them on—even things like pottery. As it has become pertinent for marketers to find these groups of like-minded individuals—rather than humongous populations with little in common other than half-watching the same sitcom—these types of massively joined networks are the only tool that makes sense.

Introducing the Power Charter

Marketers, simplify a consumer's life! The Punk Marketing Consumer Power Charter must be posted on the fridge. Preferably the one in the office . . .

---

* One of us accidently TiVo'd a show on Bravo—and the machine suggested gay programming for three weeks straight.

Punk Marketers of the world:

1. Consumers are looking to us to help simplify their lives so we will do our utmost to help them get simple.

2. Consumers have a right to expect a clear education about products being offered to enable them to make informed choices. That is our duty. Labeling should make it easy for consumers to quickly grasp what the product does *and* what it contains.

3. We are responsible for keeping the number of choices to a minimum: less is most definitely *it*.

4. Each product variant, line extension, or subbrand should be distinctive from any other we offer and meet real consumer need.

5. Me-too products that copy competitor items without trying to offer a distinct point of differentiation represent lazy thinking.

6. We need to use our marketing prowess responsibly and only when we have something meaningful to say.

7. Marketing foisting itself upon consumers is offensive. It will create antagonism to the brand in particular and marketing always.

8. There are no-go places marketing professionals need to respect at all times. That's right, Coke, *at all times*. Leave the potty alone.

9. We need to do more listening and learning from signals we get from consumers about their feelings toward marketing.

10. As marketers we will take the high ground and be a champion for consumers—never their enemies.

And, please, where oh where are those damn chocolate Pop-Tarts?

Tasty Morsels

- Less than a quarter of consumers think companies tell the truth when they market.

- Ten percent think advertising practitioners are honest.

- More than 80 percent of opinion leaders claim they won't purchase goods or services from companies they do not trust.

- Dishonest marketing will be discovered and talked about by consumers, who trust one another more than corporations (see sidebar, "Smallest Sidebar," page 132), and can irreparably damage a brand's reputation.

- Honesty is a powerful strategy to gain any and all consumer trust and loyalty.

Lies Lies Lies: Nine
The Truth about Truth
And Factoids about Facts

Let's get down to it: it's no lie to say people have little faith in marketing. Look at the data:

Only 24 percent of those surveyed in 2003 agreed that companies generally tell the truth in advertisements.[1] Newspaper and magazine ads were the only forms of ads trusted by more than half, beating TV, radio, and online. Web banners, product placements, and text ads on mobile phones were the least trusted, while recommendations from consumer associates or acquaintances or friends or lovers came out tops, with almost 90 percent claiming to somewhat-to-completely trust those POVs.

This is supported by a 2006 survey by Edelman Public Relations that found that for opinion leaders the most credible source of intelligence about a company is not the ads but a dude like me (not him, me).*

> Dear Advice Columnist:
>
> Gosh, do I have a problem. My father is serving a life sentence for murder. My mother ran away when we were just kids. Both my sisters are prostitutes in Orange County. My brother works in advertising. Now I've met the woman of my dreams and I want to be totally honest with her, but how can I tell her about my brother?
>
> (RL) Full Name Withheld

---

* Edelman Trust Barometer, 2006, which we admit before you say it is something most people outside of PR laugh at. A PR company talking about who trusts whom? Oh, boy. Especially when Edelman was busted, in 2006, for creating faux consumer blogs for demanding client Wal-Mart.

The corporate marketing director of Procter and Gamble in the UK and Ireland, Roisin Donnelly, remarked about attempts to market to young consumers: "Research shows that younger people are more likely to believe a stranger in an Internet chat room than a TV advertisement."[2] Whoa, Donnelly.

Let's get into this further. A 2004 Gallup poll of public perceptions of honesty and ethics in thirty-two professions of all types had advertising a crack above the

bottom.* Just 10 percent saw advertising practitioners as honest, scraping above lowly car salesman (9%) and below insurance salesmen (11%), lawyers (18%), congressional types (20%), business execs (20%), newspaper reporters (21%), toilet-paper rollers (50%—we're lying).

Business in general is no better off. In a recent poll conducted by the Roper Center for Public Opinion Research, 72 percent of respondents felt wrongdoing was widespread in all industries, up from 66 percent just a year earlier.[3] And just 2 percent thought CEOs of large companies to be "very trustworthy." Robert S. "Steve" Miller, CEO of auto parts maker Delphi Automotive Systems, says, "Society has come to believe the term 'crooked CEO' is redundant."[4]

To many, corporate America and its seemingly unstoppable focus on maximizing shareholder value is to blame. Yet it hasn't always been this way. A statement on corporate responsibility issued in 1981 by the Business Roundtable—an association of CEOs of some of the largest U.S. corporations—said, "The shareholder must receive good return but the legitimate concerns of other constituencies (customers, employees, communities, suppliers, and society at large) also must have appropriate attention."

Roll over to 1997 and the Business Roundtable has changed its tune, making its new priorities to CEOs to, ahem, maximize shareholder value: "The notion that the board must somehow balance the interests of stockholders against the interests of other stakeholders fundamentally misconstrues the role of directors."

As noted in an article titled "Memo to CEOs" in the June 2002 issue of *Fast Company*, this policy change meant, "The customer may be king and the employees may be the corporation's greatest asset. But the CEO's only real responsibility is to serve the interests of the shareholders."

Consumers are cynical; no wonder. They have experienced firsthand a focus on profit at the expense of everything including the death of customer service. As a result the American Customer Satisfaction index has declined in almost every single industry since the mid-1990s. (Turn to chapter 6, "The Captive Consumer.")

And why should employees feel motivated to service their customers? Their wages rose barely above inflation in the nineties (a 37 percent rise as inflation rose

---

* Yes, that was tasteless. Now continue reading.

32 percent) while executive pay shot up by 570 percent. And surprise, surprise, a recent study found that only 34 percent of employees worldwide feel a strong sense of loyalty toward their employer.

What's wrong with this picture? How can businesses hope to keep customers when customer-facing employees don't give a damn about the business? Try calling communications monster Sprint Nextel with a problem, and unless you're a corporate customer, you end up either talking to an anonymous person who clearly doesn't give a shit, or a machine that cares even less. We prefer talking to the Bangalore call center and newly-named "Todd," who has been trained to (1) speak in a clear voice and (2) care.*

On the other side of the pond, Sir Richard Branson has an idea we dub right. Instead of focusing on making the shareholder happy, his well-publicized intention is to motivate his staff in the belief that a pleasant experience for customers makes them happy and keeps them coming back for more dealings with pleasant people. This makes the business profitable and keeps the shareholders happy. Much sounder logic, right?

Consumers have wised up to the way corporations behave and increasingly use trust, or lack of it, as a guide to purchasing choices. Chris Riley, founder of now-defunct Studioriley, which created economically, socially, and environmentally healthy brands, saw how a teenager in a Nike focus group picked an Air Jordan sneaker from a pile and identified the precise factory in Vietnam where it was created.[5]

Edelman's PR-friendly survey of opinion leaders says more than 80 percent of them refuse to buy goods or services from a company they simply do not trust, and over two-thirds bad-mouth a distrusted firm to people they *don't even know*. A third will share their negative opinions on the Web.

For too long business assumed marketing can say whatever it wants and consumers will have faith: It must be true—it was on TV.

Should it matter that an actual experience of the product bears little resem-

---

* In India, it is widely reported that employees, though paid less than U.S. counterparts, are treated with respect, admiration, and tons more. They are picked up and driven home, encouraged to decorate their offices to "look just like the company they support," and get food and other perquisites like child care. Makes caring a little easier, that we know.

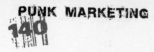
Lying *from* the Sun

Sometimes you do things and think to yourself, "Well, I know it's bad for me, but heck. No big deal." In the case of lying marketers, we wonder if they sleep at night when they tell you it's going to be okay or are just thinking, "It's not me, it's the company."

Case in point: As sun worshippers, the two authors are always wondering how much damage they are doing to their epidermises and what their hides will actually feel like at, say, age sixty. A recent class action suit has made us feel worse. Brought against five leading U.S. suntan-lotion makers, the lawyers are accusing them of lying about products protecting skin from "harmful effects of sunrays." Targeted brands include Coppertone (Schering-Plough), Banana Boat (Sun Pharmaceuticals and Playtex Products), Hawaiian Tropic (Tanning Research Laboratories), Neutrogena (Neutrogena Corp. and Johnson and Johnson), and Bullfrog (Chattem Inc.). The lawyers are seeking the elimination from packaging of such sought-after marketing terms as *sunblock* and *waterproof*. The sharks argue that claims about skin protection by these brands are misleading, citing that they do not actually block all of the sun's harmful rays. Just because you're not getting burned doesn't mean you're not getting . . . burned.

Too much exposure to the sun is bad; okay, we get it. Authorities on the subject will argue this and even say the use of sunscreen has increased the cases of skin cancer because of the false feeling that if we apply it, we can stay in the sun longer without worry. Further, it is said that sunscreen can actually increase the risk of certain cancers, primarily colon cancer and breast cancer, because some elements of the sun's rays are beneficial and are blocked by those lotions. You may repeat that sentence again.

Sure, there may be benefits from the sun, but the facts remain that claims of sunscreen makers are false. We're sold a sense of security that has put ourselves at higher risk as a result.

blance to the promise made in the marketing? Nah, right, because by then you've already got 'em. Our competitors play the same game, so it's not as if our empty promises are worse than anyone else's, you see, Mr. Trade Commissioner. This logic is what makes buyers tune out the marketing maelstrom. They are tired of being handed bold-faced fibs.

We think life's complicated enough without having to sort through marketing messages to determine who is lying and who may be faithful. Those disclaimers at the ends of ads and the horrible use of ™ and sm for every line of text make everyone suspect everything is a fabrication—or worse, protected lies.

Companies that aren't 1,000 percent honest in advertising claims will be found and killed off. Never forget how Blockbuster Inc. began dying a painfully slow and public death because of nonstop anger from heretofore loyal consumers pissed off by its summarily less-than-honest (and loudly proclaimed) promise it would no longer charge fees if DVD or video rentals were returned late. Just as the offer was rolling out, some folks realized the gambit was up and so Blockbuster amended its marketing and suffered horrendous publicity and a loss of credibility. Then they had to refund to thousands of former customers in forty-seven states that sued them for deception to a (name that) tune of over $600,000. See our sidebar (back one page) on suntan-lotion companies being taken to court for out and out lying.

The auto industry is littered with noteworthy examples of those who use truth and those who abuse it. Isuzu Motors' ingenious advertising campaign in the late 1980s took a swipe at automakers' ads that implied their vehicles could pretty much do anything. The fictitious spokesman Joe Isuzu—played by sitcom actor David Leisure—made ridiculous claims about Isuzu cars while on-screen a scroll appeared telling viewers, "He's lying." Joe became one of the most popular marketing characters of the time.[6]

On the other hand, Ford Motor Company took heat for bending the truth in a subtly shameful way. In ads from 2005 it made much of its nascent relationship with Volvo Car Corporation* to boost its own safety credentials and used a nefarious "truthiness,"† that the two car divisions shared the same crash-testing facilities, to imply that both have the same standards of safety. Hmmm, not even slightly true.

A Ford spokesperson told *USA Today* that yeah okay fine, Fords and Volvos appeal to different types of buyers with different budgets. This could imply that Fords aren't built as safely as Volvos—despite what the ads say. Hey, Joe? Is that you over at Ford?[7]

Volvo has also had its share of problems for advertising that doesn't match any reality we know. In the 1980s it parted ways with longtime agency Scali, McCabe,

---

* Which it bought out in 1999.

† We give props to television character Ste-*phan* Col-*bare* for coining this term.

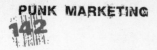

Sloves after the media revealed how a commercial with a monster truck driving over a line of cars and crushing them all, save the Volvo, had been faked. Oh, Sven, shame on you. The pillars on the Volvo had artificially been strengthened while those of the other cars were weakened. The irony was that Volvo was and *is* tougher and would probably have withstood the impact; yet some schmuck decided it looked more dramatic if the effect was exaggerated. What's worse is, trust in one's own product didn't exist.

I Chopped the Cherry Tree (But I Did Not Kill No Deputy)

Our bud the Internet makes it possible for consumers to find out what they want about a company and its people and products with a snap. Businesses better be careful what they choose to hide from their customers, as the truth is a few clicks away, and you know those mice love to run about all crazy like.

As George Washington found, being way honest is a sure way to get into the history books. Sure, he chopped down that helpless tree, but he came clean about it quickly. Likewise consumers respect a GW-like firm that is just as honest. Honest in how its products are made, who its partners are, what its margins are, who works for them and how they are treated.

The trick is to say so before consumers force you.

Health-care-oriented companies totally suck at this. A product recall is the worst thing to happen to them, and most of them are the last to tell us about it (cue Bausch & Lomb's "solvent" crisis, 2006). As marketing pros we are shocked about how slow such huge corporations are in talking about safety issues with a public whose own personal safety is, along with beer, all they care about. The leaping-to-action part of the equation is often a "wait to see" policy, rather than one of the few times they should be explaining their asses off.

A major target of consumer backlash, Nike was forced to change most of its manufacturing processes after an enormous uproar about the sneaker ruler's dependence upon third-world sweatshops. Starbucks decided to rethink its coffee-growing policy too, since they were called out for not using Fair Trade coffee (though they still get guff today for not offering it as heralded Brewed Coffee of the Day).

In all our striving businesses, just as in whatever personal lives we still possess,

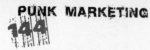

Words That Mean Nothing

We Punk kids want you to lose language that smells anything like a buzzword. Here are biz terms and phrases we all need to stray from, starting with THING. Try stretching yourself by replacing it in a sentence—you should appear smart(er) or at the least less of a poseur. Others include this hard-earned list:

Great, sounds good, meet-up, game-changing, dialed up/dialed down, leveling *any* playing field, nation as a suffix, it's not Project Anything nor Uncle Someone, win-win, win-win-win, something with mama tacked on—or 'zilla afterward—yeah right, your call is important to us, ROI, your/his/my demons, having a moment here, Done!, interface or dialogue, turnkey, leading edge, challenge (just say problem!), critical mass, first mover, rules changer, HD radio, bold, cursory, plug, clever as opposed to smart, any press is good press, free media, kewl!/coolio?, my bad, cause and effect, eat good, "liaise," metrosexual (confusexual is our word), couch-jumper, Best of Breed (*best of bleed* is all right), best practices, Booyah!, synergistic, mission critical, scalable, next generation, value add, seamless, e-tailing, core competencies, empower, reality TV, out of pocket, off the grid, going for the jugular, guilty pleasure. And don't *even* say this to yourself: meet projections.

Final note on a long subject: Say what you mean. Others will nod and think, "Golly gee. I don't need to translate him. *Praise the Lord.*"*

we must accept our faults and attempt to change them. Encouraging feedback from customers and taking suggestions seriously is a crucial way of demonstrating not only that you're listening ("Yes, go on") but that you're making steps to be all you can ("My name is Richard. I'm a parenthesis–a-holic").

The days of a wooden suggestions box are but a fond memory. Consumers will write blogs about a bad experience before a good and make it available to as many salivating types as they can. Search "I hate Sprint" on the Web and almost two million entries pop up.

Some blogs on companies or brands have followers in the tens of thousands.

---

* Oh, and can someone explain. Is it *cool* or *hot*? Advise.

Pity the foolish company that ignores consistent feedback! Bill Gates: "Your most unhappy customers are your greatest source of learning."

The most trusted global company on Edelman's 2006 survey? Microsoft! Coincidence?

Come On, People, Now. Use Truth as a Weapon

A smart marketer can use trustworthiness as a point of differentiation. One of our favorite agencies, Crispin Porter + Bogusky (CP+B), used truth directly in the marketing they created for the State of Florida's effort to reduce teenage smoking. They created a now notorious brand, Truth, to represent the importance of getting facts in antithesis to "the lies perpetrated by Big Tobacco."

The campaign was backslapper *AdWeek*'s Best Campaign of the Year back in 2000, but more important was that teenage smoking in Florida dropped for the first time. Prior to the campaign, teen smoking had been increasing each year for ten consecutive years, and within three years after the campaign began, that trend reversed.

eBay's whole business model is built upon honesty and trust. The auction site would not have become nearly as successful without a user-feedback system allowing potential buyers and sellers to see who is trustworthy and who is pure scum. If a seller doesn't get a high score, it's unlikely anyone else will do business with him; the system keeps people honest at a cost. This also supports eBay founder Pierre Omidyar's optimistic contention that people are ultimately good.*

In fact, the authors are slowly developing a Web community that has trust at its core. Each user will earn a "trustworthiness quotient" based upon other people's online interactions with them that over time reflects the views of many people, not just of a few biased ones. Imagine the potential of getting an accurate picture about people you might want to befriend, date, or do business with not just from the fiction they make up about themselves but by what others think of them!†

---

* Google's notorious mantra, "Don't be evil," doesn't assume people are good—it asks them to be so. O logic, my lionheart.

† Software, says Google's CEO Eric Schmidt, will soon "hold politicians to account." He calls it "truth predictor."

Financial Times, October 4, 2006.

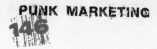
We're open for business from potential investors. Just e-mail at punkthink@ punkmarketing.com.

Use This with the Grand Jury

1. Consumers are tired of not being told the truth in marketing, and since they can see it clearly themselves, all marketing that does not pass muster is summarily ignored. (Yes, we like Dijon too.) To win back consumer trust, marketers need be clear and honest about their products—no exceptions, thank you. All disclaimers must be avoided. Rid ye of what is called mouseprint,* before it gets rid of ye.

2. A focus on profit at the expense of *all else* has left employees feeling disloyal and consumers cynical. Companies need to consider putting emphasis onto making their employees feel fine and dandy so that customer satisfaction and profits follow.

3. Opinions from consumers are no longer consigned to the suggestions box. Like it or not, they are broadcast on blogs and podcasts and sites, by lovers and fiends alike. Rather than pretend it ain't so, Flo, corporate entities *must* embrace feedback—don't be so sensitive—to demonstrate they can listen, are listening, and doing something about it.

4. Marketers can use their own good upbringing (e.g., honesty in front of the cookie jar) as a way to stand out from thine enemy, by noting that the other guys have bad habits that get in the way of their being open with *their* customers (who should be yours).

We only hope you trust us. We know. We've been lied to too.

---

* **Example:** Warning! Everything in this book is made up.

Punk is . . .

Making creativity a part of everyone's jobs, not just the domain of the department named after it.

Knowing that what you do passes the bullshit test and is meaningful, honest and interesting and, if it isn't, doing something else instead.

Realizing people don't care about your business, and certainly not *your* marketing, unless you give them a good reason. Better be a damn good one.

[to be continued]

Tasty Morsels

- Fifty percent of U.S. households will own a device like TiVo by end of 2008 that lets them skip TV advertising and in some cases even keep the darn recordings on a personal network on a server.

- Seven billion dollars of TV ad revenue will switch to other forms of advertising by then.

- What was once straightforward product placement in movies now typically involves a complex drama between advertiser and studio/producer.

- Sixty-three percent of advertisers are using product placement of some form or another.

- Product placement is valued at $3.4 billion a year, but since TV makes it part of an ad buy, its real value is probably way less.

- Eighty percent of consumers say they don't mind product placements, but the numbers who do (12%) keep doubling each year. Information is dangerous . . . so stop talking about it!

- While the benefits of a direct product placement are in no way monetized, integrating a brand into a piece of entertainment can lead to stunning results.

As Seen on TV

Place It, Baby, Place It

While the thirty-second TV spot has lost favor in all marketing circles, announcing its death is pretty premature. It's true when people get a digital video recorder, or vaunted DVR, the majority of people merrily roll through ads,* but even now only a minority of people own DVRs. (One of the reasons, we feel, is the word *video*; folks hear that in the name and say "I got a VCR, man. Why'd I need D *video* R?")

That will change when the machines start being given away with boxes of Tide. It is predicted almost half of U.S. households in a year or so will have some sort of device allowing them the pleasure of jumping over ads.† Cable operator Cablevision recently launched a highly controversial "network DVR" so consumers won't even need a box at home to do TiVo-like things. If ads are skipped at the rate they are for current owners of DVRs, then half of households having the ability to skip through ads represent $7 billion of wasted TV advertising money,[1] translating to a boat filled with executives now gunning for you advertising holdouts! No wonder marketers, ad agencies, and TV networks are so darn nervous.

---

* According to a 2002 study by Oregon firm CNW Marketing Research, 72.3 percent of them.

† Forrester Research estimated DVRs and VODs will be in almost 50 percent of U.S. households in 2007, from a 2002 report titled "Will Ad-Skipping Kill Television?"

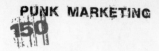

Predictably, Hollywood studios and the powerful TV networks have joined forces to fight Cablevision's move in the courts, arguing that it effectively puts all of the content "on demand," something cable operators currently only do with express permission of content providers.*2 We think they are just plain petrified.

The death of TV advertising may be greatly exaggerated, Mr. Twain, but it's down with more than a bad cold.

Consumers have never liked pesky TV commercials (except for the few that hit us in the cultural stomach), but in the early years they decided en masse to tolerate them. A 1951 study we've been holding on to from Social Research Inc. found it to be "very common in our society to dislike [television] advertising" and that viewers regarded them with "the stoical air appropriate to a necessary evil."3

Viewers back then disliked noisy and clichéd commercials, the studies say. Yet opinions varied by social class. Most tolerant were lower-middle classes, who felt it necessary to pay attention to sales messages "because the advertiser pays for the program." You can imagine black-and-white families dutifully watching their Westinghouse sets; how quaint. "Shhhh, the ads are on" moistens our rolling eyes.

At that time an advertiser paid for and actually produced the shows—one sponsor per program, please. Many have fond memories of the fifties and sixties programs (some of us in reruns) when *Playhouse 90* was presented by, egads, a cigarette company! It was only when costs rose that it became inconceivably expensive for a single advertiser to fund something.

Then, when the singles left the scene, the price was shared by many advertisers, all of whom still got a lot of leverage over the programming since no one knew another way to offer them the goods. It wasn't until the last part of the fifties that television networks realized what they had and took control. Till then all those programs were in the evil hands of "creative" ad agencies. What a world that must have been . . .

---

* These two forces of nature ganged up on Replay when they invented a DVR that automatically skipped the commercial segment, making watching NBC like viewing HBO. They shouldn't have bothered with a legal fight; if they'd have just lowered the volume of the ads to normal, the machine would have been thwarted.

And in the late sixties everything changed again when the remote control gave viewers power to change channels without leaving the armchair. It may seem unbelievable to the young Punk but there was a time when you had to leave your potato position and walk to the TV and turn the dial. Yes, Virginia, there was a dial—and the stations went to something called a "pattern" from around 1 a.m. to 6 a.m. . . .

An engineer at Zenith Electronics Corporation in 1950 developed the first clicker, dubbed Lazy Bones, and then in 1956 the first practical wireless device, the Zenith Space Command, rolled out for special use. According to data from the Consumer Electronics Association it wasn't until—we mean this—1985 that more televisions were sold with than without one.[4] (In 2000 the average household owned four remote controls, most of them living inside the love seat.) A change in

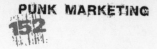

viewing habits to "channel grazing" followed, and program makers saw they had to get those trigger-happy viewers into a show quickly and keep them interested using such techniques as fast cutting, special effects, and even expensive opening scenes.

Commercials were always something that the networks had little if any control over—even if they didn't like them. It's fascinating to Punks that broadcasters don't simply reject a commercial that *they know* a viewer will outright hate. Why not at least charge a premium for such boring monstrosities? They are the villains in the story of chapter 10, knowingly responsible for the defection to other channels *or activities* during commercial pee breaks.

Perhaps that will change. Research tools are now available, such as MediaCheck, developed by PreTesting of Omaha, that determine exactly when a viewer switches and, if during a break, which ad was the camel's back or the last straw or some other cliché. And dear old Nielsen is trying to measure actual commercial breaks during shows, which is not uncynically all that matters to network executives.

As always, irrefutable research forces change, even though gut instinct and common sense told us how to solve this a long time ago. We have all known for decades that bad ads lead us to tune out, but the facts to back us up have been missing. Until those diabolical fools at TiVo let the cat out of the bag we'd tied to a rock.

Recently released data on viewing habits of owners of TiVo-type devices first sounded alarm bells in the marketing community and made senior management of those companies who did nothing but advertise on TV start reconsidering that reliance. A typical conversation went something like the following:

CFO: "Phil? Phil? How come we're spending so much money on TV ads when research shows that nobody's watching them?"

CMO: "Well, Bill, you see, television is such an evocative medium, and when we pretested our spot, gee whiz, the core target got the message that We Care."

CFO: "Uh, okay. But TV rates have been going up and up. And if people are fast-forwarding during breaks, surely we're just wasting money, right?"

CMO: "I must talk to the agency and get them to think outside the box of TV. We need a solution that relies less on commercials."

Lo and behold, a lightbulb went ding. The CMO calls the agency—probably the media-buying agency, not the ad agency, for it is they that control how senior decision makers at major advertisers spend their marketing budgets. And that's how dialogues like the one we envision above played out.

Products Re-placed

The easiest to "get" branded entertainment is something we all hear about every day, product placement. This sneaky little technique unobtrusively features a brand in the action. It's been around for years. You can watch Turner Classic Movies (TCM) and see brands stuck in old Spencer Tracy movies—even Shakespeare famously included a certain ale in his great works (didn't he?). Among the most notorious examples is E.T. eating Reese's Pieces in his life story, *E.T.: The Extra-Terrestrial*, which led to a giant increase in sales of the confectionary delights and a pissed-off, arms-folded stance from M&M's; they had said no way when first asked.

There are a number of sensational and surprising examples of placement in movies. In the early days of film, products got into movies through the powerful prop masters, who acquired free stuff for the shoot via specialty brokers who acted on behalf of advertisers. Money did not change hands back then—but the free loot reduced production costs and made the prop masters' jobs a wee bit easier. Careful to note: paying for this was never spoken about.

We will stop being romantic; once again, follow the money. There were certainly times when cash changed hands and made the difference. Even before it was done de rigueur, a movie couldn't get made if someone didn't toss some coin the producers' way for an obvious push. The excellent Australian release *Strictly Ballroom*, the first from Baz (*Moulin Rouge!*) Luhrmann, supposedly relied on a bit of funding by the Coca-Cola Company, who stumped in exchange for prominent placing of a product. In a key emotional scene where two sexy leads dance on a rooftop, a large neon Coca-Cola sign provides all the lighting!

In the 1978 classic *Grease*, Coke signs in the drive-through appeared blurry because of a deal with Pepsi. It's called a positive setup. However, an unusual twist on product placement is the more insidious way in which an advertiser will pay a moviemaker to feature his competitor looking bad. Such a practice is rare—and more rarely will anyone admit to it—but can be witnessed in several films. Look at how Coca-Cola bottles were used in Affleck bomb (tautological, indeed) *Pearl Harbor* as receptacles for blood in a military hospital while the Pepsi bottles were on-screen minutes later in their more familiar use as receptacles for soda. We have no concrete proof that Pepsico Inc. arranged this, but who would admit to such a thing! All you have to do is rent this clunker and see for yourself. Judge, jury.

In recent years, movie product placement has become a sophisticated affair where a prop master's role has been superseded by studio cheeses and production companies "liaising" (see sidebar "Words That Mean Nothing," page 144) with equally giant advertisers and their media agency representatives ("suits"). Along with all those fancy-named individuals are several specialist outfits that act as well-paid go-betweens between both parties to broker a deal.

In deals like this, a product "being placed" is one part of a complex arrangement that may include the advertiser agreeing to help promote a movie. This is more useful to the studio than cash as marketing budgets are tight (you're nodding) and new movie releases struggle to break through a cluttered movie season.

Help from an advertiser's budget, or use of a partner's distribution channels, can help increase awareness and make for healthy box office.

Avon Cosmetics struck a deal with the producers of 2004's *After the Sunset*, starring playthings Pierce Brosnan and Salma Hayek. Hayek had been signed as the new spokeslady for Avon, and therefore an arrangement with New Line Cinema made sense. The program included Avon's launching of two makeup lines, notably Bronze Goddess and Pink Paradise, styled after Hayek's makeup in said movie. The cosmetics company held a contest where lucky winners received a vacation in the Bahamas, where the movie was based. There was a charity component—always helpful for press—and Hayek helped the Avon Foundation promote the movie *and* the cosmetics. In a burst of genius, it was discovered that Hayek's pet charity was domestic violence against women, so New Line held a sensational charity premiere with a silent auction's proceeds earmarked for women in need.

Although most deals are done movie by movie, long-term partnerships between advertisers and studios are common too. The biggest was a multiyear partnership between NBC Universal and Volkswagen Cars of North America ("V-Dub"). In consideration of a teeny 200 million smackers, the car company had right of first refusal for its products to be featured in a slew of movies and TV programs created by the studio.

Some movies have strongly featured a brand despite there being no cash arrangement, such as FedEx in Tom Hanks's volleyball movie, *Cast Away,* or BMW's colorful MINI Coopers featured in both fast-edited editions of *The Italian Job.**

A "new classic" example in this realm is the 2004 cult flick *Harold and Kumar Go to White Castle,* where two bizarre stoners are hell-bent on scoffing down the greasy burgers after an unending bout of the munchies.† In this wild case study the fast-food chain made no up-front arrangement with the Bill and Ted–like duo but was pleased by the attention and so developed postrelease collectible cups, store displays, branded bags, tray liners, and even some radio support. The film's stars, director, and screenwriters were inducted into the—yes—White Castle Hall of Fame, which honors those whose stomach lining is fine after eating too many WC sandwiches.‡

Clearly Hollywood is open for business when it comes to working with marketers who can pay the freight—and it's not just the domain of the blockbusters anymore. Independent, small-budget films put that indie pride aside and welcome any help an advertiser offers. This is no longer considered selling out but rather what would happen if a tree falls in the woods in a highly competitive environment . . . !

All of this applies to movies destined to premiere on DVD too. Before long, films will be released digitally, and an advertiser's marketing muscle can help a movie break through and be chosen for download.

While there is no system for a marketer to create a partnership with a movie producer, you can get an assist from media buyers and talent agencies and just plain people who have friends. For a fee.

---

* There is a rumor in the car industry that BMW heard the Wahlberg flick was going into production and rushed MINI into production before it was due. Hollywood rules.

† Ask your dad.

‡ Coming in after the fact is typical. In Robert Redford's *Quiz Show,* Geritol was the brand "sponsoring" a tawdry fifties game show, but only after the movie was hot did Geritol start taking it seriously—after articles referred to Geritol as defunct!

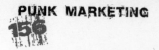

David Wirtschafter, president of the William Morris Agency, believes the true value of relationships between marketers and Hollywood is only realized when the two are brought together early in development (and via agents like his team).[5]

By getting to the table early a marketer makes full use of an association with a burgeoning production and can launch a brand along with a movie, which is something requiring a fair amount of lead time.

Chrysler started working with Paramount Pictures for forgettable actioner *Sahara*—starring threesome Penélope Cruz, Matthew McConaughey, and Steve Zahn—two years before the film debuted; you could say the movie was launched *for* the Special Edition Jeep Wrangler. Commercials for the car used snippets of the three leads running around the desert like chickens, produced by Ant Farm, the same company that made the flick's nifty trailers.

It was all tidy—and it was done better because Chrysler knew better. About two years earlier Chrysler executives learned what to ask for from everyone while stitching up a tie-in with Paramount's 2003 *Lara Croft Tomb Raider: The Cradle of Life*, a multititled sequel with Angelina Jolie-Pitt-Aniston. Chrysler/Jeep VP of marketing Jeffrey A. Bell (or Jeep Veep to friends) revealed he first asked Angie to say, "It's a Jeep thing. You wouldn't understand," for a commercial, but eventually—after a rumored five months of negotiations with the star, Chrysler, director, and a ton of others—settled for one line in an ad that didn't even mention the name of the truck.[6]

Lesson is abundantly clear: A star does not want to compromise his or her box office earnings to make some advertiser happy.

TV Lands Placements

If movie placement has been around for a while, its role in TV can be called back to the future. In the Golden Age of Television artistry, advertisers in the United States produced and paid for shows as vehicles for brands. *Colgate Comedy Hour, Texaco Star Theater, Kraft Television Theatre* and *Ford Theatre* were everyday fare. Even Lucy's shows got money for products within. (Early TV's product participants had *no idea* how good they had it: Mr. Max Factor has a credit at the end of each episode of *I Love Lucy*, a business decision that lives on in infamy as endless reruns, not to mention those DVD sales, see no end in sight.)

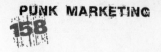
TV broadcasters, seeing a potential decline in revenue through the soon-to-tank sales of commercial airtime, have again embraced the placement of products into their programs. The never-ceasing spurts of reality (hear us cough) TV provide more opportunities for brands to be featured; it adds to what producers call realism. Or money.

We beseech you to stop using *reality* and *show* in the same sentence. Simon Cowell and those other two who pretend to judge *American Idol* are seen drinking from prominently displayed Coca-Cola cups, and Chef Rocco on *The Restaurant* never leaves his scene without the American Express card.

An interesting variation on this familiar scenario occurred in 2004 when Wal-Mart Stores Inc. struck gold with Walt Disney Company's ABC Television. Enchantment, a fictitious cosmetics firm that existed for a while in the plot of *All My Children*, launched a wanton fragrance in Wal-Mart stores. It's not for sale in the stores now, but you can still find the odd bottle on eBay to smell like a bitch in heat.

Back to *American Idol*'s Coke-swilling. Such product placement is disallowed in the UK, where a code adhered to by all public broadcasters strictly forbids "undue prominence of any brand." But in the United State there are no regulations because in the United States there are rarely rules about anything unless the right wing doesn't dig it. We're done—rant over.

Today's rules hardly exist but you can't go too far. (The axiom in Hollywood is "There are no rules, but you break them at your own peril.") The broadcaster or cabler gambles on how far to go before the consumer says stop that. So far the people at home either haven't cared or noticed,* but organizations like consumer watchdog Commercial Alerts are not happy. Plus, TV writers are lobbying for product placement to have stricter guidelines because they've got ethics!

In November 2005, Writers Guild of America west issued a demand for some sort of producers' code of conduct. About three-quarters of the members said the lines between advertising and content need to be more firmly drawn and want there

---

* A 2005 study by Mindshare , a part of the WPP Group's media-buying division Group M, reported that 80 percent of consumers are okay with product placement in TV shows.

to be disclosures at the beginning of shows saying which advertisers were paid to be involved.[7]

In the report, conglomerate advertiser Procter and Gamble was singled out as an advertiser turning product placement into product drama. In tween sensation *What I Like About You* on the WB, the two lead characters, both of whom play actresses, auditioned for an ad promoting P&G's Herbal Essences shampoo. The ad they went after then actually appeared in the ad break.

Many scripted shows are working hard to repurpose brands, not only to add some degree of realism but to fund what have become tight production budgets. (In an episode of *Monk*, a product was used as a murder weapon!)

But we're not talking big money. It's too damn difficult to measure effectiveness, making it difficult to price. Methods of measurement are as numerous as firms trying to establish methodology, and each wishes to become the industry standard. Some use the price of a thirty-second spot as point A, and others are adamant that sport sponsorship rates are the best start point.

While some advertisers cite lack of industry standards as the reason they won't dip a toe in the water, many don't think a standard is desirable. They want instances judged case by case. The value a marketer places on having its brand featured in a program is up for debate. While placing something into a show is one way to get in front of those pesky TiVo-toting avoiders, it's only a bandage on the problem and sometimes totally cheapens the entertainment. Then you *hurt* the brand.

Two reality shows—*The Restaurant* on NBC and season one of *Blow Out* on NBC's Bravo cable network—costarred products to such an extent that viewers thought they were watching an infomercial in prime time. For the hair care program Bravo recognized how overt marketing had left viewers cold; and despite loss of production dollars, they decided to make the second season without any placement deals. Bravo to Bravo!

A paradox marketers and programmers face is how to do product placement to the satisfaction of both parties without cheapening the entertainment. The placement of a product must be subtle and seem natural. Yet to be effective in getting consumers to act or think differently it is almost impossible to be either.

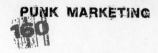
Brand Integration

A new branch of branded entertainment aims to address this conundrum, and that's brand integration. The idea is that a product is closely tied to the action and helps move the story along. This is not your product getting a cameo or some walk-on part; it's the costar if not the star itself! Take it in. The guy who first saw potential in this role was TV impresario Mark (*Survivor*) Burnett, beginning with special guest appearances of refreshing Sierra Mist soda or icy cold bottles of Coors Light in the island-dumping show. He followed this up with full-fledged leads in episodes of his Trump card, *The Apprentice*.

Ice cream, jeans, toothpaste, office products, and yummy grilled burgers were all center stage in ways that made sense for *Apprentice—and made the show better*. Viewers were in on the deal—they knew brands paid to be on—but didn't mind because *Apprentice* teaches us how to succeed in business, so isn't Sales 101 a part of that?

We wish we could have been at the initial pitch meeting (file that in Things We Wish We'd Thought of Somehow, Damn It to Hell). What a proposition from Burnett and his boy: Everyone gets happy! Advertisers are thrilled beyond recognition being there, and unlike those old-hat placements that could hardly be measured, see results within days—nay, hours—of airing!

Burnett was thrilled. Not only did he get license fees for his show from NBC, he saw a hefty fee for showcasing brand names to the tune of $1.5 to $5 million each.

Remember, the marketers saw increases in purchases due to *The Apprentice*! After a new Crest toothpaste was featured alongside star The Donnie—and a short commercial promoted a contest at crest.com—Procter and Gamble claimed 4.7 million hits on the site, the highest level ever for a P&G launch.

In another episode, contestants created a new flavor of ice cream for New York–based Ciao Bella Gelato Company, and within hours the phrase "Apprentice ice cream" became the third most searched term on Yahoo! while the flavor sold out by afternoon the next day.

Another effective use of brand integration is the Sears Holdings Corporation, featured broadly in ABC's surprise hit *Extreme Makeover: Home Edition* (a sequel to ghastly create-a-face program *Extreme Makeover*). Families down on their luck have their homes rebuilt for them, thanks to Sears in the guise of Kenmore home appliances and manly Craftsman tools! Sears commercials run in all the breaks and show host Ty Pennington (who came to life on TLC's makeover oldie *Trading Spaces*) gives the hard sell. It worked on many levels. To the viewer Sears provides to people in need; the company saw a spike in Web traffic, store visits, and money.*

Similarly, schoolteachers—those in need, part two—were helped by automaker General Motors on a hyped 2004 *Oprah* when 276 new Pontiac G6 cars were gifted to every member of a teacher-filled studio audience. It raised awareness of the car and perhaps enhanced their brand, but GM said later that sales actually decreased from the previous year. And in rare bit of bad PR for Oprah, many refused the cars because they couldn't afford to pay thousands of dollars in taxes on their gifts. Yikes.

Just as in dating, so long as everyone's having a good time, you put up with a lot. Viewers, producers, marketers, and broadcasters are willing to embrace branded integration. Bravo's reality show that pitted would-be fashion designers against one another, *Project Runway*, scored Gap Inc.'s Banana Republic as a sponsor. The prize for winning was a stint as a designer for the big Banana; and like many of the successful brands integrated into *Apprentice*, the stores marketed the hell out of it. On one episode during season one, the competitors on *Runway* were tasked with making a dress for Banana Republic, and the winner got in-store display for days following the smock's debut. Real nice.

With clever integration a show's producers can hit upon a winning formula to get brands to star as a crucial element in an entertainment vehicle without distracting from the story itself. Marketers must assess opportunities incredibly carefully to ensure that any investment is viable! Success depends on any number of key ingredients, but one in particular: the programming has to be quality and the product should add to the story instead of becoming a nuisance. (Hello? Consumers are smart?) You cannot be responsible for taking viewers from the scripted moment to a message for a product that irks them. Stop looking pretty and get involved with producers; get yourself enmeshed in the experience and make it more than a one-hit-wonderful moment.

---

* Sears research quoted in "TV's New Brand of Stars," *Newsweek*, November 22, 2004, claims viewers are 25 percent more likely to visit after watching *EM:HE*.

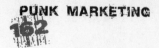

Here are the ways:

The quality of the show!

Success stories of brands integrated into *Extreme Makeover: Home Edition, The Apprentice,* or *Project Runway* would not be possible if the programs weren't appealing, or fun. And yet it's difficult to predict who will be worth getting into bed with because there are so many variables; it's called a risk!

Get in at the beginning, pay a little, and maybe the piece will flop, but if you get a hit, you will probably get rewarded for your loyalty and prescience. We suggest a deal with the show producers in which the marketer gets a guarantee of ratings with refunds or make-goods if the numbers fall short. Toyota Motor Corporation reportedly paid millions to be integrated into Burnett's boxing reality flop *The Contender* and ended up getting almost half the cabbage back when the show failed to meet targets.

The addition to the entertainment!

For a brand to make the show more instead of less entertaining, the subject or plotline must be relevant to whatever business you are tossing in . . . or it can't be anathema to your business itself . . . or you can't seem stupid and out of place. (Oh, the ridiculous examples we've thought up, but we won't divert your attention here.)

Yes, Sears worked fabulously in *Makeover* because their home-building products make sense in rebuilding a home. Make every homeowner use Visa, and it won't work.

Banana Republic naturally slid into *Project Runway* as a fashion brand in a show about fashionistas. If Glade Air Infusions tried to place its brand it would be a stinky fit at best, unless the *Runway* designers created collections from scented fabrics. How about no?

In reality—former definition of reality—it is rare to find an outing that is perfect for a brand-integration exercise. Programs whose timing is perfect such as *The Apprentice* are going to be fewer and farther between.

The *Apprentice* was "Fired!" for the fall '06 season because the franchise had lost steam (Martha's version was lackluster with "There just doesn't seem to be a place for you") and viewers got weary of its repetitiveness. Despite Burnett's classy production values and a strong dramatic premise, viewers were sick of Donald's hair flying in the wind.

The creation of a marketing program!

A TV show is not an appropriate place to sell a product outright, unless it's at 3 a.m. and involves Ginsu. Brands that integrate into programming can help consumers become interested in what you have because you made a big deal about the association. This means promoting your "insider status"; adding a product's-been-placed Web presence both on the network's site and your own; and also a physical component such as an in-store mention of your participation.

When, on *The Apprentice*, competing contestants designed a desk organizer especially for Staples Inc., the winning creation was made available in stores within days. All of them sold out quickly, and even if Staples had made no money on this, the increase in store traffic would have made up for it.

The staying involved!

Getting the most of a brand integration deal requires having a champion marketer who toils endlessly alongside the program producers to ensure that your product is portrayed correctly–this end up!–and that each aspect of the integration makes the product look good. Oh, and it would be nice if the show looked good too.

Don't make it a one-off, either. Try to do more than one outing to see if this really works for you! You have a responsibility to ensure too that the product is featured and the credit is given; and you also better be sure you don't *step on* producers but rather work with them so the final cut is something people want to watch.

What is key: don't be heavy-handed.

Despite Trump's exaggerated enthusiasm for featured brands, this par-

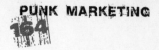
ticular gig did not make the product endorsements seem like purchased time.*

Love Is a Many Blurred Line

Another development is creation of mini-shows one minute in length to run between traditional programming as advertised-supported commercial time. Walt Disney Company's ABC Television has experimented with mini-movies sponsored by Procter and Gamble. And Monster.com was sponsor of *Office Romance,* which ran on the SOAPnet cable channel (also Disney's) over six weeks in 2004. Inside the latter was a related Monster promotion that awarded one winner the opportunity to be the president of SOAPnet and program the tiny network for a day.

Such initiatives further blur the line between advertising and programming. Once episodes were twenty-two or forty-four minutes long, excluding ad time, and commercials were thirty seconds or sixty seconds, but now the programs look a lot like ads and the stuff in between the shows are, well, other shows! (One snarky ad agency announced the one-second ad for radio recently. Goes like . . .)

Now that broadcasters have entered into the territory that was the traditional domain of the ad agency, it's not surprising that as well as creating programming for a brand to be featured in, and sponsored minis between shows, networks are creating actual commercials for their advertisers as a high-stakes version of what cable companies have been doing for the locals since their advent.

Should Madison Avenue be shaking in its boots?

You answer for a change.

---

* Are you surprised to read here that Trump gets a cut of products successfully sold via "his" show!?!

Use This to Impress Your Seatmate

1. Product placement is hardly new, but recent data detail how people who own DVRs gloriously let them skip TV ads and has led to an explosion in interest in how to get brands *into* the entertainment. We marketers shouldn't wait for data to support what was blindingly obvious: consumers will avoid irritating marketing if it's easy. (Why else are TV-DVD combos so hot now?) Let's all think of new ways to engage consumers before a gun is at our heads.

2. When it comes to moviemaking and product plugs, the earlier the marketer gets involved—via a talent agent or media buyer or even your cousin who's sleeping with a producer—the stronger the relationship.

3. Product placement on TV has increased with the boom in those freaking reality TV hours. Willingness by executives to feature brands prominently to make up missing pennies in decimated budgets has led to some heavy-handed placements that reflect poorly on everyone, including the whole damn industry. TV people are awful at product placement because most use it as a blunt tool with little demonstrable value for a marketer unless it's so seamless that the program is protected. When viewers shout, "Give me a break," you've failed.

4. Brand integration means you develop a placement scheme in which the product is given a truly relevant role to the on-screen action and adds to the flow and value of said entertainment. To make it work in a marketing program, you want viewers to do something with their interest in the brand, such as go and buy it.

5. "Content is king" is not a cliché—or if it is, tough titties, because it's true. Whether talking a deal to promote a movie or an integration into a hit TV episode, marketers should never ("Never ever ever?" so says Chris Rock) weaken the value of a program in the interest of branding. You could make some bread, surely, but you'll lose either a customer or that job you hold so dearly.

And we're sorry we called you Shirley.

Tasty Morsels

- Marketers are once again experimenting with creating their own TV shows just as they did over fifty years ago in the Golden Age of Television.

- For the right type of content a broadcaster may be willing to air a program created with a brand hoisted within and give up some ad inventory for the privilege.

- Advertisers like Grey Goose vodka ("Sip Responsibly") are funding TV shows with zero brand mentions on air. Are they crazy? Action-sports brands Vans, Burton snowboards, and Quiksilver are financing movies about their respective sports.

- Other available formats for marketer-created content include DVDs (nearly all U.S. households own a DVD player), mobile phones (ditto), gaming devices (not so much), and the always-on Internet (have to ask?) via short films, podcasts and other downloadables, games, and a whole lot of stuff that five years ago would have confused you during this bullet.

Eleven

At Last, a Job in Hollywood!
You Are the Content

Through product placement and brand integration, marketers are able to be a part of the entertainment, and not just in easily skipped over ad breaks. But marketers can do more by funding an entire production created with their brand in mind. Oh, yes, Hollywood, beware. Madison Avenue wants your job.

Ah, that's not true. In most cases the content ends up being created and produced by people from the entertainment industry anyway, because those whores will do anything for pay, like us. The branding is the issue here. Oh, and the money.

So without taking up time blabbing about history—we're on to the future here!—suffice to say the notion of advertisers financing content with their brands the star is not new. It's as old as TV itself. In fact in the 1940s and 1950s the advertising agencies, not the broadcasters, produced programming on both radio and TV, and the ad clients had total say on what stayed and what went. Only later, as once-cheap productions became sophisticated with extravagant budgets to match, no single marketer could afford to support a weekly show. Broadcasters started to underwrite the production and offered multiple advertisers places in the breaks. We already told you that.

The Producers sans Mel!

Now we've come full circle: evidence mounts that TV commercials are not always a smart way to influence consumers, so marketers experiment with content

167

they call their own. But the game is different because marketers can play not only in the halls of television, but in the movies, music, via sporting events, and on the Web.

BMW Films is cited as the start of contemporary branded entertainment, introducing in 2001 a series of high-profile Web shorts made by and featuring top Hollywood talent. This was a brave play for the automaker that garnered much publicity ("It's so new!"), which made the outlandish expense worthwhile. It led to a slew of copycats, none of whom has enjoyed the same success or word of mouth.

Marketers can now take up where they left off half a century ago creating their own content that will draw consumers to them like moths toward the moon. It is possible today because of the fragmentation of the media. A decade and a half ago, the idea of your own show meant hijacking one of the major networks and trying to reach tens of millions. It was unjustifiably expensive to pull off. Yet the numbers of TV networks are nearing *a thousand* so the possibility of reaching a niche audience through cable has become a decent idea. The airtime costs are lower because so are the audience numbers, and marketers can target to the precise buyer they want to reach. Yes, you.

The North Face Inc., a manufacturer of clothing and gear for adventurous types, reached outdoor enthusiasts through a five-part series airing on NBC Universal's NBC Sports network at the turn of the decade. *The North Face Expeditions* were classy documentaries narrated by sex enthusiast Sting, with highly skilled adventurers "tackling the planet's most challenging landscapes." This program displayed North Face equipment during these varied adventures in a fitting way right in context of the action.* North Face demonstrated brand values authentically, lending its products credibility and, more important, awareness.

Nike Inc.'s street basketball series, *Battlegrounds*, produced by production powerhouse @radical.media, ran on Viacom-owned MTV and turned out to be a pretty good case study for both the inventive marketer and old-style cable company. *Battle* explored the cultural phenomenon of streetball, which is an urban form of

---

* Having the adventurers stop to drink a Mountain Dew would, for instance, have been unnatural and more like traditional product placement.

basketball usually played in playgrounds, intertwined with hip-hop music. In each episode two streetballers featured as "players" in their hometown basketball courts went one-on-one in their quest to be a tournament champion and winner of that sweet $50,000 prize. And they got Nike products to boot (or to sneaker)! It made a hot showcase for Nike's authentic involvement in the urban community, and the shoe giant was able to make a bit of its investment back through sales of DVDs of the show.

One fascinating success, *Iconoclasts*, also produced by @radical.media, began on the Sundance Channel in 2005, largely with support of Grey Goose vodka, a brand owned by Bacardi & Company Ltd. The six-part series reportedly cost $15 million to produce and much to the bafflement of cynical observers, paired innovators from distinct fields with, uh, no Grey Goose products anywhere. Since, uncannily, Sundance is commercial-free, there could be no advertising on the cable channel. Sacrilege to even think of!

But Grey Goose desired to promote *outside* the channel. Through a partnership with the Condé Nast Media Group, the vodka connection was revealed through carefully crafted print ads, off-network TV spots, and consumer PR. They held launch parties for *Iconoclasts* in twenty markets where signage was prominently displayed and GG served. Edited highlights of the wild L.A. event were aired before the shows . . . so viewers did at least get the connection.

And the Grey Goose Tastemakers sweepstakes bestowed a trip to Miami's South Beach (as opposed to Staten Island's South Beach . . .) for the winning submission of a cocktail recipe featuring Grey Goose products. See? It kept the content of the series intact and away from the hands of the Goose while communicating odorless values that liquor leader considers its hub: ambition, creativity, and style.

The series was so beloved by Sundance founder Bob that he even agreed to appear in an episode with stubbly costar Paul ("Butch") Newman.

Yet even with big bucks thrown at them broadcasters claim it still must be outstanding entertainment to get on the air. Blah blah. Based on the evidence so far, it is debatable whether the networks are sticking to their guns. Read on.

In NBC's *Meet Mister Mom*, a reality show that ran for almost half a season in 2005, the opening montage featured a teenage girl sporting a State Farm Insurance T-shirt (could that be a sponsor?), something a character of her age wouldn't die

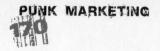
wearing. Seconds later the montage pauses on a JCPenney store (could it?) that gazes lovingly into the camera. In its review the *New York Post* said it was "possibly the most boring reality show in history" and referred to the part where a State Farm agent (agent?) proudly hands a check for $25,000 to a participating family, calling it the "most shameful product placement ever."[1] Boo plus hiss equals yuck.

NBC was not silly enough to run any more of this exercise in shoddy product placement and likely wasn't canceled before for fear of upsetting *Mom*ertisers.

Why anyone in 2007 thinks the consumer is stupid enough to buy something forced onto TV episodes proves how stupid some marketers still are. As Nike's love affair with MTV demonstrated to an industry or two, it *is* possible to create compelling programming and say something positive about a sponsor. As Goose's sunny dance provided evidence of, consumers can make subtle connections between show and product if a brand steward does some thinking.

Heck, to some an episode is paltry compared with the origination of an entire channel with your products! That's what Volkswagen-owned automaker Audi did in Britain during late 2005, when it launched the Audi Channel on British Sky Broadcasting, today reaching over 20 million British subjects. The programming à la Audi is strictly infotainment and has content beyond auto obsession: there is golf and polo and celebrity talk. Future plans include interactive features for viewers on how to find dealers (cars), request brochures (cars), set up test-drives (cars), and then price a machine (cars).*

Some marketers have also become moviemakers so as to demonstrate brand values. Movie director Stacy Peralta's cult skateboarding film *Dogtown and Z-Boys* was backed by skateboard apparel company Van Doren Rubber Company (Vans). As in the case of Grey Goose and *Iconoclasts*, the role of Vans in the movie was pretty nonexistent. In *Dogtown and Z-Boys* there's credit for Vans at the end and in a glimpse in some seventies footage of shoes being worn by a fairly well-known skater. But they leveraged the flick association in online promotions and in store displays.

Of course most brands don't operate in such exciting arenas, so opportunities

---

* Audi Channel is in partnership with their clever longtime ad agency, Bartle Bogle Hegarty Ltd., and TV production company North One Television.

to create something adventurous are fairly limited. A film about window clean-ing funded by Windex might, we guess, appeal only to obsessive-compulsives. Although watching skyscraper-window cleaners high up on shaky platforms could be sort of fun.

But there can be opportunities for marketers to create films on DVD to comple-ment other pieces of entertainment.

As always, though, stick to fab content so consumers will watch without ques-tion. The quirkily entertaining shorts *Meet the Lucky Ones*, funded entirely by Ford's Mercury division, originally appeared as a series on a Web site and were subse-quently distributed through online megastar Amazon inside the box to over a mil-lion customers who bought a DVD from them in summer 2004.

In fact, Amazon saw the light in 2004 and began releasing its own line of short films to market its wares and the brand itself.* Its series of five shorts that made up Amazon Theater during the holiday shopping season in 2004 involved, like BMW Films before them, top Hollywood talent. Produced by Hollywood megabrothers Ridley and Tony Scott and starring Minnie Driver and some other hardly in-demand actors, all products from the shorts were available for sale on-site. If a viewer clicked on an end credit—say, a handbag—they were transported to the page where they—ta-da!—bought a handbag. Amazon thus demonstrated to consumers that you could get more than books and tchotchkes and did what TV networks had hoped to do since the day the Internet rolled in: displayed a product you *could* use a rat, we mean a mouse, to buy!

I'll Show You Mine

Other retailers have upped the ante on exclusive content to drive sales of products at their stores. Both Wal-Mart and Target sell "music exclusives" to drive people into the stores and to their sites. Target sold an EP of tunes that diminutive singer Rob Thomas (Matchbox Twenty) created for the chain in exchange for pro-

---

* Even a "product placement talk show," *Amazon Fishbowl*, starring former *Politically Incorrect* comic Bill Maher, who is now correctly called an ultimate sell-out. A funny one, naturally.

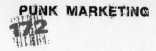
motional support for his latest commercial release, similar to a deal they made with nose-ringed Lenny Kravitz the previous year.

Wal-Mart had the same intent and struck a deal with TV channel Black Entertainment Television (BET) so the box company could sell "exclusive programming and other content" from BET on DVDs only at Wal-Mart. The new BET Official brand created for the alliance kicked off with a companion DVD to a CD released by cocky superstar rapper Kanye West, which contained never-seen-before footage of him.

Best Buy has made arrangements with some of the chart-topping-est music acts around—bigger than Thomas and West—to get music lovers into their stores. The Rolling Stones' heavily promoted 2003 *Four Flicks* four-disc DVD set was a mouthful *and* in their stores for four months before anyone else could sell it. This benefited both the aging rockers and the electronics store.

Still, this deal, while adding millions to Mick and Keith's overflowing coffers, did not go down well with other music retailers; in Canada, HMV stores pulled all Stones CDs and DVDs off the shelves as retaliation. (In 2005, Canadian Alanis "Ironic" Morissette did an exclusive presell of a ten-year rehash of *Jagged Little Pill* at Starbucks, and Canadian retailers felt the sting again. All of Canada booed and Morissette's CDs were put in the back.)

Both these were in our estimation extreme cases of cutting off noses.

Starbucks Corporation is so immersed in the content game that it often seems more a music company than a coffeemaker. It has been producing and distributing exclusive music for several years, hoping to give people a reason more than their coffee addiction to come inside. The Ray Charles *Genius Loves Company* release won eight Grammy Awards including album and song of the year. Through its shops and the Hear Music subsidiary (and a deal with XM Satellite Radio) Starbucks proffers CDs from artists who might not see prominent shelf space at another retailer.*

Starbucks is an ideal venue to showcase music that they find consistent with

---

* We add here that was the original intent. Today it makes deals with dozens of mainstream artists to feature their discs near the Starbucks chocolate grahams. It did not accept a 2004 Bruce Springsteen album because it included a song that went against their values.

the values of the chain, but for Starbucks it is not clear what those values are. In mid-2006 the chain released Diana Ross's *Blue*, a collection from the 1970s of Miss Ross singing standards quietly shelved by Motown until now. When asked why the store wasn't playing it in rotation like everything else on the shelves, a manager commented to one author, "It's just not that good."

Recently, Starbucks has extended this push for content to include movies. In 2006 they offered customers ads, contests, and essentially, propoganda—and eventually a DVD—surrounding a new movie, *Akeelah and the Bee*, from studio Lionsgate Entertainment, about a young girl and her spelling prowess. Unfortunately, even with Starbucks prodding visitors through daily words spelled out on cards and napkins and cups and door signs, the movie was a serious bust, taking in a monosyllabic $6 million in the first weekend. ("Your word is flop." "F-L-O-P.")

It's not just large retail chains such as Best Buy and Starbucks that have valuable real estate available for content producers keen to find ways to promote something.* In 2003 former president of Coca-Cola Steve Heyer said in a speech to the advertising and entertainment industries:

> Look around you, the Coca-Cola Company has more impressions than any other company on the planet. You see our brand on cafés, concession booths, and hot dog stands. Our brands light up Times Square and Piccadilly Circus, but also neighborhood delis and ballparks. People wear the brand on T-shirts and ball caps. They display it on coolers and beach balls and key chains—just about anything you can think of. . . . In total, Coca-Cola benefits from 2 billion plus brand-communication opportunities every day in the U.S. alone."[2]

Yes, that was long, but he said it so well. Brands can provide a means of distribution that you can't shake a stick at. That's a serious concept for those in various entertainment industries who want to reach consumers who dig their brands.

---

* Book publishers are anxious and ingenious when it comes to finding new places to sell. Read car washes, stationery stores, porno shops, movie theaters, lemonade stands . . .

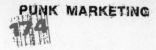

A space on a Coke can is how many times more valuable than an ad break on *American Idol* . . . ? Let's all say it together: It is tons more!

Marketers with smaller brands than the Can Company can think along the same lines and consider what they have that could offer value. As long as the consumer benefits, why not go for it?

Use This at Boring Conferences (as if there were any other)*

1. It is difficult to get a TV program developed around a brand to air on any respectable network. It can be done, but requires that a broadcaster's ad sales department keep the advertiser happy and that the broadcaster's creative folks feel good about it; and everyone kisses and hugs and says, yeah, this is terrific and will get the audience we all want and respectable numbers at that. To make it work requires an extraordinary team effort involving brand, an agency (ad, media, or whoever else drives that deal), network, talent, and G-d. All stars need align and everyone must share a vision: We will not play with the audience. We know how fickle they are and how quickly they will turn on us.

2. Whether a TV show or another, there should not be any dropped-in, heavy-handed marketing messages. *Meet Mister Mom* was a colossal failure because it seemed like a skit! It was chock-full of messages from the advertisers funding the crap. Then there is Sundance's *Iconoclasts*, a quality piece that makes people think nicely about its peacock sponsor, Grey Goose. No references were left in about the brand whatsoever. It did a lot of good off the air for the vodka bottler. Educate thyself! Get creative!

3. While action-sports brands have funded cinematic movies about a sport, bigger opportunities for most exist in a DVD format. Everyone owns a player and there

---

* There *will be* an exciting Punk Marketing conference. (Stay in touch.)

are ways for marketers to make a short reflecting a brand's core values to be distributed to people who dig those beliefs.

4. Retailers are "doing deals" with content producers—of music, TV, film, and online—so their beloved customers can gain access to new and exclusive entertainment in exchange for some promotional muscle. This principle is applicable to any piece of real estate a marketer owns including that ole desirable packaging. It's the old advertising model turned upside down!

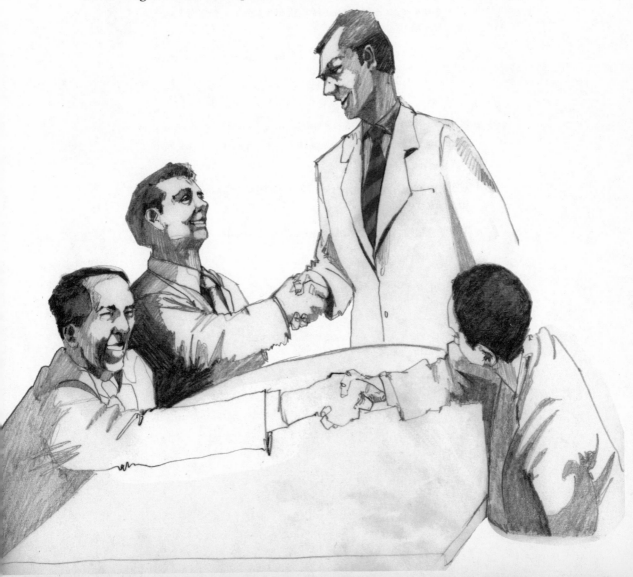

Tasty Morsels

- The video-game industry is projected to be worth $55 billion by 2009.[1]

- There are 100 million gaming households in the United States.[2]

- The age of the average gamer is thirty-years old.[3]

- Active male gamers spend an average of 12.5 hours a week playing video games compared with less than 10 hours watching TV.[4]

- On average, a gamer spends 25 percent of leisure time playing video games.[5]

- Thirty-eight percent of gamers are female.[6] Girls, girls, girls.

Twelve

Game On
No One Is a Loser

Computer games came of age as a legitimate form of entertainment with the right to sit at the grown-up table on the day Microsoft sold $125 million worth of *Halo 2*'s within the first twenty-four hours of release on November 9, 2004, more than beating previous notorious record-holder *Spider-Man 2*—yes, a movie—from its opening weekend.

On that glorious day video games could no longer be considered the sole territory of adolescent schoolboys. With those numbers it was clear they were reaching a broader part of the consumer market, and Hollywood bolted up from their stupor. With over $10 billion in sales per year the market for computer games and game consoles in the United States is worth more than movie-ticket sales.

Studios have since forged alliances with game publishers or started their own game divisions or made acquisitions. And big film directors such as Ron Howard, Steven Spielberg, and James Cameron want a piece of the action. Cameron just joined the board of new gaming company Multiverse Network Inc., which was started by Netscape veterans in 2004, to create massive multiplayer online games (MMOGs) surrounding film projects. His first offering will be released as a game *before* the film to give people the chance to, as is MMOGs wont, become a character in the newly created universe of the new Cameron joint, then run to see their world in narrative form when the film gets its release.

In Hollywood, green bills shout. That an MMOG such as Vivendi Universal's *World of WarCraft* pulls in sixty million a month in subscription fees has not gone unnoticed.

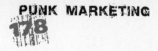

Yes, sir, a lot of heretofore ignored money is to be made in games, and it only gets truer each year. Once upon a time a title might sell well for mere months, giving a tiny window for games publishers to recoup costs. Movies—even a box office lemon—have multiple opportunities to make bank through DVD sales, rentals, TV cable, network deals, pay-per-view, sequels, prequels, and Vick's NyQuil (oops).

But with unpredictably successful franchises like Microsoft's *Halo* series and unstoppable *The Sims* from leader Electronic Arts (EA), the proposition starts to look like a party we had better get an invitation to.*

* Carrie Fisher once famously said the two saddest words in the English language are: What party?

Especially considering how game production budgets are still around $20 million, whereas a movie budgeted at less than $100 million is an independent experiment, those are cheap pants to get into. Lest you forget, marketing costs for a game are typically a fraction of those for a movie. (*M: I: III*'s marketers spent $100 million to show us Cruise's pearly whites while jumping on Oprah's couch.)

Halo 2 had a tiny marketing spend compared with those flicks it ran roughshod over as it skipped into the record books. Yet Punk Marketers know that not having as much money means you think more than spend.

It probably seems odd to imagine movies competing with computer games—passive experiences vs. active—but they're both jostling for consumer time and money, so you better believe it's so. As film and games converge, the combined industries hope there will be less conflict and more synergy; whoever wins will pay the other's freight.

Watching *The Godfather* films may tempt you to play (and buy) *The Godfather: The Game*, released in 2005 by EA. And likewise, playing the video game *Lara Croft Tomb Raider*—reading the comic books or, uh, gazing at her online—might make you want to see her on a ninety-five-foot screen. Especially with those breasts.

Yeah, that's good in theory. A successful game does not an enjoyable movie-watching experience make. Or vice versa! There are few examples of supersuccessful movie/game franchises. *Sin City* was one—and that may have been more because of Jessica Alba's appearing in the movie at a time when her Q Score was at a high.*

The growth in games has definitely been at the expense of other entertainment forms. Audiences for prime-time TV and butts in cinemas have steadily declined largely because the core eighteen-to-thirty-four-year-old males have been spending more time playing out video addictions. In fact, three-quarters of households that include an eighteen-to-thirty-four-year-old male have a video games system.[7] And for teen boys, video games represent a full 15 percent of their media intake.[8]

But it would be a mistake to think only kids and young-adult males play along. Although kids do use video games more frequently—with 61 percent of kids under

---

* The firm Marketing Evaluations/TVQ Inc. is famous for their Q Score system, which measures the appeal of specific actors, TV shows, and movies (the head-scratching reason Jenna Elfman keeps getting cast at all).

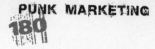
fifteen years old saying they play daily—it's a fact that more gamers are adults than kids. Just because we love numbers: only a third of *all* video game players are younger than eighteen;* just under 40 percent of gamers are women; and if you calculate those referred to as casual *online* gamers, the balance is in favor of women. Clearly video games represent a remarkable manner for us to reach consumers of all shapes and sizes.

Finally, there are three ways marketers can integrate video games into marketing strategies (write these down): in-game advertising, sponsorships, and "advergaming." We thank you for reading our prosaic preamble. We now move on to the meat!

In-Game Advertising: No Delusions

Game developers used to beg permission from brands they included on a "set" so the game was given a more realistic environment. Those naïve days. Now the tables have turned topsy, and advertisers that see the outrageous benefit of having a brand on a game monitor that a core demographic is salivating over (e.g., living inside) will shell out *muchos dólares* for the privilege of a product placement inside the hot or up-and-coming titles. The returns and results are pretty scrumptious.

Video game *Tony Hawk's American Wasteland* from Activision Inc. is a vehicle for superstar skateboarder Tony Hawk *and* the Chrysler Jeep brand. Research from Nielsen Entertainment tossed out a startling stat: players reported seeing a skillful 3-D rendering of a Jeep inside AW *twenty-three times* within the first twenty minutes.[9] Hawk's costars in the game were Jeep Wranglers, Grand Cherokees, and Jeep Libertys, which may seem like overkill until you learn that 96 percent who recalled the cars according to the Nielsen data had no problem with their appearance ("They fit right in").

And now, the pièce de résistance: more than half the players said they'd recommend Jeep to a friend and almost two-thirds would consider buying one on the day they get off the couch.

------

* Thirty-five percent, according to the Entertainment Software Association.

The Jeep placements in *American Wasteland* were, as the consultants say, good for Chrysler (win one) and good for Activision (win two). Conjoined with placement deals from Nokia and Motorola, Activision made a sweet 10 percent of production costs with cabbage spent by product placements.

Another example of a heroic brand inside a game is in Ubisoft Entertainment's *Tom Clancy's Splinter Cell Pandora Tomorrow*, in which not one but two Sony Ericsson phones are featured. The "real" star of the game, a character named Sam Fisher, tries to wage his own *Death Wish*–like war against terrorism, and his Sony Ericsson P900 smart phone's high-tech fabulousness helps combat the forces of evil and save our asses. The player cannot move forward without commandeering either a P900 or the ever-popular T637 camera phone to complete the many complicated missions of Mr. Sam.

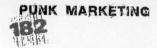

A Real Live Conversation

AD EXECUTIVE 1:
"We put a guy in a chicken costume and sit him in a room with a video camera. People can watch him on the Internet and tell him to do 'whatever' and the guy *has* to do them. Within reason of course. We do it by taking thousands of videos of the 'chicken,' so everyone thinks they're actually telling him to do things."

AD EXECUTIVE 2:
"And this will help us sell more chicken sandwiches?"

AD EXECUTIVE 1:
"Who the hell knows, but it'll sure be funny!"

SIDEBAR

Okay, so this is a completely fabricated transcript, but the idea is true. It was called Subservient Chicken, put out by Burger King via our friends at CP+B. It became a viral marketing phenomenon with plenty of rip-offs soon after including Subservient President, Subservient Hezbollah, and The Subservient Donald. It had little connection to the business of Burger King and its new TenderCrisp Chicken Sandwich, but it worked. They were after a consumer market of young adults, mostly guys, who were smart enough to know where to find them and bold enough to try something outrageous to get their attention. Burger King has since continued this path of quirky advertising via CP+B, focusing less on romanticizing its artery clogging products and more on building a relationship with the consumer. Sure, it's scary to take chances, but when it hits it hits big.

Fight the fear.*

In a first-of-kind deal between handset maker and games publisher, Sony supported the launch of *Splinter Cell* with an online photo contest, world-premiere events in Hollywood and New York, a large consumer e-mail campaign, and whatever was handy for them to glom on to. While there was a demo of the game on Sony's consumer site, it was, as with most unmanageable Web conglomerates,

---

* SubservientChicken.com. Say, hi, from us.

impossible to locate. (SonyStyle.com, the monolithic corporate site, was recently voted by an ad magazine the "worst site of its kind.")

Game publishers will stop at nothing to woo marketers with money who might place brands onto console titles and, as with all nascent industries, now find public conferences everywhere to help. (Businesses that take off are notable for the suddenness of expensive "symposia" at which to mingle.)

The L.A. Office Roadshow Gaming Boot Camp is intense.[10] At a recent Boot Camp, Midway Games Inc. huddled with beverage, confection, snack-food, and sporting goods companies to find hard money for its planned game based on DreamWorks Animation's animated *Over the Hedge* (which features goofy songs by Ben Folds). This was a safe bet for many new to this brand-on-game action; everyone wants badly to reach a demo of eighteen-to-thirty-four-year-old guys.

But the challenge for marketers who want to integrate products into video games is that they often feature graphic violent or sexual content. Will the association be good for their image? In EA's *Burnout Revenge*, players can drive *and* crash a delivery truck for burger chain Carl's Jr. Doesn't seem to be a problem for parent company CKE Restaurants, Inc., but UPS wouldn't go near it with a brown stick.

So now you know. Game placements by 2010 will be worth $700 million, according to patriotic researchers Yankee Group.[11] The real growth is likely not to come from stand-alone console games, however, but from those played online, since in that field advertisers have a nifty way to run flights of ads or placements based on location of player, time of day, or even predicted mood.

When played during the evening, a virtual fast-food store on the Main Drag switches from being all sandwiches to sausage pizzas. Or a virtual soda in China might have a different name from the one downed in France. Or, say, for a movie opening in L.A. and New York, ads could be inserted in the game only for folks playing from those cities. And so on.

Massive Inc., an agency that launched in 2004 specializing in such in-game ad placements, has since been bought by Microsoft for lots of bread. They sell ad units in online games in the form of billboards, posters, vehicles, pizza boxes, soda cans, screen savers, and TV screens, among countless and growing other categories (we think someone's underwear will wear a logo soon). At 2005's video game monster show Electronic Entertainment Expo (E3), Massive's CEO, Mitchell Davis,

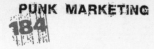
told the attending crowd that in-game ads can boost brand recognition by 23–35 percent, compared with just 6–7 percent for a decent TV campaign. Using Massive's not-small technology, it's possible to have full-motion stopgap commercials during games like *Anarchy Online* and perhaps appearing on a plasma-screen billboard a character strolls past.

Such possibilities should have particularly salivating appeal to movie studios, who promote new or impending releases using a trailer that only lasts fifteen seconds or so; the trick is to keep gamers on board. Remember, they can easily avoid watching the ads by simply "walking away" from it (or, heaven forbid, shutting down).

And wouldn't you know? The smart Massive does not charge advertisers unless the ad is viewed—just like regular old online.

Virtual-game spots from Massive can be bought in online games of almost all major publishers, and with the arrival of the new generation of Internet games consoles—Microsoft's Xbox 360 and the Sony PlayStation 3—Massive and competitors are now capable of opening new doors and monitors on the consoles.

In addition to the funky flexibility it offers advertisers on how, where, and when they can promote brands, tracking effect is effortless. Massive has created a relationship with researchers Nielsen Interactive so a paying advertiser is able to see data every day on an intranet and can make corrections to their strategies daily, hourly, minutely.

IGA Worldgroup, another big name in in-game advertising, seeks ad-friendly opportunities within new-release video games; its job is to find ways for advertisers to control and update in-game ad campaigns to match the ones that run and evolve in other formats. IGA's network, called Radial (as in run-flat tires), enables audio, video, and 3-D objects to be seamlessly placed, and then replaced, in the gaming action.

Elsewhere, not only can you see a pizza in the game you're playing, you can also order and eat one for real without leaving the gaming experience. In Sony Online Entertainment's game *Everquest II* players can type in "pizza pizza" whenever hunger strikes to place an online order with Pizza Hut to arrive in half an hour (or your slice is free).

You still need to get out of your chair to open the door, which sucks, but gives an indication where in-game advertising is going. Another example, from Nike Inc., was the deal with the large and in charge Take-Two Interactive's 2K Sports so that in the latest version of the publisher's *NBA 2K* basketball game, not only are virtual players wearing Nike products, but the players gawking on can buy personalized versions of the shoes for themselves through Nike's iD customization tool.

Soon payment for products consumed while playing will be added to a monthly subscription charge for games in what are now commonly called micropayments. Now, if we could only find a device to slice and hold the pizza for us, then turn it just so; we don't want to interrupt the game!

(We Are) Game to Sponsor

A 2003 MTV documentary, *True Life: I'm a Gamer,* was a revealing look at the professional video game player's (pro gamer's) life. There was twenty-one-year-old Fatality, then the number one ranked PC gamer in the country, who raked in more than $150,000 in tournaments in one year, and twenty-three-year-old Craig Kinzler, *Golden Tee Golf* World Champion, who claimed to have won more than $125,000 in the previous two years.

There are live video game tournaments where players compete against one another—including the rough 'n' tumble World Cyber Games, the Global Gaming League, and the Cyberathlete Professional League—each of which has for some time been attracting corporate sponsors directly dependent on the videogame industry. But recently other companies with no reason to buy in have become fascinated by the dollar signs they see in the others' eyes. They view these hard-edged competitions as a way to connect with a coveted, ever-so-evasive demo.

In September 2005, Johnson & Johnson became the first of its kind to buy in when its Tylenol subsidiary announced it would sponsor a professional team called Ouch (nicknamed Pain Alleviation Inc.), which would stand in tournaments for the game *Counter Strike.** In such tournaments, crowds watch as teams or individuals compete at game consoles or computer terminals—the ultimate geek fest—while action is displayed on monitors and announcers provide a lively Cosellish commentary.

---

* Neither of us honestly believes the players need Tylenol because they've struck their heads on a counter, although who knows.

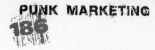

The Nag Factor

Kids are powerful. You need not have one to realize this. While parents like to think they have a strong influence on their children, the reverse is true. Marketers know this and every year rely on something called the Nag Factor to push products.

The Nag Factor, a popular advertising procedure, was first employed in a 1984 Tonka toys commercial. It's simple: kids see something they want on TV, in a magazine, on a billboard, and they nag, nag, and nag a parent to buy it until one or both fold. According to a national survey commissioned by the comically named Center for a New American Dream, American children ages twelve to seventeen will ask their parents an average of nine times for products they have seen advertised until they give in. Some ask as much as fifty times. We think, why should that be a problem for a child? Kids will nag—they have the time. Kids!

And here's the kicker: the survey also found that 55 percent of kids are successful in getting *anything* they want from their parents. Cool!

The Nag Factor is so successful since most marketers are blind to any moral obligation thanks to the enormous profits the nags bring in.[*] It is estimated that kids who are still living at home influence, on the low end, $500 billion of their parents' purchases. Advertising spending aimed at kids is at an all-time high at roughly $230 billion a year, or $2,190 per household, according to McCann-Erickson.

There may be hope for parents though. According to marketing consultants Yankelovich Inc., in a 2005 study sponsored by Disney (natch), the Nag Factor is clearly showing its age and irrelevance. In a shocking twist, it has missed several emerging trends among parents and kids. The study cites a trend toward shared preferences as part of a broader trend called Zapping the Gap, which refers to the generation gap, a term Yankelovich coined forty years ago.[†] Parents and kids, they believe, are now more likely to start discussions about the things they want in life more from a place of commonality rather than conflict. (Cue a Carpenters song.) The gap that today's parents experienced in their youth has diminished since kids now

---

[*] In October 2006, the Campaign for a Commercial-Free Childhood, petitioned Wal-Mart to shutter its new Toyland micro site that encourages kiddies to "review" new offerings.

[†] Sometimes we wonder if consultants spend more time naming their studies than anything else.

have more in common and share more with their parents, mostly due to shared destinations on our pal the Net.

Still, advertisers are relentless when it comes to preying on kids. It is hard enough to raise well-adjusted young'uns without the TV telling them they are way inadequate if they don't own (insert hot gizmo). But who is to blame? Are we failing as parents by letting ads have more influence on our children than we do? Or is the media just too powerful at selling products and self-esteem so the playing field is anything but flat?

We will nag you further about it elsewhere in the book. For now, hang your head in shame for allowing anyone to talk *you* into anything.

SIDEBAR

A biggie like World Cyber Games can attract a million gamers to compete, a vast majority from countries in Asia or equally faraway places. In South Korea, an astounding 30 percent of the population is registered to play online games; naturally, Korea hosts World Cyber finals. As if that weren't mouth-widening enough, two TV channels are dedicated to competitive-video-gaming broadcasting 24-7 in South Korea. You thought they only had car companies, huh?

In 2005 in China, a female player died after intense play of *World of Warcraft,* prompting Chinese gamers to hold an online funeral service . . . sponsored in part by . . . * We suppose that's the ultimate example of terminal illness.

The launch of worldwide e-sports competitions gave a big boost to the field in early 2006. World Series of Video Games is U.S.-based, created by Games Media Properties, an opportunistic venture of the William Morris Agency. Intel Corporation and MS's Xbox 360 were on board as sponsors before the press release was dry.

Broadcasters are starting to give serious coverage of video gaming tournaments. DirecTV launched a league in 2006, and its executive vice president of Entertainment, Eric Shanks, told *Hollywood Reporter,* "The key to compelling content is how you produce it. No one wants to see the back of some guy's head and a

---

* Even we are not that tacky. Almost.

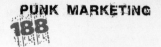
mouse."[12] Good point, Eric. DirecTV's Massive Gaming League (MGL) aims to turn video gaming into a real sport and its best players into pop heroes.

Image consultants, stand by your phones, please.

Advergaming: It Makes Us Hot

Not only can marketers place ads in and around video games—and sponsor people in competitions—but a smart one can create an advergame! Such typically online ventures are free for users to play and relatively small in scope compared with those by the giant publishers such as Electronic Arts or Activision. Advergames are designed to engage consumers in a fully branded experience, so as to collect useful intelligence for future marketing campaigns. The games cost up to $100,000 to produce, as compared with the many millions of dollars for a retail game, but the value is real.

Online travel agent Orbitz—a group effort of airlines American, Continental, Delta, Northwest, and United—hosts a gaming site featuring games such as *Island Hop* and *Beach Valley Pong* for multitudes of bored office workers to play while day-dreaming how to shoot their bosses.[13] In each there is a link to the Orbitz site that will take you away from it all! The games aren't merely for fun; they are part of a promotional campaign in which lucky gamers win vacations. Play *Dunkin' Mascots* (sadly, no paid relation to Dunkin' Donuts) and you get to toss a school mascot through the basketball net and are qualified to enter a sweepstakes for a grand prize of a beach vacation for two!

Similarly, plastic-brick maker The Lego Group hosts games online that promote its notorious building blocks and communicate a message about playfulness that we can't get enough of.

Blockdot Inc., owned by Media General, Inc., that made a game for Lipton Cup-a-Soup, saw its product get tons of acclaim when it came upon the scene in 2005 and attracted millions of game plays in what was the brand's first advertising in a decade. The impressive *Beat the 3PM Slump* helped reposition Cup-a-Soup as an ideal snack at work when you were looking for a pick-me-up in the mid-afternoon. According to the setup: *It's [now] 2:59. The 3PM Slump is about to descend upon the office to drain you of all [your] energy, [ability to] focus, and motivation. Worse yet, your* boss . . . *scheduled your performance review for 3:15. At long last, here's your chance to* Beat the 3PM Slump *head-on, and [allow you to] sail through the rest of your afternoon.* The game was part of a campaign that included TV commercials, radio promotions, and newspaper insertions.

Marketers hire Blockdot to create advergames and pay a fee to have them hosted on Blockdot's hugely popular game site Kewlbox.com to get traceable exposure for games.* Kewlbox.com offers a diverse array of popular nonbranded or advergames and attracts half a million gamers a day, thus giving the marketers a chance to reach a real community that spreads the word. Get traction with a group who would never go to your corporate site.

Redmond, Washington–based games maker WildTangent Inc. has its own advergames department plus its own popular portal called Wild Games, so consumers can pay a subscription and play. The twist with Wild is that its relationship with computer makers Dell Inc. and Hewlett-Packard (HP) places it on a special desktop console automatically updated whenever a new game is issued. (Mind you, this is automatically bundled onto tens of millions of computers!) With WildTangent, marketers can place messages on banners within these auto-downloaded games–sold for profit after the demo expires–or place their brands as product placements within virtual worlds.

With the mobile gaming industry at $1.5 billion by 2008,[14] and over 100 million U.S. game-capable mobiles today, it's no surprise that advergames have also been created for download on phones or PDAs, usually as part of a larger marketing campaign.

Microsoft has released mobile advergames on AvantGo–a free service that allows user access to thousands of Web sites on their mobile devices–to promote its Office 2003 suite. One, from April 2005, was *Microsoft Trivia Challenge,* in which players are asked softball questions (including some about Office software) and race against the clock. After playing, an interstitial ad appears with those cringe-worthy dinosaurs from that creaky print campaign.

---

* That is a top 50 gaming destination.

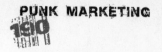
The Coca-Cola Company's *Coca-Cola Christmas Quest* game forces players to help Santa deliver Coke on time for the holidays. Joyride over rooftops in his sled as Santa catches each Coke bottle thrown to/at him from a truck down below. Once each is caught, he must deliver by dropping them down the chimneys of the residents' houses. Blue Sphere Games Ltd, *Christmas Quest*'s creator, created a game for Ford Motor Company's Land Rover division where the Sports Tourer effortlessly covered long distances comfortably and with exhilarating as opposed to *devastating* driving performance.*

Quirky games on your cell phone are good to dive into if you're selling soda, but you've got to wonder whether they will sway potential Land Rover buyers to choose it over competing Lexus, Mercedes, or BMW cars. Another case of falling in love with a new medium without thinking through the logic. Or are we too cynical?

Merge with Oncoming Traffic

Music is crucial to the gaming experience, and the labels have started to see gaming as a way to promote their product. A week after the launch of *Tony Hawk's American Wasteland,* the band on the sound track, Fall Out Boy, sold seventy thousand albums without radio play.[15] In Japan it is commonplace to find original music for a video game sold independently. It's not long before consumers will be able to buy music online without leaving the game in the same way they can currently buy pizzas and sneakers.

You won't blink when we say the worlds of reality TV and video games are converging. Mark Burnett–*Survivor* and *The Apprentice* dude–has formed a partnership with Time Warner Inc's meandering AOL to create an MMOG that plays out like a regular TV series. Burnett's much-hyped *Gold Rush* is a real-life treasure hunt testing players' knowledge of pop culture in which members of the public race one another to find hidden stores of gold throughout the United States using clues buried on AOL sites and in a song, a TV show, a blog, etc. When announcing the show in 2006,

---

* Range Rover has been running an ad that talks about "devastating performance." The ad agency needs to go to grammar school.

Burnett crowed, "It will be a fun, interactive game and it will be in my style with a big opening." Colorful AOL spokesperson Ruth Sarfaty said the conglomerate was aiming to attract online gamers and reality TV fans simultaneously.

Gold Rush has similarities to *The Runner,* developed by untouchable duo Damon and Affleck in mid-2001 for Walt Disney Company's ABC Television, shelved before airing because ABC felt it would compete with the Taliban. (Yes, it is ridiculous how safe some people remain.) A contestant raced across the United States pursued by members of the public enlisted as agents and viewers hoping to get a million in cash. Burnett has also been trying to resurrect the chase concept at Yahoo! While the TV version was ahead of its time with contestants being tasked with brand interaction *during the action,* marketers will be everywhere inside Burnett's online *Runner II.*

The gradual blurring of lines between video games and other forms of entertainment is a start. As the stature of games grows into a serious form of entertainment they will have an increasingly significant influence on popular culture and on the money folks. Smart marketing types see consumers as even more enamored of the new media of consoles and online gaming, with some devoting their lives to MMOGs—no exaggeration.

Perhaps it's no coincidence that ballyhooed *Second Life*, a "complete metaphysical universe where players create an alternate role for themselves," is most successful in inclement-weather cities.[16] Players of *Second Life*, developed by Linden Lab of San Francisco, can buy virtual goods such as music, art, films, clothes, even secondary games that "neighbors" and "friends" can see and hear, but no touching (not yet).

In a scary footnote, players are able to turn creations into real goods that they can sell! Sounds complicated because it is. At the *Second Life* site it vividly proclaims: "In *Second Life*, all Residents retain Intellectual Property rights over everything they create in-world—in *Second Life*, and offline. Turn a series of screenshots into a graphic novel, and sell the rights to a real life comic publisher. Prototype a fashion line, create real world versions of it, and sell them in a local clothing boutique. Shoot a machinima*

---

* A film using low-end, as opposed to professional quality computer-generated imagery (CGI).

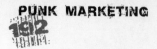
movie short in-world, and sell it as a pilot for a cable network. Not only is all this permitted—it's encouraged."

Watch this space as folks use stay-at-homes as guinea pigs for launching virtual products that after the trial balloon go right out to market. Strange days ahead? The Borough of Queens, New York already used *Second Life* to produce a digital plan of land near LaGuardia Airport and asked players to redesign it. Elements of the best are being incorporated (for free and with a ton of press coverage) into the real design![17] And please attend our book readings, held breathlessly in *Second Life*.

Use This to Kick Some Ass

1. Playing video games is a major leisure activity, not just for boys at home but for adults of both sexes—anywhere and everywhere. With its rise in importance as an entertainment medium, it brings opportunities for marketers to reach consumers through carefully targeted campaigns.

2. In-game advertising is a phenomenal growth industry driven by placement opportunities in the online games. Marketers can target their messages here through online mapping of where and when the game is being played, fine-tuning (and changing) strategies on a dime.

3. Corporate sponsorships of video game tournaments and those who participate in them are used both by companies directly involved in the video game industry and those in outside fields as well. For the first time, tournaments are being created especially for the United States and broadcast on cable TV; so the involvement of mainstream marketers will only increase.

4. Marketers commission games that communicate brand values in altogether engaging ways. This is true interactivity so you have to "play" along. Popular advergames can be hosted on a product's site and also via online gamer portals that attract tens of millions who are loyal to the games they play—and whoever is lucky enough to be a brand that clicks with them.

5. Video games influence popular culture as a whole. Virtual worlds in MMOGs

draw out millions—and in the near future marketers will use them to test out new concepts before launching them in the real world (why live there?).

So what is a gamer? Let's turn to Answers.com—a helpful site launched by one Punk author that thinks being clueless is so 1995: she or he is "plucky," "unyielding in spirit," "resolute," and "willing." Those are the attributes everyone wants in a customer, since those ultra-spirited folks are the most talkative, share everything with the world, give good word of mouth. For those who think gaming is a gamble for marketers, in this paragraph we call you wrong.

We're willing to wager.

Punk is . . .

Unmistakable.

Questioning colleagues on assumptions—to their faces.

Setting yourself impossibly high goals and thinking of crazy ways to get there. This will free your mind to bigger possibilities.

Thirteen

It's More Than Just Us
Hard as That Is to Believe

> Punk was just a way to sell trousers.
> —Malcolm McLaren, Punk Svengali

Talking to Alex Bogusky, creative chief at Crispin Porter + Bogusky (CP+B), you are struck by how he takes everything in stride. His aura of self-conviction borders on arrogance, and yet he gets away with it, in no small part due to stellar work guided during his time at the agency. As Winston Churchill mumbled about archrival Clement Attlee, "Mr. Attlee is a very modest man. Indeed he has much to be modest about." With Alex he has much to be arrogant about.

CP+B caught heat in 2002 because of its work for BMW's MINI car and Swedish retailer IKEA. The agency had actually been doing incredible work for some years before that, with lauded campaigns for AND1 basketball shoes, Giro and Bell Sports bicycle helmets, and Shimano bicycle components. But the Truth antitobacco messages broke ground in the way they transcended traditional thinking to solve an almost impossibly tough marketing problem: reducing smoking among teenagers.

While the campaign was lauded at award shows and by youth experts and "cause marketers," the larger marketing community sniffed, just a PSA. The Truth campaign didn't mean the agency had what it took to handle mass-market brands. Plus they were far away from Mad Ave in Coconut Grove, Florida, which confirmed they were just an offbeat agency and way too groovy to be considered mainstream.

CP+B heard this and opened an office managed by one of us in Los Angeles. The CP+B corporate thinking was if they had presence on both coasts, suddenly they'd get recognition as a national agency and be handed a shot at more cash-giving national brands. By the time the office opened, CP+B had already won IKEA and MINI, making it an unnecessary gesture.

The MINI ads sure made heads turn. This was the turning point for CP+B, since forward-thinking marketers fit snugly into the profile of people they aimed this campaign toward. Marketing executives saw the outdoor and print of the little cars right in their own neighborhoods and in magazines they actually thumbed through. Also, editorials placed about the car "being hard to find" indicated to other hungry advertisers that unconventional ideas eschewing conventional car-launch tactics (e.g., no TV spots) might be the ticket to high-end success.

CP+B wasn't doing anything different from what it had for four or five years, and yet for the first time marketers of those mass brands were going "Oh."

Pulpit of the Media Agnostics

CP+B stands for a different approach, one that competing agencies cannot fathom how to replicate. One difference is its media-neutral or media-agnostic stance.* To CP+B no one medium—as in the hands-down favorite, television—is more important than any other when it comes to effective communication. In fact anything is considered fair-game media, and not only that for which there are already established and conventional ways to purchase and/or measure them.

A format could be an online game (Burger King's Subservient Chicken), a label on a beer bottle (Molson's twin labels on opposing sides of the bottle), or a kiddy ride at the mall (those MINI rides with full-sized-for-them cars instead of boring carriages). Anything.

Within the bounds of traditional agency thinking, the above ideas would hardly ever fly.

---

* *Agnostic* in this context means doubting that a particular question has one correct answer. Traditional solutions are not the answer to every marketing problem.

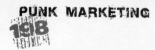

Believe in Yourself. Believe in Trends More!

When you've got one example, it's a "noticeable situation." When you've got two examples, it's a fact. And when you've got three examples—welcome to a trend.

In other words, a trend is something that is still just beginning to happen—the use of those tiny devices to check our e-mail; the tendency for movies to be built around con-sumer products like Ray-Bans or a particular type of Mercedes—and is happening in a significant enough way that it portends real and widespread change.

The trends enjoyed by a few today will be experienced by many tomorrow, and virtually all next week. And a good trendspotter knows how to separate the wheat from the chaff, how to distinguish today's passing fancy or fading passion from tomorrow's hot new item du jour.

In lots of businesses—media, entertainment, marketing, fashion, and all stock-market-related professions—knowing the latest trend is a prerequisite for success (or even survival). The message is clear: you miss out on a trend, you're out on the street.

We asked a friend, a journalist, why she thought we are so fascinated by trends. "Simple," she said. "The trends happen without fail, and we find ourselves in the middle of them, and we want to identify what is happening."

The most important rule in spotting trends is the rule of talking to experts. Here's how:

1. Pay attention to people you believe in. Get in touch and ask questions.

2. Ask the right questions. Have total belief in your sources and make them know this.

3. Find visionaries who can teach you new ideas, and try to tell them one thing they weren't aware of. People who are true visionaries know they can take a new person's idea to another level. So they are thankful to respond to your call/e-mail. It's important to learn to recognize the difference between true visionaries and slick BS. For more on *slick* see Bad Pitch Blog (BadRelease.com), where one of us holds court regularly; there you will meet Slick, our mascot.

4. Be aware of where life is going. Pay attention to the signs that something—big change—is on the horizon.

5. Great trendspotters are always evolving, learning, and growing. Remember that Italian class you're always thinking of taking? Right.

6. Don't just read the Arts section. Be well-rounded. In marketing, and in life, nothing succeeds (even success) like a person who is knowledgeable and, er, interesting. And stuff.

Today we welcome a new wave of U.S. agencies that genuinely embrace non-traditional media. Anomaly, Droga5, Strawberry Frog, SS&K, Amalgamated, Toy, and Mother have all opened to give the Mad Crowd a run for its money. These are thriving, healthy companies winning accounts such as Coca-Cola, Heineken, Ben & Jerry's, Oxygen (the TV network, not the gas), and Señor Richard's Virgin Mobile.

In some cases there are European roots. Anomaly was the brainchild of British adman Carl Johnson; StrawberryFrog got started as a "bunch of crazy hippies" in Amsterdam; and Mother launched in London, where it is still a leader in the business.

There are Revolutionary agencies on the West Coast too. Wieden + Kennedy in Portland, Oregon is an indie without a Mom or Dad, and with offices in New York, Amsterdam, London, Tokyo, and Shanghai. They have been doing thrilling campaigns for decades and have been "out-there," embracing alternative media as a prime way to connect with consumers. While continuing to do some of the best TV for bigwigs such as Nike, they are one of a few mainstream agencies to have succeeded using new marketing tools such as branded entertainment (see chapter 11, "At Last, a Job in Hollywood!") and alternative reality branding (ARB).

Wieden + Kennedy's New York office created Beta-7 for the ESPN NFL football game, an ARB campaign talked about elsewhere in this book that played out on the Web as a real story (see chapter 7, "Now It's Story Time").

Farther down the coast from Portland to Sausalito, you have Butler, Shine, Stern & Partners, who are behind an impressive campaign for Converse sneakers (see chapter 2, "Kill the Middlemen") in which consumers were asked to forge ahead to make ads they loved (so diabolical since they'd be *forced* to watch them). In December 2005 they beat formidable competition to win the MINI account, which Crispin Porter + Bogusky had resigned months before for Volkswagen's business.*

Whizzing down the Pacific Coast Highway to L.A. you find agencies supporting our Revolution. Santa Monica's Conductor is owned by Marketing Content Partners

---

* BMW disallowed CP+B to bid for the big-boy account—dumb-ass reasoning that one couldn't do both MINI and BMW; CP+B took their toys to another German automaker, Volkswagen of America Inc., and are now creating advertising for them that is pushing sales through the sunroof.

LLC and is a cheerleader of our beloved storytelling approach, developed while marketing movie releases such as *Spider-Man* and *Spider-Man 2*, and for the National Hockey League, Unilever PLC, and Miller Brewing Company.

In Venice, CA, you see the offices of 86 The Onions, a strangely named smaller agency with big, easily comprehensible ideas. Managed by creative genius Chad Rea, who has an impressive pedigree in breakthrough advertising learned at the feet of the cheeses at Mother in London and KesselsKramer in Amsterdam, 86 has enjoyed stellar years working for the South Beach Beverage Company (SoBe), ESPN, and extreme-sports TV channel Fuel TV Inc. The extremely broad approach to marketing at 86 presupposes no one idea or solution; like a true Punk, they are 100 percent agnostic in approach. Here's a salute to being godless, open, and while we're at it—good.

A few miles south you'll stumble into the city of El Segundo and the creative guys and gals at 72 and Sunny (always!). They will have you at hello for a Web-based film they did on behalf of skateboarding apparel maker DC Shoes titled *Hoops*, wherein skateboarders prove to be all-round athletes with excellent and surprising basketball skills. The Xbox ad called *Standoff* has dozens of ordinary people pulling imaginary guns on one another in a shoot-out, the implication being they are caught up in lifelike video games. It was quickly pulled by softy Microsoft for being too violent, but an homage to the ad itself was created as a flash mob (see chapter 5, "The Sell Phone") by University of Florida students and posted on YouTube.

Consumers won't let a good thing die. We like that about them. Huzzah!

For an agency* to be truly media agnostic and walk from the Altar of TV it has to do more than shout, "I believe in you, other forms of advertising! I believe in the power! Yes, I believe!" No, faith alone is not enough to move mountains when it comes to stubborn and lazy habits. One's media planning better be totally in sync with the creative that is put forth. A media plan can't be developed in isolation of ideas, one must feed seamlessly into the other, and in an era when planning and buying agencies are so often separated—usually at birth—this is not a simple matter.

---

* For pure PR providers, see www.PunkPR.com.

At CP+B, the media department toils in cahoots with their creative, and both report to Chief Alex. This is unusual. This also pays off.

Other successful media agnostic agencies will not necessarily have media departments report to the creative chieftains, but see that media planning and creative development is a partnership rather than a source of problematic friction. Chad Rea of 86 The Onions told us, "More often than not a marketer will come to us with some traditional ideas on content distribution. This is a good starting point, but rather than limit our thinking, we turn on the proverbial faucet and let the ideas flow, thinking about all aspects of their business." They simply do not limit their ideas, see? Kill the format hounds!

One of his agency's novel marketing solutions is "the world's smallest, most powerful dance club that takes place inside a traveling VW microbus," says Rea, which is what they did to promote a tiny but potent energy drink called Upshot (they came

up with the name too). Another was to create adhesive bandages for action-sports network Fuel TV that had slogans, such as "You should see the ground," on them and were handed out in Fuel-branded tins—a refreshing alternative to the T-shirts and caps that are usually handed out at the sports events Fuel TV covers. At the events, scantily clad nurses offered to kiss people's boo-boos.

To become an agnostic, an agency has to be able to produce the ideas it comes up with. It's all well and good to say, "Hey, gang, let's take seats out of a sports stadium and toss a car in there," as CP+B did for MINI, but making it happen is a game only the brave, strong and committed can play.

The team at West Coast CP+B where Mark was managing director proposed without laughing the building of a desert island in the Hudson River off Manhattan Island to launch Scripps Networks' Fine Living to the New York market.* You cannot buy desert islands off the rack; damn those yellow pages! We didn't know where to find one, either. It was a mean feat to begin with, but meaner still with a bizarrely small budget and three months before Fine Living's big day.

But we made it happen (why else would we be crowing?), and on that morning we unveiled a sand-covered island, complete with a single palm tree and a cutely adorned tiki hut, inhabited by a couple and their dog, floating on the river and getting media attention.

The CP+B team battled inclement weather, a bossy Port Authority, that nosy mayor's office, as well as the crazy logistics of building an island off of a concrete jungle, but you know what? The results put Fine Living on the cable map in a wholly unexpected way.

What's the Big Idea?

Notions that are strong and gorgeous are developed using a different process from what the traditional—dinosaur—ad firms are wont to use.

---

* Coauthor Mark was in fact the respectable managing director of CP+B's L.A. roost from 2002–2004. The island idea was realized by creative team Robin Fitzgerald and Valerie Powell, under the direction of Mark's fair friend Sally Hogshead. We give credit; we do.

Here's how most agencies work: A creative team of two are handed a brief from which to create something for a media type that has been dictated (TV, print, radio, homing pigeon). The team members work in isolation and present ideas to a creative director in a competition; he gives "his"* feedback, and then they skulk away again to refine their efforts. It's an alpha-male environment; it's eat or be eaten when it comes to their ideas chosen to be presented to that client.

Then there's Toy, a New York agency we give respect to, cofounded by Anne Bologna and Ari Merkin. Bologna describes the duo's creative process as "very free-form and not at all linear." In the early stages, the ideas are not tied to any particular media. Only later when the ideas are more fully developed do they decide how they can best bring them to life. Bologna says the methodical process seen with most marketing organizations kills a blossom while still on the vine! "It takes away the nervousness you feel with big ideas!" she exclaims.†

---

* We say *his* with intent: unfortunately, the majority of creative directors are still male. The *New York Times* in late 2005 looked at an *AdWeek* chart ranking the top thirty-three agencies; only four have flagship offices with female creative directors.

† Or, maybe no one is feeling nervousness today because we are so hopped up on Prozac/Paxil! We are too busy gazing out the window.

Punk Predictions

If the future *is* unknown and terrifying, it's partly because it seems to be arriving so *fast*. Nobody but a few techno geeks can keep up with *all* the latest computer technology—but all of us have to keep up with *some* of it. Maybe we're not all movie executives charged with investing millions in the latest blockbuster—but we *do* want to know how trends in movies are affecting our slang, our fashion, and our Saturday nights. And what will be the big thing in the next ten years? An economy in which we can buy our life online and can even stop people from intruding on our privacy with a click and a PayPal or Google Checkout purchase.

But we, the Punksters, spend half our time thinking what options are open to us—as consumers, as citizens, as employees—as we try to map out our lives. So with our tongues only partially in our cheeks we imagine a marketing world ten years hence.

Influencing consumers is going to be harder than ever in ten years. Imagine buying products because you said "Aha!" through TV commercials that interrupt their entertainment. Hardly. It's a thing of the past. As TiVo and its competitors reach critical mass, the marketers will pull the rest of their dollars from TV advertising with the exception of a presence in a few major televised events, such as the Super Bowl and major awards shows, for which they spend a mere fortune. The cost of thirty seconds of time during the Super Bowl will be approaching $8 million by 2017.* That's a boy band salary's worth of moola! And whether it's worth it or not, it'll never be questioned. This is never fired for buying IBM territory.

On the other hand once disliked infomercials will soon become the norm, appreciated by consumers for their high production values and liberal use of celebrities. Cindy Crawford and Chuck Norris still look too great to be real. And because they seem so forthright and without fault, they'll be selling something you might actually want! Following new rulings on disclosure, shows like *The Apprentice* that showcase brands will have been classified by the FCC as infomercials and will appear on specialty networks sandwiched  between knives and tummy tuckers. Can't get enough of those Norris gizmos.

Samsung, Motorola, Nokia, NTT DoCoMo, and Apple will battle it out to be the superpower of strange-looking and difficult-to-choose mobile devices, each offering an array of functionality and content in sleek and Slivr-like packages, so small they'll fit in your ear or a

---

* We made that figure up of course.

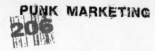
tooth or inside your skin. The "service" (a word loosely used) providers have become monsters, many merging with other, often smaller providers—likewise, film and game studios are becoming one now—to ensure that they have a hold on anything unique to offer to their subscribers, most of whom have opted out of service contracts as they have realized it was they the consumers who had real say.

Almost half of the population will have created a bit of content on his or her computer. It could be a blog, podcast, home reality program, movie, or cartoon strip (see disisdad.com for example), distributed to friends or enemies or Romans, and it's bound to be sponsored by a brand keenly interested in his or her like-minded network of friends. Massive multiplayer online games (MMOGs) will be the most popular leisure activity by far with almost everybody having at least one virtual alter ego that lives the life they wish they had in reality. Within online alternative worlds players will be able to consume entertainment and brands without having to go to the trouble of traveling to the store or movie theater (all of which have now been converted to video gaming salons). MMOGs will have incorporated social networking sites in the realization that there is little difference between the characters video game players create for themselves and the profiles MySpace users create.

There will be a superleague of Iconic Brands like Apple, Nike, and BMW that touch consumers' lives in multiple ways, not just as hardware (computers, shoes, and cars) but also in the form of their own stores and the content they create—these will be showcases for the best in design and contemporary culture, each with its own coffee shop (proudly serving, yes, Starbucks coffee) and a big white area for their users to create content. The Iconic Brands themselves will continue in the tradition of entertainment experiments (e.g., BMW films) and be providers of music and film.

Creativity will have earned its rightful place in business as the one thing that stops products from becoming commodities. And the most successful corporations will have learned (through hiring *us*) how to rethink the organization so that creativity is employed right from the start.

All marketing will be Punk one day with the exception of a few "traditionalists," as they are known, who are left fighting for the chance to create a Budweiser commercial for the next Bowl.

Oh, and the man to the right is not Matthew Perry.

SIDEBAR

That anxious "aha" feeling, as when you're watching *Gilmore Girls* (Lorelai is too much), is exhilarating. Merkin and Bologna are not process slaves. They go with their intuition and trust the team to develop ideas in a free-form style, inviting in outsiders from other industries. Merkin develops big stuff in the way that Alex Bogusky does, with what we call "democratic creativity." It flies in the face of conventional wisdom and involves all the creative in a single department displaying raw selves on sleeves and collaborating without competition to *do something* magnificent.

At CP+B, multiple creative teams are briefed on an assignment and then build upon one another's ideas over time. Bogusky will review everybody's work regularly and, when he sees a germ of a great idea, will tell all of the teams to work on *that* one to make it better until the next big idea appears from one of the teams. And then all energy is shifted toward that. There might be TV in the final mix of ideas, but there are just as likely to be events, new product ideas or extensions, packaging designs, guerrilla stunts, and in-store concepts as well.

Collaborative processes are in direct opposition to competitive processes where ideas are thought up and subsequently killed by a committee. Yet it is the best way to work, according to research.

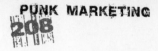

GET Your Creative On

Over the years creativity has been assigned a limited role in business in general and marketing in particular. For the most part agencies do not influence decisions that affect a marketer's business beyond the little ones right when the objects are being brought to market. Only a decade or so ago an advertising guy would have called himself a partner with his marketing client and nosed his helpful self into everything from new-product development to retail distribution.

Not today. Through the years most ad guys, like the doctors they visit with a sigh, began to become specialists, and annoying ones at that. They got uppity and focused their expertise on a small set of skills, leaving other specialists to work on everything else that wasn't in their purview.

Advertising agencies no longer have the wherewithal to think broadly, and that is a mistake. Clients think them irrelevant in discussions about business because they've made themselves so.

Tsk, tsk. Lost their place at the big-boy table.

So guess what's going to happen? The creativity marketing agencies offer will become even more marginalized. This is bad news for every marketing professional, who is told budgets are under terrible pressure to shrink.

We put forth that without creative advisers to jump up and rudely challenge and provide fresh thinking to guide business decisions, everything we do will become more formulaic and less effective and pretty much depress us.

We boys have begun our own campaign to put genuine inspiration back into business. We offer a Punk campaign to reintroduce ingenuity into all aspects of marketing and into business, period. We're calling it GET the Creativity Back (GTCB), a movement. Please take the time to get bumper stickers and T-shirts on our mini-site at punkmarketing.com/whoareyoukidding.

Here is a whiff of what GTCB will represent:

Same Old Song Award will go each week to marketing that copies other successes.

Risk Takers Gallery of those who found they were in trouble for trying something different and failing. To them a big wet kiss.

The Salmon for mavericks who go against the stream. (We will hand out a salmon to the lucky woman or man who fights back against the current . . . and his/her

family. No more turkey giveaways.) Wanna mail Punk to friends! Find the thirty-nine-cent stamp on our site.

Creativity is almost impossible to define. According to consumer-insight researchers at Lucid Incorporated, every person recognizes he or she has it, but its meaning varies widely. Anna Sandilands and Anna David, who quit Starbucks Corp. in 2004 to found Lucid, have appealing perspectives on creativity, both from their experience at the coffee lords *and* from an astounding 2006 research project on behalf of Apple Computer Inc.

There they found that people not labeled (and pressured to be) professional Creative Types usually have fresher and less formulaic views on what being creative is. A lawyer they interviewed saw his mountain-bike riding as highly creative because it gave him inspiration for legal cases.*

Lucid also found that for all people—regardless of their jobs and whether they are thought of as ingenious by others—*to create* is as basic a need as food, water, and sleep. Even if the result of their creativity—a poem or a cake—doesn't turn out perfect, and the process was a nightmare, it is rewarding to them because it exercises a part of their brains they feel fulfilled for having used. So next time you're at a museum pretending not to be bored, remember you're a better person now!

Those Lucid talked to cite time constraints as the reason for limiting creativity. It seems all of us would benefit from time for real thought, so put the book down right now. Put your feet up and ponder the stars and the sun and that gorgeous bit of chocolate you munched upon last night. Daydream, believe it.†

Corporations do not nurture creativity! Even at an innovative company such as Starbucks, so say Lucid's founders, any artistic aspect is not brought in until the key

---

* One of us thrillingly interviewed Gregory McDonald, author of the outrageous *Fletch* detective series, about to be rereleased by Hollywood (directed by *Scrubs'* Bill Lawrence, probably starring Zach Braff) to the wonderment of those who remember the eighties. Greg explained how he walked his garden and thought through a plot before writing a single hilarious word.

† You know, it's funny. Mark and Richard get so much *tsuris* for wasting time, and now these nutty researchers are telling us to sit around. Hey—can we catch a break?

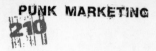

people *upstairs* have nailed down the business end, at which time it is often too late to influence key decisions.[*]

Problem? In many firms creativity is seen to be an add-on rather than a must-have and is treated with Rodney Dangerfield levels of respect. And everyone, we must remind you, has an opinion and an asshole, so Wilde said to no one in particular. We are all so eager to share our opinions on creative work that is now being managed to death so it becomes a useless melting pot of poor and superb. (There is too such a thing as a bad idea.)

Teresa M. Amabile, Edsel Bryant Ford Professor of Business Administration at the Entrepreneurial Management unit of Harvard Business School, argues that every intelligent person has potential to be creative at their job, regardless of whether they toil in Marketing, HR, Finance, or Lunch Meat Selection. And accounting too, but that's dangerous to say in public. . . .

From Lucid's lucid insights it appears encouraging people to be creative in their jobs makes folks feel better about the daily grind and gives real value to those who have to "think different" for a living.

Whatever, so long as people stop treading on the toes of others trying to do something hard, fast, and innovative.

Big corporations aren't organized so that the people with ideas are respected for them. Recommendation is to bring in the outsiders, whose businesses revolve around being an Idea Factory. Plus those who haven't drunk your Kool-Aid will tell you your shit stinks. Get those folks into the process as early as possible. Bring 'em in, put 'em on pedestals, chain 'em to a desk, give 'em M&M's.

A Hard Stop

Besides, no one has ever formalized just *what* creative is! It's not on any job description we've eyeballed. Obviously, some work environments are more conducive to creativity than others. For instance, a high-pressure work space of go-go-go

---

[*] Say what you will about the sameness of this coffee emporium, they certainly bedazzled the naysayer with their ability to change with the ever-evolving times. And sorry, deli coffee is too inconsistent for addicts! Besides, what other mainstream company's logo features a naked, smiling woman?

will distract from the focus required to make one's mind roar. There is also a school of belief that creativity has a direct correlation with joy: people are happy when they have an idea, and because they also have better ideas when they're happy.

Guess van Gogh should have left that ear on.

Use This in Place of the Charmin

1. There are some new wave agencies dedicated to being media agnostic by not assuming that TV spots and other traditional media formats are the end-all solution to marketing problems. Thinking the alternative is no simple matter. It requires changes to how media is planned and willingness to execute on something "impossible" to bring to life (good things). Results make it worthwhile. Damn, do they ever.

2. The biggest challenge to creating something that is a heretofore untold marketing solution is in creating an environment at work in which big ideas develop. Collaboration among all the relevant parties is contrary to how it's usually done, but evidence from agencies doing it already and from studies suggests this is the only real way to create something of lasting value.

3. Creativity in advertising, in marketing, and in business as a whole has been allowed to flounder and, jeez, is always relegated to the end of process by which a product is brought to market. It needs to play a bigger role earlier on. Marketers need to embrace creativity in every single aspect of business and get the help of smart outside advisers not afraid to push boundaries and thinking.

4. Trite is sometimes acceptable. A happy work environment where employees feel valued and respected is conducive to creativity; the more people use a creative muscle, the more strongly developed it becomes. Be happy for real—just not what Bobby McFerrin said!

Oh, and apologies to everyone we insulted in the book. Because we meant it.

Who Are Your Leaders?

Richard Laermer

A frequently quoted authority on media and hype, Laermer is an author and PR firm CEO who co-hosted TLC's series *Taking Care of Business* in 2005.

His journalism career began back in 1980; he appeared in the *New York Times, NY Daily News,* Reuters, *USA Today, Chief Executive, Us Weekly,* and more. Laermer's books include *Full Frontal PR: Building Buzz about Your Business, Your Product, or You,* and *trendSpotting,* described as "an invaluable trend reference guide for the new millennium." The next is its sequel, titled *2011.* Other books include *Native's Guide to New York* and *Get On With It.* His columns on marketing and PR appear in *Ad Age, AdWeek,* and *PR News.* Laermer was a media commentator on National Public Radio's "Marketplace," and his new radio program that breaks down how media really works, "Unspun," runs nationwide.

Laermer founded RLM pr (www.RLMpr.com) in 1991. His "Aha!" moment occurred when he recognized PR folks were hardly grasping intricacies of its clients' businesses. As a consultant, Laermer speaks to corporate groups and at conferences on how to make money from pending trends; and his BadRelease.com blog, co-hosted by Kevin Dugan, is the PR industry's watchdog.

He lives in California, but resides in New York.

Mark Simmons

Simmons is a Brit who has taken the United States by storm twice in an unyielding eighteen years of marketing. Bringing healthy cynicism and a soupçon of common sense to the party, his reputation is that of a savvy marketer and creator of powerful promotion who constantly pushes boundaries. He has invented techniques running his own agency Anti-Corp and at the maverick hot-shop Crispin Porter + Bogusky (CP+B).

After stints at London's top ad agencies, Simmons rushed to the United States to carry out global advertising responsibilities at Coca-Cola where he ran all advertising in Latin America and Sprite advertising worldwide. Anti-Corp followed, the agency dedicated to turning tradition on its head using unknown marketing techniques to outthink rather than outspend client competitors.

In 2002 he landed in California to run the West Coast office of CP+B, which soon became the most highly awarded agency on the planet.

Simmons, whose town is Santa Monica, California is currently a marketing consultant who helps agencies, marketers, and nonprofit organizations create campaigns that break through.

Learn more about the Punk Marketing world by dialing up punkmarketing.com

(Sign on to the semi-irregular PM newsletter by writing to editorofsnooze@punkmarketing.com.)

Notes

Prologue: Welcome to the Revolution

[1] "Brand Killers," *Fortune*, August 11, 2003.

[2] Harris Interactive and Teenage Research Unlimited surveyed 2,618 people age thirteen to fourteen in 2003 on behalf of Yahoo! and media services company Carat North America.

[3] Cable Television Advertising Bureau.

Chapter Two: Kill the Middlemen

[1] "Ads for the People, by the People," *Advertising Age*, March 2, 2006.

[2] According to data from Information Resources Inc., in "Marketers' New Idea: Get Consumers to Design Ads," *Wall Street Journal*, December 14, 2005, after a three-year decline, fifty-two-week sales of Ban rose 13.6 percent following the campaign.

[3] "Blog Buzz Helps Companies Catch Trends in the Making," *Washington Post*, March 3, 2006.

[4] "Three Minutes: Fired Google Blogger," *PC World*, February 16, 2005.

[5] "Super Bowl Ads May Be Downright Amateurish," by Laura Petrecca, *USA Today*, November 13, 2006.

[6] "The MySpace Generation: They Live Online. They Buy Online. They Play Online. Their Power Is Growing," *BusinessWeek*, December 12, 2005.

[7] In terms of number of page views, according to "News Corp. (hearts) MySpace: The media giant recently bought MySpace, the popular networking site for youth—and it looks like a grand slam," *Fortune*, March 29, 2006.

[8] "MySpace Generation," *BusinessWeek*, December 12, 2005.

Chapter Three: Brand Not Bland

[1] "Critics Target 'Omnipresent' Ads," *USA Today*, March 16, 2001.

[2] "OXO's Favorite Mistakes," *Fast Company*, October 2005.

[3] Ibid.

[4] "Shopping Rebellion: What the Kids Want," *New Yorker*, March 18, 2002.

[5] Written by Robin Fitzgerald, art-directed (and stamped with her hand!) by Valerie Powell, with creative direction by Sally Hogshead.

Chapter Four: Who's Eating Your Lunch?

[1] "Branding: Five New Lessons," *BusinessWeek*, February 14, 2005.

[2] "Ad Icon P&G Cuts Commitment to TV Commercials," *Wall Street Journal*, June 14, 2005.

[3] From the marketing site Brand Channel in articles "Innocent Drinks—Savvy," March 22, 2004, and "Growing Pains Small Brands," June 20, 2005.

[4] "Tesco: California Dreaming?" *BusinessWeek*, February 16, 2006.

Chapter Five: The Sell Phone

[1] Cellular phone industry revenue was $115.1 billion in 2005 according to market researcher iSuppli Corporation.

[2] The Yankee Group.

[3] American Advertising Federation.

[4] According to data from Intrado, Switzerland's University of St. Galen, and the International Telecommunication Union, February 2005.

[5] "Ads Take Aim at Cell Phones," *InformationWeek* , August 8, 2005.

[6] "Cell Phones Emerge as New Advertising Medium," *TechNewsWorld*, November 16, 2005.

[7] "The Billboards That Speak to Your Mobile," *Financial Times*, August 27, 2006.

[8] According to research and consulting firm Strategy Analytics in February 2005.

[9] "Slingbox Plots a Revolution," *Red Herring*, January 6, 2006.

[10] "Sad, Lonely? For a Good Time Call Vivienne," *New York Times*, February 24, 2005.

Chapter Six: The Captive Consumer

[1] JD Powers & Associates, March 2006.

[2] "AOL Subscriber Defections Continue, Top 1 Million," *Washington Post*, June 4, 2003.

[3] An independent measurement jointly taken by the University of Michigan and the American Society for Quality.

[4] According to a poll by IPSOS North America in July 2005, 47 percent of customers said they would change if it weren't for those fees. From "Locked in a Cell," a U.S. PIRG Education Fund report, August 2005.

[5] The average costs for the Big Five cell phone companies before they became the Bigger Three, according to figures from "Balance Swings to Customer Retention," *Wireless Week*, January 15, 2006.

[6] "Cheap Is New Cell-Phone Mantra," *Wired News*, July 11, 2005.

[7] Consumer Intentions and Actions Survey, March 2006.

[8] International Communications Research on behalf of Accenture, May 2005.

Chapter Seven: Now It's Story Time

[1] From a March 3, 2003, Volvo press release.

[2] Simon Pride, European account director at MVBMS Fuel Europe, quoted in a March 3, 2003, Volvo press release.

[3] "A New Kind of Car Chase," *BusinessWeek*, May 16, 2005.

Chapter Eight: Leave Me Alone, Will Ya!

[1] Professor Sheena Iyengar of Columbia University and Professor Mark Lepper of Stanford University, 2000.

[2] David Glen Mick, Susan M. Broniarczyk, and Jonathan Haidt, *Journal of Business Ethics, 2004*.

[3] Professors Sheena Iyengar and Wei Jaing.

[4] Professor Barry Schwartz of Swarthmore College in Pennsylvania, published in *The Chronicle of Higher Education*, January 23, 2004.

[5] Mike Bernacchi, marketing professor at the University of Detroit Mercy, as quoted in *Detroit News*, May 2005.

[6] 2004 Yankelovich Monitor.

[7] "In Marketing, Less Can Be More," *International Herald Tribune*, June 14, 2004.

[8] PhaseOne's Advertising Environment Study.

[9] "The Mind of the DVR User," Forrester Research report, September 8, 2004.

[10] "Marc Smith: Inbox out of Control? You're Not Alone," *Financial Times*, April 11, 2006.

Chapter Nine: Lies Lies Lies: The Truth about Truth

[1] Forrester and Intelliseek's online survey of members of consumer opinion service, PlanetFeedback.com, December 2003.

[2] "Young People 'No Longer Believe TV Ads,'" *Media Guardian*, August 2, 2004.

[3] Roper poll conducted July 28–August 10, 2005.

[4] "Take Your Best Shot; New Surveys Show That Big Business Has a P.R. Problem," *New York Times*, December 9, 2005.

[5] "The Good Brand," *Fast Company*, August 2004.

[6] "He's Retiring (Yeah, Sure)" *Time*, June 1990.

[7] "Ford Touts Volvo Safety Link in Ads but Not in Trials," *USA Today*, January 16, 2006.

Chapter Ten: As Seen on TV

[1] A 2002 survey of national advertisers conducted by Forrester Research and the Association of National Advertisers estimated that $7 billion of TV ad revenues would be lost by 2007.

[2] "Cablevision Faces Network Battle," *Financial Times*, June 1, 2006.

[3] Lawrence R. Samuel, *Brought to You By: Postwar Television Advertising and the American Dream*.

[4] Christine Rosen, "The Age of Ego Casting," *New Atlantis*, fall 2004/winter 2005.

[5] "Secret Agent Man," *New Yorker*, March 21, 2005.

[6] "Lessons Taught by 'Lara Croft' Help Paramount and Jeep to a Smooth Ride across the 'Sahara,'" *New York Times*, March 10, 2005.

[7] Writers Guild of America west survey from March 2005.

Chapter Eleven: At Last, a Job in Hollywood!

[1] "'Mom' Is Stuck in the 1950's," *New York Post*, August 1, 2005.

[2] AdAge.com, February 6, 2003.

Chapter Twelve: Game On

[1] PriceWaterhouseCoopers, "Global Entertainment and Media Outlook: 2005–2009," August 2005.

[2] Forrester Research Inc., quoted in "Rated M for Mad Ave," *BusinessWeek*, February 27, 2006.

[3] "State of the Industry Address," by president of the Entertainment Software Association, Douglas Lowenstein, at the Electronic Entertainment Expo, May 18, 2005.

[4] Nielsen Entertainment figures, 2004.

[5] Nielsen Entertainment figures, 2004.

[6] Entertainment Software Association, from www.theesa.com/facts/top_10_facts.php.

[7] Nielsen Entertainment, 2004.

[8] Knowledge Networks/SRI, 2004.

[9] "Rated M for Mad Ave," *BusinessWeek*, February 27, 2006.

[10] "Fair Game?" *PROMO Magazine*, November 1, 2005.

[11] A Yankee Group press release, April 17, 2006.

[12] "DirecTV Has Its Finger on Pro Gaming Button," *Hollywood Reporter*, February 1, 2006.

[13] "It's a Game. No, It's an Ad. No, It's Advergame," *New York Times*, September 21, 2005.

[14] From a 2004 study, "U.S. Wireless Gaming Forecast and Analysis, 2004–2008: Gaming . . . Together," by IDC, provider of market intelligence owned by International Data Group.

[15] "Video Games Drive Music Sales," *USA Today*, January 26, 2006.

[16] According to the founder of Linden Lab, who created *Second Life*, in "A Survey of New Media," *Economist*, April 22, 2006.

[17] "Second Life for a City Park," *Wired*, May 2006.

Index

A Bathing Ape, 40, 50
A Clockwork Orange, xxiv
ABC Television, 85, 158, 161, 164, 191
abc.com, 85, 91
About Inc., 31
Academy of TV Arts & Sciences, 85
Activision Inc., 180–81, 188
Ad Skipper, 37
Advergaming, 188–90
Advertising Age, 21, 212
AdWeek, 110, 145, 204*n*, 212
Aeromexico, 95–97
After the Sunset, 154
agency fees, xv–xvi
airlines, 95–97
Air Jordan XIII Retro Lows, 51
Ajegroup, 62
Akeelah and the Bee, 173
Alba, Jessica, 179
All My Children, 158
Allen, Woody, 100
Alltel, 102
alternative-reality branding (ARB), 111, 113,
    115–18, 199
Amabile, Teresa M., 210
Amazon, 124, 131–32, 171
American Airlines, 96
American Consumer Satisfaction index, 137
American Idol, 80, 158, 174
American Association of Advertising Agencies, 67
American Society for Quality, 99
Anheuser-Busch, xvii*n*, 80
Anderson, Tom, 37
Anomaly, 199
Answers.com, 193
Anti-Corp, 213
AOL (America Online), 11, 28, 29, 97–98, 124, 190–91
AOL.com, ancient e-mail access, 98
apology, 211
Apple Computers Inc., 19, 36–37, 40, 43, 72, 85,
    205–06
Apprentice, The, 160–64, 205
Articles of the Revolution, 1–17
Artificial Life, 88–89
Art of the H3ist, 108, 115–17
asking "why not," 2
assumptions, challenging your, 2
AT&T, 77*n*, 101
AtomFilms, 22

attention economy, 72–73
attention, giving your undivided, 9–10
Attlee, Clement, 195
Audi, 115–17, 170
Audi Channel, 170
AvantGo, 189
Avon Cosmetics, 154
AwardAwards.com, 43

Babe, 21
Bad Pitch Blog, 198, 212
Banana Boat, 140
Banana Republic, 161, 162
Ban deodorant, 23, 25
Banco Walla-Marti, 105
Banana Republic, 161
Bartle Bogle Hegarty Ltd., 170*n*
Battlegrounds, 168–69
Bausch & Lomb, 142
BBC, 31
BBDO, 77*n*
Beanie Babies, 40, 55–56
Beat the 3PM Slump, 188–89
Beav (*Leave it to Beaver*), 16
Bebo, 123
Bell, Jeffrey A., 156
Bell, Alexander Graham, 84*n*
Berkshire Hathaway Inc., 25
Better Business Bureaus, U.S. Council of, 99
Bezos, Jeff, 55
Best Buy, 172-73
Beta-7, 117, 199
big bad enemy (BBE), 75
big businesses, 60–62
Billionaire Boys Club, 50
Biomat, 69
BlackBerry (a/k/a CrackBerry), 9, 17, 72–73
Black Entertainment Television (BET), 172
Blockbuster, 28*n*, 141
Blockdot Inc., 188–89
BlogAds, 31–32
blogs, 11–12, 18, 19, 27–33, 38, 144–45
Bloomsbury Books, 56
Blow Out, 159
Blue Sphere Games, 190
BMW, 66, 155, 195, 197, 199*n*, 206
BMW Films, 8, 11, 168, 171
Bogusky, Alex, 195, 197, 200–01, 204, 207
Bologna, Anne, 204, 207

book publishers, 173*n*
Booyah!, e.g., bad word, 144
Borax, 24–25
Braff, Zach, 21, 209*n*
brand integration, 160–64, 165, 167
brands, interaction between consumers and, xx–xxiii
brandscape, changing, xviii, xx–xxi
Branson, Richard, 7, 62–63, 139
Bravo cable network, 132, 159, 161
British Airways, 63
Broniarczyk, Susan, 125–26
Brooks, Dan, 27
Buca di Beppo, 52–54
Budweiser, 206
Buffett, Warren E., 25
Built NY, 45
Bullfrog, 140
Bungie Studios, 113
Burger King, 83, 182
Burnett, Mark, 160, 163, 190–91
Burnout Revenge, 183
Burton, 166
Bush, President George W., 27
Business Roundtable, 137
Butler, Shine, Stern & Partners (BSSP), 22–23, 199
Buy.com, 6
Buyerlings, Mr. and Mrs. Buyer and the, xxv
Buzz-Oven.com, 36
buzzwords, 10, 144
BuzzMetrics, 28
BYO Lunch Bag, 45

Cablevision, 149–50
Cadillac, 25, 33
California Public Utilities Commission (CPUC), 99
Cameron, James, 177
Campaign for a Commercial-Free Childhood, 186*n*
Cannes Lions International festival, 69
captive consumers, 92–106
    airlines, 95–97
    customer service, 92, 103–5
    mobile/PDA users, 98–103
Carpenters, 186
Cartoon Network, 87
Cast Away, 155
CBS News, 27
CBS Television, 127
cell phones, 76–92
    advertising on, 80–82
    as true life partner, 79
    attention economy and, 72
    consumer satisfaction with service, 98–103
    entertainment on, 82–89
    gaming on, 88–89
    mobile TV, 84–88
    product design and, 45–46
    text messaging, 80–82
    zero talking, 9–11
CEOs (chief executive officers), 137, 139
Chanel, 48
Charles, Ray, 172
Charles Shaw wine, 68
Chief Executive, 212
children, and The Nag Factor, 186–87
choice. *See* consumerism
"Choose, Choose, Choose, Choose, Choose, Choose, Choose," 125–26
Chrysler, 66, 156
Churchill, Winston, 195
Ciao Bella Gelato Company, 160
Cingular Wireless, 45, 99–101
Citibank, 131
CKE Restaurants Inc., 183
Clash, The, dedication page
Clerks by Kevin Smith, 73*n*
Clorox, 48
clutter, 129–32
The Closer on TNT, 15*n*
CNBC, 85
CNN, 15, 85
CNW Marketing Research, 149*n*
Coca-Cola (Coke), 7, 26, 36, 51, 61–62, 63*n*, 133, 153–54, 158, 173–74, 190, 199, 213
Colbert ("Col-*bare*"), Stephen 141
cognitive pollution, 43
Coke Zero, 51
Colgate-Palmolive, 48, 121–23, 128
collaboration (collaborative processes), 203–7, 211
collaborative filtering, 124–25, 131–32
Columbia University, 128
Commerce Bank, 105
communication issues
    age of zero talking, 9–11
    attention economy, 72–73
computer gaming. *See* gaming
computer-generated imagery (CGI), 191*n*
ConAgra Foods, 28
Conde Nast Media Group, 169
Conductor, 109, 199–200
Considered from Nike, 44
consumers, xxvii, 13. *See also* captive consumers
    interaction between brands and, xx–xxiii
consumer-created content, 18–38
    blogs, 27–33

films, 19–27
  social networks, 35–37
consumerism, 120–33
Consumer Electronics Association, 151
Consumer Reports, 99
consumer satisfaction, 98–103
Contender, The, 162
content, xxvii, 13, 165, 167–75. *See also* consumer-created content
Continuous Partial Attention (CPA), 10, 72–73
contracts, 93, 97–103, 105
control, giving up, 4, 6
convergence, xxvii, 13
Converse, 22–23, 33, 199
Copeland, Henry, 32
Coppertone, 140
Costanza (George, *Seinfeld*), 10
Cotton, Tom, 109
Couric, Katie, 27
Cowell, Simon, 158
Coq Roq campaign, 83
Counter Strike, 185
crash cam, 117
Crawford, Cindy, 205
creativity, 13, 207–10, 211
Crest, 160
Crispin Porter + Bogusky (CP+B), 7, 95–97, 145, 195, 197, 200–01, 203, 204, 207, 213
CTIA-The Wireless Association, 101
Current TV, 18, 33
Curry, Adam, 32–33
customer service, 102–05
Cyberathlete Professional League, 185

Daily *Show with Jon Stewart,* 87
Daily *Source Code,* 33
Damon and Affleck, 191
Dangerfield, Rodney ("No Respect"), 43*n*
Dannon, 112
David, Anna, 208–09
Davis, Mitchell, 183–84
Dawn and Drew Show, 33
DC Shoes, 200
del.icio.us, 132
Delphi Automotive Systems, 137
Denton, Nick, 31
design, 43–48
Design and Art Directors (D&AD), 43
Desperate Housewives, 85
Di Cesare, Chris, 113, 115
Diddy, P ("Dud"), 62
Diet Rite, 63

Digital Chocolate, 88
DirecTV, 88, 187–88
disintermediation, 21
Disney Mobile, 87
distress marketing, 4
Donnelly, Roisin, 136
Dove, 2
Dijon, 146
Draganska, Michaela, 126, 128
Driver, Minnie (vroom!), 171
Dugan, Kevin, 212
DVDs, 170–71, 174
DVRs (digital video recorders), 120, 149–50, 152–53
Dyson, 58, 64

Early-termination fees (ETFs), 92, 101, 106
EarthLink, 33, 41*n*
Easter Bunny Hates You, 22
Easy Money, 43*n*
eBay, 6, 145
Edelman Trust Barometer, 135*n,* 139
E! Entertainment, 87
EFFIE Award winner, 23
86 The Onions, 200-01, 203
Electronic Arts (EA), 36, 88, 178, 183, 188
Electronic Entertainment Expo (E3), 183
Ellen DeGeneres (her show), 53
Ellis, Tim, 111
Ellwood, Mark, 72–73
e-mail rules, 9–11
End of Detroit, The (Maynard), 66
Enpocket, 81
Entertainment Software Association, 180*n*
Enron, xx
Epinions.com, xxvi
Erotigo, 90
ESPN, 199-200
E.T.: The Extra-Terrestrial, 153
E*TRADE, xvii*n*
Everquest II, 184
Evolution of Dance, 22
exposing yourself, 6–7
Extreme Makeover: Home Edition, 161–64

FaceBook, 18, 36–37
Factor, Max, 156
Fall Out Boy, 190
F.A.O. Schwarz, 54
Fast Company, 137
FastLane blog 29–30
Fasulo, Mike, 21

Federal Communications Commission (FCC), 130, 205
FedEx, 155
Fiesta, 4
Fine Living, 203
Firefox, 25–26
Fireflox Flicks video contest, 26
Fisher, Sam, 181
Fitzgerald, Robin, 203n
flash mobs, 89
Fletch, 209n
Flickr, 35, 132
Florida, State of, 7, 145
Fly2Korea.com travel site, 84
Forbes, 55
Ford, Henry, 4
Ford, Lee, 27
Ford Motor Company, 66, 109–10, 141, 171, 190
Forrester Research, 149
Fowl Mouth, 83
42 Entertainment, 113, 115
Fred Segal shopping mall, 50
Friends, 97
Friendster, 37
FriendWise, 35
Fuel TV, 203
Full Frontal PR, 212
Furbies, 54
Future Shock (Toffler), 123

Gallup, 136
Gain, 24–25
game tournaments, 185–88
gaming, 176–93
    Advergaming, 188–90
    on cell phones, 88–89
    in-game advertising, 180–85
    music, 190–92
    sponsorships, 185–88
Gap, 12, 161
Garden State, 21
Gates, Bill, 7, 145
Gawker Media, 31
GEICO, 25
General Motors (GM), 25, 29–30, 66, 83, 129, 161
GET the Creativity Back (GTCB), 208
Geritol, 155
Ghostbusters, 22
Gillespie, Brian, 69, 71
Gilmore Girls, 207
Ginsu, 163
Glade, 162

Global Gaming League, 185
Godfather, The: The Game, 179
Godiva chocolates, 125
Gold Rush, 190–91
Got Milk?, xvii
Google, 22, 30, 36, 145n, 205
Gore, Albert, Jr., 18, 33
Grease, 153–54
Grey Goose, 166, 169, 174
growing pains, 71–74
GSM Association, 102
Game Show Network (GSN), 29
Gurasich, Spence, Darilek & McClure (GSD&M), 44

Haidt, Jonathan, 125–26
Halo 2, 108, 111, 113, 177, 179
Hanks, Tom, 155
Harold and Kumar Go to White Castle, 155
Harry Potter book series, 56
Hawaiian Tropic, 140
Hawkins, Trip, 88
Hayek, Salma, 154
HBO, 150
health club contracts, 97
Healthy Choice, 28
Hear Music, 172
Herbal Essences, 159
Heyer, Steve, 173
Hieatt, Dave and Clare, 70
Hirneise, Linda, 95
HMV, 172
Hogshead, Sally, 203n
Honda, 66
honesty, 6–7, 134–46
Hoover, 58, 64–66
Howard, Ron, 177
Howies, 70, 75
Hurley International, 73–74
Hyundai, 66

Ibele, Tyson, 19, 21
IBM, 205
Iconic Brands, 206
Iconoclasts, 169–70, 174
Idont, 116
iFilm.com, 22
IGA Worldgroup, 184
Iger, Robert, 91n
IKEA, 195
ILoveBees.com, 113
I Love Lucy, 156
IM-ing (instant messaging), 36, 73

Industrial Design Excellent Awards (IDEA), 43
infomercials, 205
in-game advertising, 180–85
ING Group, 131
Innocent Ltd., 71
In-N-Out Burger, 74
Intel Corporation, 187
Internet service provider (ISP) contracts, 97–98
INVIDI Technologies, xxiii–xxiv
iPod, 19, 43, 73, 82–83, 85, 116
ipsh!, 80–81
Isdell, E. Neville, 26
Isuzu Motors (and Joe), 141
Italian Job, The, 155
It's JerryTime!, 85
iTunes, 85, 125, 132
iTunes MiniStore, 125

Jackson, Michael, 113*n*
Jackson, Janet, booby, 127
Jain, Dipak, 128
Jamba Juice, 71
J.D. Power & Associates, 95
Jeep, 156, 180
Jefferson, Thomas, 53
Jen, Mark, 30
JetBlue Airways, 95-96
Jetsons, The, xxvi
Jobs, Steve, 85
Jolie, Angelina (Pitt), 156
Johnson, Carl, 199
Johnson & Johnson, 185
Jones Soda, 51
Jonze, Spike, 111
Juno, 97

Katien, P. J., 23, 25
Kellogg Company, 80
Kennedy, Maureen, 71
Kerry, John, 3
Kewlbox.com, 189
Kinzler, Craig, 185
know thyself, 12
Kohl's, 12
Kool-Aid, drinking of, 210
Krispy Kreme, 52

La-Z-Boy, xxiv
L.A. Office Roadshow Gaming Boot Camp, 183
labor wages, 137, 139
Laipply, Judson, 22
Lara Croft Tomb Raider, 156, 179

Lawrence, Bill, 209*n*
Lego Group, 188
Lemelson-MIT Invention Index, 77
Letters to the Editor, 53
liaising, 144, 154
lies. *See* truth in marketing
Lifehacker, 31
Linden Lab, 191
Lionsgate Entertainment, 173
Lipton, 188–89
LiveDigital, 35
Lost, 85*n*
Lowry, Adam, 47–48
Lucid, 209–10
Luhrmann, Baz, 153
Lunch Meat Selection job, 210
Lutz, Bob, 29–30

McDonald, Gregory, 209*n*
McDonald's, 60-61
McKinney-Silver, 115–17
Mac, 37
Macomber, Pete, 26
Madonna, dull, 50-51
Maher, Bill, 171*n*
MAKE LLC, 21
Manifesto, Punk Marketing, 1–17
Marketing Content Partners, 199–200
marketing, dishonest, 135
Markoff, John, xxvi*n*
Marlboro, xx
Mary Beth's Beanie World, 55
Marx, Karl, 1
Massive Gaming League (MGL), 188
Massive Inc., 183–84
massive multiplayer online games (MMOGs), 177–78, 190–93, 206
MasterCard, 96
Masters, George, 19
Matchbox Twenty, 171
Mathlouthi, Tawfik, 62
Maynard, Micheline, 66
McCann–Erickson, 186
McFerrin, Bobby, worrier, 211
media agnostics, 197–203, 211
media-buying firms, xvii–xviii
MediaCheck, 15*n*, 152
media fragmentation, xx–xxiii
Meet Mister Mom, 169–70, 174
Meet the Lucky Ones, 109-110, 171
Mehta, Nihal, 80–81
Mercury Mariner, 109

Merkin, Ari, 204, 207
message is the message, 11–12
Method Home, 47–48
me-too products, 41, 133
metrics, 16–17, 184
Metacafe, 18
M:I:III, 179
Mick, David, 125–26
Microsoft, 30, 72, 84, 113, 115, 131, 145, 177, 183, 189
middlemen, 18–38
Midway Games, 183
Miller, Jonathan F., 29
Miller, Robert S. "Steve", 137
Mindshare, 158
MINI Cooper (Cutest Car Ever), 155, 157, 199, 203
M&M's, 153, 210
mobile devices, 76–92. *See also* cell phones
    consumer satisfaction with, 98–103
    punk predictions, 205–06
    zero talking, 9–11
mobile TV, 84–88
Moen Inc., 45
Molson, 26–27
Monster (Monster Worldwide), 164
Morissette, Alanis, 172
Mother, 199, 200
Motorola, 40, 45–46, 205
Mountain Dew, 168*n*
mouseprint [mouseprint], 146
movies, 19–27. *See also specific movies*
    product placement in, 153–59
Mozilla Corp., 25–26
MP3 Players, 18
MSNBC, 31
MTV, 168–69
Multiverse Network, 177–78
Murdoch, Rupert, 35
music, in games, 190–92
music exclusives, 171–73
Must Pee TV, 130*n*
MVBMS Fuel Europe, 111
MySpace, 18, 35–37, 132
MyNetworkTV, 35
Mystery of Dalarö, 111

Nag Factor, The, 186–87
narrative marketing, 108–18
Native's Guide to New York, 212
NBC Television (NBC Universal), 150, 154–55, 159, 168, 169–70
Near Field Communications (NFC) tags, 84
Netflix, 28

NetZero, 97
Neutrogena, 140
Newman, Paul, 169
News Corp., 35
Newsweek, 161*n*
NY Daily News, 212
New York Times, 25–26, 66, 89, 131*n*, 204*n*, 212
New York Times Company, 30–31
New Yorker, 38, 53
NHL (National Hockey League), 109, 200
niche branding and marketing, 66–71
Nielsen, 16–17, 28, 180, 184
Nigo, 50
Nike, 8, 22–23, 40, 44, 51, 73–74, 139, 142, 168–69, 184-85, 199, 206
Niketown, 51
Nissan, 66
Nokia, 45*n*, 79
Norris, Chuck, 205
North Face, The, 168
North One Television, 170*n*
NTT DoCoMo, 205

Office, The, 36
Office Romance, 164
Ogilvy, David, xxv
OhmyNews, 32
Ol' Roy, 68
Olympics, 2006 Turin, 88
Omidyar, Pierre, 145
Omnicom Group Inc., 80
Oprah, and Oprah, 161, 179
Orbitz, 188
Orkut, 123
originality, 44
Ouch, 185
OutKast, 64
outthinking the competition, 8, 11
Over the Hedge, 183
OXO International, 47

Pace Productivity, 72–73
pandering, 4
Paramount Pictures, 37
PayPal, 205
Pearl Harbor, 154
Pennington, Ty, 161
Pepsi (PepsiCo), 62, 153
Peralta, Stacy, 170
Pesci, Joe , 43
pet frog, Web character, 109
Philips Electronics, 102, 130

Pigeon Dunk sneakers, 51
Pirates of the Caribbean: Dead Man's Chest, 108
Planet of the Apes, 50
Plaxo, 30
Playhouse 90, 150
podcasting, 18, 32–33
PodShow, 18, 32–33
Pop-Tarts, 121, 133
porting telephone numbers, allowance of, 99-100
Powell, Valerie*, 203*n*
Prevention magazine, 55
PRIMEDIA Inc., 31
Primer, 21
Procter and Gamble (P&G), 36, 48, 58, 66–67, 69,
    74, 136, 159-60, 164
producers, 167–71
product choice, 120–33
product design, 43–48
product placement, 148, 153–59
        movies, 153–56
        TV, 156–59
        "most shameful ever," 170
        positive set-up, 153
product recalls, 142
product scarcity, 48–51, 54–56
product uniqueness, 51–54
Project Runway, 161–64
Project Wanamaker, 15*n*
Public Interest Research Groups (PIRGs), 101
punk definitions, 17, 39, 106, 119, 147, 193
PunkMarketing.com, nonstop action, xxvi*n*, 17
Punk Marketing Manifesto, 1–17
Punk Marketing Consumer Power Charter, 132-33
Punk Marketing Revolution, xv–xviii
        Articles of the, 1–17
        ...don't stand in the way of, 87
punk predictions, 205–06
punk rock, xxiv, xxv
Purina, 68
Purist Hatbox Toilet, 45

Quality, no longer a differentiator, 75
quantity vs. quality, 15–16
Quiksilver, 166
Quiz Show, 155*n*
Q Score from TVQ Inc., 179*n*
Queens, The Borough of, 192
QWERTY keyboard, 80
Qwest Communications, 83

R
@radical.media, 168

radio frequency identification (RFID) tags, 81, 84, 91
Rashid, Karim, 48
Rather, Dan, 27
Razr V3, 45
Rea, Chad, 200-201, 203
reality TV, 158–64, 190–91
Real Simple, 130–31
RBC Capital Markets, 84
Reebok, 50, 80
Recovery Road, 102-105
Redford, Robert, 155*n*, 169
regular Joes, 32
Reitman, Jason, 22
Reitman, Ivan, 22
remote controls, xxiii, 151–52
Replay, 129, 150
resoluteness, 2–4
results, making it worthwhile, 211
Restaurant, The, 159
Reuters, 212
Revolution. *See* Punk Marketing Revolution
Revolution showerhead, 45
Reynolds, Glenn, 38*n*
Riley, Chris, 139
risk avoidance, 1–2
Ritson, Mark, 129
RLM Public Relations ("Richard and Co."), 132, 212
Robertson, Cliff, 77
Robertson, Pat, 37
Rolling Stones, 172
Roper Center for Public Opinion Research, 137
road warriors (pseudo), 82
Rock, Chris, 165
Ross, Diana, 173
Rowling, J. K., 56
Runner, The, 191
Ruskin, Gary, 43
Ryan, Eric, 47–48

Sahara, 156
Sakamoto, Ryuichi, 45*n*
Samsung, 40, 84, 205
Sandilands, Anna, 208–9
SanDisk, 116
Sarfaty, Ruth, 191
Saucony, 69, 71
SC Johnson, 48
scarcity, 48–51, 54–56
Scali, McCabe, Sloves, 141-42
Schmidt, Eric, 145*n*
Scoble, Robert, 30
Scott, Ridley and Tony, 171

Scripps Networks, 203

Sears, 44, 160–61, 162

Second Life, 191–92

Sega Games, 117

Sesame Street (.com), 87

72 and Sunny, 200

service providers, big jokes, 85

Sex Pistols, The, xxiv, xxv

Shames, Laurence, 85*n*

Shanks, Eric, 187–88

Shopping.com, 6

Short Messaging System (SMS), 80–81

Silas & Maria, 50

simplification, 132–33

SIRIUS Satellite Radio, 109*n*

Sims, The, 178

Sin City, 179

sitcom plot suggestion, 89

Sky News/Sky Broadcasting, 31, 170

Slingbox, 87

SlingPlayer Mobile, 87

small, acting, 58, 62–71

Smart Communications, 26

Smith, Marc, 131

Snarf by Microsoft, 131

SOAPnet, 164

Sobolewski, Mary Beth, 55

social networks, 18, 35–37, 132

Social Research Inc., 150

Solemates, 44

Sondheim, Stephen, 56*n*

Song Airways, 6*n*

Sony, 19, 21, 31, 46, 181–83, 184

South Korea, 83–84, 187

Southwest Airlines, 95–96

Spider-Man 2, 113

Spielberg, Steven, 177

Spitzer, Gov. Eliot , 98

sponsorships, 129, 185–88

Sprint Nextel, 45–46, 87, 102, 139

standards, setting, 14–16

standing out, 40–58
    product design, 43–48
    product scarcity, 48–51, 54–56
    product uniqueness, 51–54

Staples Inc., 163

Starbucks, 51–52, 61, 101, 128–29, 142, 172–73, 206, 209

State Farm Insurance, 169

stealth-marketing, 57

Stengel, Jim, 67, 69

Stephens, Darrin, xvii

Stewart, Martha (ex-con), 163

Sting, 168

Stone, Linda, 72

Stonyfield Farm, 112

storytelling, 108–18

StrawberryFrog, 199

Streisand, Barbara, 55

Strictly Ballroom, 153

strong stands (resoluteness), 2–4

Studioriley, 139

Subservient Chicken, 182, 197

Sundance Channel, 169

Sundance Festival, 21

suntan lotions, 140

Super Bowl, 33, 127, 205

SUVs, 3*n*, 109

*T*agged, 35

Take-Two Interactive, 184–85

Taking Care of Business, 212

Target, 12, 104, 171–72

targeted marketing, xxiii–xxv

tease (teasing), 7–8

technology seduction, 11–12

Technorati, 28

Tesco PLC, 73

television, makes all true, 139

text messaging, 80–82

Thank You for Smoking, 22

Thriller, 113*n*

Thomas, Dave, 104

Tiger Electronics, 54

Time Warner Inc., 97

tiny, acting, 58, 62–71

TiVo and TiVoing, xx, xxiii, xxvi, 4, 125, 129, 132, 148–50, 152–53, 159, 205

TLC (nee Learning Channel), 29

TM Infringement, 19

T-Mobile, 101

"Todd," newly-named answerer from Bangalore, 139

Toffler, Alvin, 123

Tom Clancy's Splinter Cell Pandora Tomorrow, 181–83

Tony Hawk's American Wasteland, 180–81, 190

tools of the Revolution, 16–17

Tokyo Sex Pistols, the, 50

Toy, 204

Toyota Motor Company, 66, 162

Trader Joe's, 68

trends, believing in, 198
    big deal trends, 11, 50, 145
    trendspotting, 84, 123

trendSpotting, 212

True Life: I'm a Gamer, 185
Trump, Big D, 160, 163-64
Truth anti-tobacco campaign, 7, 145, 195
truth in marketing, 6–7, 134–46
Turner, Ted, 2
Turner Classic Movies (TCM), 29, 153
24 Conspiracy mobisodes, 85
TV (television), 120, 129–30, 148–66
    brand integration, 160–64
    mobile, 84–88
    product placement, 148, 156–59
Ty.com, 56
Tylenol, 185

Ubisoft Entertainment 181–83
uniqueness, 51–54
Unilever, 2
United Airlines, 109
Unspun, 212
Upshot, 201, 203
urinals, product placement on, 129
USA Today, 33, 43, 141, 212
Us Weekly, 212

Van Gogh, Vincent, 210
Van Leeuwen, Ernie, 71
Vans, 166, 170
Vaughn Whelan & Partners, 26–27
Verizon Wireless, 87
Versus (Outdoor Life, Network), 29
V CAST, 87
vibrating phones, 9
Victoria's Secret, 37
video gaming. *See* gaming
video on demand (VOD), 88*n*
Virgin Group, 7, 58, 62–63, 75, 139
Virgin Cola, 63
Vivienne, virtual girlfriend, 88
VoIP (Voice over Internet Protocol), 9, 102–3
Volkswagen, 27, 154–55, 201
Volvo, 111, 141–42
Vonage Holdings Corp., 102–3
Von Dutch Originals, 12

Wahlberg, Marky Mark, 155*n*
Walken, Chris, 111
Wall Street Journal, 23, 67, 91
Wal-Mart, 12, 44, 68, 103–4, 105, 158, 171–72, 186*n*
Walt Disney Company, 158, 164, 186, 191
Walton, Sam, 68
Warner, Ty, 40, 55–56
Washington, George, 142

Washington Post, 28
Webber, Harry, 26
Wendy's, 36, 104
Web 2.0, xxvi and *n*
WETNoZ International, 44–45
What I Like About You, 159
White Castle, 155
"why not" questions, 2
Who, The, 55
Wicks, Jim, 46
Wieden + Kennedy, 117, 199
Wi-Fi phone, 102
Wild Games by Wild Tangent Inc., 189
Willard Bishop Consulting, xxi–xxii
Williams, Pharrell, N*E*R*D, 50
William Morris Agency, 187
Wireless Application Protocol (WAP), 81–82
Wirtschafter, David, 156
WiseNut, xxvi
World Cup (FIFA), 88
World Cyber Games, 185, 187
World of Warcraft, 177–78
World Series of Video Games, 187
World Trade Organization, 61
Writers Guild of America west, 158

Xbox, 82, 113, 115, 184, 187, 200

Yahoo!, 30, 160
Yankee Group, 183
Yankelovich Inc., 186–87
Yoplait, 112
yogurt tops, branding of, 112
YouTube, 18, 22

Zafirovski, Mike, 46
Zenith Electronic Corporation, 151–52
zero talking, 9–11
Zucker, Jerry, 85
Zucker, Orrin, 85

FINAL WORDS

Delivered by Someone Else (But of Course)

So think before you do what they say
It's your life so go your own way

—Sham 69 (British punk band circa '76)